Which A levels?

The guide to choosing A levels, Advanced Diplomas and other post-16 qualifications

Alison Dixon

Lifetime
Publishing

Which A levels? The guide to choosing A levels, Advanced Diplomas and other post-16 qualifications

Seventh edition

Published by Lifetime Publishing, Mill House, Stallard Street, Trowbridge BA14 8HH

© Nord Anglia Lifetime Development South West Ltd, 2010

ISBN 978-1-904979-41-8

Cover design by Caroline Curran

Printed in the EU by SS Media Ltd

Contents

PART THREE – ALTERNATIVES TO A LEVELS

Advanced Diploma subjects (England only)

APPENDICES

INDEX

ACKNOWLEDGEMENTS

With thanks to Jo Wincott and the following staff from Sandon School, Chelmsford, Essex, who helped me with the preparation of this edition:

Michelle Adjula, Andy Davis, Maxine Dodd, Caroline Flawn, Margueritte Gill, Clare Horan, Kieran Hope, Sue McCollum, Adrian Morris, Helen Salmon, Steve Wadwell and Clive Wilton.

The Sandon School is a specialist maths and computing college based on the east side of Chelmsford. With a flourishing sixth form, it serves the local communities of Sandon and Great Baddow and attracts students from a number of neighbouring villages. With results consistently above the national average, it has a good reputation in the community and is oversubscribed. www.sandon.essex.sch.uk

Thanks also to Peter Staines, Margaret and Harry Kroto, Stuart Evans, Dr Rob Bowler of the Royal Society of Chemistry, Raye Scott of WJEC and Alice Moran and Sharon Czudak of CILT, The National Centre for Languages.

Finally, thanks to everybody who gave me quotes.

Part one

A brief introduction to post-16 options

Part one
A brief introduction to post-16 options

THE NEXT TWO YEARS

When you complete your GCSEs, or equivalent, you must choose your next step. You might want to continue studying full time at school, or go to a different sixth form or college. You also have the option to continue your studies part time through an Apprenticeship.

YOUR CHOICE OF QUALIFICATIONS

Many people who decide to continue studying after GCSEs opt for A levels. Detailed information on A levels, including descriptions of over 50 A level subjects and where each could lead, is given in **Part two** of this book. However, remember that there are various other alternative qualifications at the same level (level 3). You could, for example, consider BTEC Nationals, OCRs or, in England, the new Advanced Diploma. It is possible to combine these qualifications with A levels, so your choice of qualifications is wide. For more information on options other than A levels, see **Part three** of this book.

To find out more about different levels of qualifications and how they fit together, see the Qualifications and Credit Framework provided in Appendix 1 at the back of this book.

Besides continuing with full-time study, your other options include work and training, such as Apprenticeships, or voluntary work.

APPRENTICESHIPS

Apprenticeships are available in many career areas. They offer structured training with an employer, leading to further qualifications. They generally fall into one of three categories:

- Apprenticeships – equivalent to GCSE level
- Advanced Apprenticeships – equivalent to A level
- Higher Apprenticeships – equivalent to a foundation degree.

Apprenticeships are open to anybody over 16 and there is no upper age limit so they are a realistic alternative to studying full time. You might even progress to higher education as part of, or after completing, an Apprenticeship.

See www.apprenticeships.org.uk for details of the National Apprenticeship Scheme where you can search online for vacancies. Your local Connexions/careers service will have information about Apprenticeship opportunities in your area.

WORK NOW, STUDY LATER?

Some people decide to have a break in full-time education and then resume their studies as a mature student. Many students also consider a gap year between completing their sixth form study and going on to higher education. Gap years can consist of anything from work (paid or voluntary) or travel, or a mixture of both. In general, admissions officers in higher education are fine about gap years as they feel that students benefit from increased experience and maturity.

However, for some subjects, such as mathematics, where a break may affect progress, or for longer courses, such as medical studies, it is always advisable to check with admissions tutors for their advice.

WHAT TO DO NEXT

The decision is yours and yours alone. Help and advice are available from your careers teacher or personal adviser/careers adviser in school or college and at your Connexions or careers centre.

You will need to consider all the alternatives and all the issues surrounding A levels and other post-16 options. Parents and friends can also offer advice, although they may not have the latest information. To help you to decide, ask yourself some basic questions.

- Why am I interested in studying further?
- Would I benefit from further study?
- Would I learn better through a mixture of work and training?
- Do I really understand what is involved in further study?
- Do my teachers think I am right to continue in full-time education?
- Do I know what is available?
- What am I good at (including skills and knowledge outside the classroom)?
- What do I really enjoy?
- What would I do after further study? Go on to university or college, or into an Apprenticeship/job that includes further training?
- Do I have any clear ideas about a career or the future?

SCHOOL OR COLLEGE?

You can study for A levels or equivalent at school, or at a sixth form, further education or tertiary college.

Some schools make a distinction between the sixth form and the rest of the school, offering special privileges and facilities. Colleges, on the other hand, are often run in a similar way to higher education institutions, where there is a greater emphasis on self-motivation and there is also a much wider age range of students. Often, teaching is done in the form of lectures (where a large group listens to a teacher) or tutorials (small group discussions). If you are considering a college, you should

visit and ask questions about how A levels or equivalent courses are taught there.

Whichever option you choose, both schools and colleges place great importance on your ability to complete work on time and your commitment to the course.

HIGHER EDUCATION

What is it and how do I decide whether it is for me?

Higher education is not just at a university. It can be at a college of higher or further education or studied by distance learning (including via the internet) and can be part time as well as full time. You can study locally or in another part of the country. Your course might last anything from two to five years and could include work or study placements in the UK or worldwide.

What are the benefits of higher education?

This is a difficult one as there are so many advantages to higher education – it depends on what you want to get out of it. You will be going somewhere new, studying a subject you like, or a new subject, in depth. You will be meeting a whole range of new people and will get the chance to do new things. You will be learning lots of useful skills for life in addition to what your course teaches you. It is also worth remembering that graduates can earn on average 20 to 25% more than non-graduates – and this is higher with degrees in subjects such as engineering, maths and sciences. You will of course have to weigh up the financial implications as well.

What courses are available?

Degree courses: these are courses that people automatically think about when they are thinking of higher education. They usually last three or four years, full time (longer if you are studying subjects such as medicine). They can also be studied part time, sometimes while working in a related job.

HNC/HND courses: Higher National Certificates (HNCs) or Diplomas (HNDs) are work-related qualifications, available in everything from accounting to film production. HNCs are the part-time equivalents of HNDs. Students often study HNCs part time over two years, while they are in employment.

HNDs take two years to complete on a full-time basis (or three years with a work placement). HNCs and HNDs can allow entry into the second or third year of a degree course.

Foundation degrees: these are degree level qualifications designed with employers, and combine academic study with workplace learning. Some have been designed to tackle particular skills shortages.

They last two years full time (or they can be taken part time) and could progress to further or higher study or enable you to go straight into work. For more information about foundation degrees, go to www.findfoundationdegree.co.uk. You can also search for foundation degree courses on the UCAS website.

To find out what grades and subjects different universities require for each course, you should look at university prospectuses and websites and other higher education guides. *University Degree Course Offers* (also known as *HEAP*) is one of the best known of these, and UCAS publishes a yearly official guide to university and college entry (called the *Big Guide*). The UCAS website has entry profiles giving you the requirements for entry to most courses and you will also find information about higher education entry in each of the A level and Diploma subject entries in this book.

If you are thinking of studying art and design at university, you usually have to study an art Foundation course at a college of further education or art school, then move on to your degree studies. Entry to college or art school depends far more on a strong portfolio (collection of artwork that you have produced) than specified grades for A levels or equivalent.

The degree that you take can have an impact on the careers that you can enter. Make sure that your choice of degree is appropriate for the career in which you are interested.

Part two

A levels

Part two

A levels

If you are considering taking A levels, think about some of these questions.

- Do I know the full range of options at 16+?
- Why do I want to do A levels?
- How demanding are A levels?
- How can I do well at them?
- What subjects should I study?
- Should I study at school or college?
- Have I taken advice from personal advisers/careers advisers, teachers, parents and friends?

HOW ARE A LEVELS STRUCTURED?

In the first year of a two-year A level programme, students usually take four or five AS level subjects, which can be kept as 'stand-alone' qualifications, or used to form the first half of full A levels (the second half being referred to as A2). Students can choose which of their AS levels to continue and build into two, three or more A levels.

Most A levels are modular and consist of four units: the first two units will form the AS level and units three and four will comprise the A2 level.

The following A levels have six units: biology, chemistry, electronics, geology, human biology, music and physics. Science (OCR) has three units as it is only available at AS level. Biblical Hebrew, Dutch, Gujarati, Persian, Portuguese and Turkish have two units.

Applied A levels consist of six units for a single award; nine units for a one-and-a-half A level award and twelve units for a double award. Applied A levels are available in the following subjects: applied art and design; applied business; engineering; health and social care; applied ICT; leisure; media (communication and production); applied science; and travel and tourism. Applied A levels will run until 2013 when they will be reviewed.

EXTENDED PROJECT

There is the opportunity to take an additional qualification at A level (also part of the Advanced Diploma), which is known as the Extended Project Qualification or EPQ. For this you must produce an extended piece of work, either in an area that you are studying or in which you have a particular interest.

This is a level 3 qualification equivalent to half an A level. It is graded, and carries the same UCAS points as an AS level except that an A* grade is available.

The Extended Project offers the opportunity to develop essential skills for higher education and the workplace, in a subject area of your choice.

It is an independent piece of research that you choose. You then meet weekly with a member of staff (supervisor) to discuss your progress, and they guide you and help you to develop the necessary skills to complete a successful project.

HOW ARE A LEVELS GRADED?

AS and A levels are graded A-E. An A* grade was first awarded at A level in 2010. The A* grade is not awarded at AS level but only at A2, as the more challenging material is introduced at A2 level.

CASHING IN

There are usually four modules in the full A level exam, two for the AS and two for A2, and any of these can be taken on more than one occasion. When a student has taken the two modules for the AS they are able to cash in to receive an AS certificate. That means that they inform the exam board that they want their marks added and a final grade and certificate issued. This needs to be done by their centre (school or college) on their behalf.

When the student goes on to complete the two A2 modules in that subject and cashes in for A level, then a further certificate is issued for A level.

Each time a student cashes in for an AS or an A level award, a certificate is issued and the best module marks will be used to calculate the overall grade on that certificate. Only the marks of the modules used to calculate the overall grade will be reported to UCAS. The marks or grades of any additional modules taken, but not used in calculating the overall grade awarded on the certificate, will not be reported to UCAS.

CHOOSING YOUR A LEVEL SUBJECTS

The two most important criteria for choosing subjects are:

- what you are likely to be good at
- what you are likely to enjoy.

You will find there are some subjects available that you won't have come across previously at school. Find out about them before you choose. The subjects listed in this book will be a good place to start.

Most higher education courses require certain A level grades (or alternative equivalent qualifications), and many specify the A level subjects and GCSE subjects that you should have. Think ahead to what you will be doing after A levels to help you choose the best subjects now. If you are not sure what career you will enter, try to choose a selection of subjects that will keep your options as open as possible.

Therefore, when making your choices you should consider:

- the subjects in which you are interested
- your abilities, aptitudes and skills
- how open you want to keep your career options
- which A level subjects are available at your school or in local sixth forms and colleges.

A level subject combinations

Some A levels cover common ground, for example, geography and environmental studies, or media studies and film studies. If the overlap is too great, some higher education institutions may not accept the combination. On the other hand, two complementary subjects may help a great deal in your studies. For example, doing physics without mathematics or another science would be difficult and is not generally recommended.

Some degree courses specify the A level subjects that you need. The following list shows the most popular degrees that often require specific A levels:

biology – biology and another science or maths

chemistry – chemistry and sometimes maths and/or another science

dentistry – chemistry and one or two other sciences

engineering – maths and physics (or maths and chemistry for chemical engineering)

maths – maths

medicine – chemistry and usually one or two other sciences. The majority of medical schools require A level chemistry, while others will accept AS level in chemistry, depending upon the other qualifications being offered. Some require biology at A level. (For candidates without science subjects at A level, or equivalent, it is possible to undertake an additional pre-medical year at some universities.

The pre-medical year is a preliminary course in chemistry, physics and biology.)

modern languages – usually you will need the language at A level standard but requirements vary, especially for less common languages

music – music

physics – physics and maths

veterinary science – chemistry and one or two other sciences.

ADVANCED EXTENSION AWARD (AEA)

The AEA is an examination designed to stretch the most able of A level students. It was available in 19 subjects but has now been withdrawn with the exception of the maths qualification, which will be available until 2013. It counts for points on the UCAS tariff.

FREQUENTLY ASKED QUESTIONS ABOUT A LEVEL STUDY

Do you need A levels to get into higher education?

Universities and colleges of higher education have a broad range of entry requirements, not just A levels. If you want to study a degree course at university, you will usually need to reach a level equivalent to a minimum of two A levels, and will often need grade C or above in mathematics and English, and sometimes other subjects, at GCSE.

You can get onto many higher courses with an Advanced Diploma, BTEC National or OCR level 3 National or Diploma.

Do I need a GCSE in the subject to take it at A level?

For some subjects you will be asked for at least a grade C in the subject, or in a related subject, at GCSE before you can start the course. Check the course information to find out the requirements.

Some A level subjects pick up where the GCSE leaves off, and you will find the A level hard going if you don't have a GCSE in that subject. These A levels include mathematics, physics, chemistry, modern and ancient languages. Sometimes there are exceptions to this, but you should talk it through with a teacher/tutor before committing yourself to a new subject.

Other subjects allow for a fresh start at A level, or are appropriate for students who are new to the subject. This is particularly the case for subjects that are less widely available at GCSE, such as government and politics, or environmental science. What is required in these cases is a genuine interest in the subject, and possibly some experience of related areas, for example, a geography or biology GCSE for environmental studies, or a history or classics GCSE for ancient history.

If I did well in the subject at GCSE, will I do well in the A level?

A good grade (C or above) in a GCSE suggests that you have understood the basic concepts involved in the subject and are able to use your knowledge in a flexible way. This could mean that you are likely to do well in the subject at AS or A level, but it is worth investigating whether you will study the subject in a different way and considering whether this will suit you. Ask your teachers or tutors for more information.

Don't forget that it's more to do with how you approach your studies, being honest about how much you understand, your desire to learn about the subject outside the classroom and your maturity to ask for help when you need it.

Should I choose arts or sciences?

Many students see the choices between arts and science subjects at A level as an 'either/ or' – you either study science subjects or you study arts subjects. Choice of AS levels enables you to balance arts and science subjects more. However, the division does apply to some extent if you are interested in the idea of going on to study science after A level, or are thinking of a science-related career, since the more sciences you study, the wider the range of science courses open to you. If you study fewer than two sciences at A level, you would seriously limit your future options for science courses and careers.

If you are not sure about your future plans, the study of two or more sciences at A level will allow you to keep your options open. Science A levels are widely accepted as useful qualifications for almost any degree subject, and are highly valued by employers. The most common combinations of science subjects are mathematics, chemistry and physics, or biology, chemistry and physics.

It is becoming more common to choose to combine arts and science subjects. This is partly because AS level courses provide the flexibility to combine different subjects. Also, there is an increasing number of social science subjects, such as sociology, psychology, and government and politics, that use not only essay-writing skills and critical analysis (where you look at an argument, idea or theory and question whether it is a useful or accurate one), which are normally associated with arts disciplines, but also statistics and research methods, which are normally associated with science subjects.

Even in more arts-based subjects such as English, modern languages, art, media studies, music and drama, or theatre studies, you will find that the abilities they encourage, such as essay-writing, the critical analysis of written and visual information, the development of logical arguments and the use of the imagination, will be extremely useful in the study of sciences.

Don't forget that there are some more general science courses available, such as science in society, which bridge the gap between the arts and sciences.

There are a couple of recommended books that could help you: *Careers with an Arts or Humanities Degree* and *Careers with a Science Degree* (both published by Lifetime Publishing).

Can I mix vocational and academic subjects?

Yes, it is possible to do this and it can add extra breadth to your studies. Apart from mixing academic and vocational subjects at A level, you may be able to combine A levels with qualifications such as BTEC or OCR Nationals as these may provide a better route for you. Diplomas allow for this as well.

What if I don't like the course I've chosen?

Everyone is taking a bit of a risk when they make their A level choices. You can't guarantee that you'll enjoy the subject, even if it was your favourite at GCSE. Most schools and colleges realise this risk, and set aside a certain period of time at the beginning of the academic year when you can still change your mind. The increased flexibility of the system makes this issue less of a problem than it used to be, since you can work out the final direction of your A level studies during the AS phase.

You'll have to discuss with your teacher and personal adviser/careers adviser why you have decided to change subjects. You must have a good reason to change. Some students find the change from GCSE to A level work quite a shock to the system and, instead of trying to adjust to the new way of working, assume wrongly that a change of subject would be the answer. Others know immediately that they have made a mistake in their choices when they start the course. However, the more informed you are about what an A level course involves before you start, the less likely you are to make a mistake.

How are A levels and AS levels assessed?

Like GCSEs, A levels and AS levels are designed and run by different examination boards. Each course is slightly different, and not all exam boards offer all subjects. The ways that boards assess you will involve one or more of the following.

- **Written exams** – during, rather than just at the end of, your course.
- **Coursework** – essays, projects or case studies completed in your own time during the course (or written exams, as a choice). Coursework has been reviewed and only remains in some practical, expressive and humanities subjects such as: art, computing, design and technology, English, home economics, history, ICT, media studies, music, performance studies, physical education, biology, chemistry, physics, geology, electronics and science.
- **Practical exams** – particularly for science subjects, and arts/practical courses such as theatre studies and photography.

HOW TO DO WELL AT A LEVEL OR EQUIVALENT

Organise yourself

Subjects will vary in the amount of work that is set and how much time you are expected to spend on each. Work is set so frequently, and with such strict deadlines, that it soon starts to pile up if you don't deal with it in a methodical way.

Once you get your timetable, it should become clear how much non-lesson time you will have each week. Make sure you add to your timetable:

- time for private study at school or college
- additional time for studying in the evenings and at weekends
- time off.

Motivate yourself

Being motivated is vital if you are to do well in your subject. If you get along with your teacher/tutor and like the rest of your class or group, then it is much easier to feel enthusiastic about a subject and be willing to work on it. Real motivation comes from being genuinely interested in a subject and wanting to do well at it.

You will find that there are periods when you have no lessons timetabled. These periods may seem like a good time to meet friends and chat. However, they are an essential part of your study time and are likely to be the only times you have to use the school's or college's resources – the internet, books and practical equipment. Without these periods, you may find yourself spending all your time in the evenings and at weekends trying to catch up on work. Most schools and colleges have library facilities that can be used as study areas and for researching assignments.

Take notes

Good note-taking is important. Most people develop their own system for note-taking, involving their own form of shorthand or abbreviations for words that crop up regularly, as well as a preferred way of setting out the information. If you do find that you have difficulty in understanding the notes you have taken, or in getting the information down quickly or accurately, ask your teacher/tutor for some advice and help.

Read around the subject

Read anything about your subject that is not covered by the set work. Keep up to date by reading the newspapers, magazines or websites that relate to your subject. Libraries have recent editions of useful magazines, which will help you to keep in touch with what is going on in biological research or politics, for example.

A LEVEL SUBJECTS

The rest of Part two of this book is divided into sections that cover over 50 A level subjects, listed alphabetically. Each section is structured in the same way, to make it easy for you to compare different A levels. The following topics are covered for each subject.

- **What do you study?** – gives an overview of the topics covered by the subject.

- **How do you study?** – includes aspects such as practical work, fieldwork etc.

- **Subject combinations** – advises on other subjects that combine well with that A level subject.

- **Higher education options** – covers degree and other higher education qualifications related to the subject.

- **Career options** – an indication of where the subject could lead you either after A levels or as a graduate.

- **Sources of information** – where you can find out more.

Accounting

Accountancy studies the money side of business and aims to answer questions such as: What profit has our business made? How does it compare with the previous year? Can we afford to expand/take on more staff?

The course stresses the importance of discipline in terms of accuracy and presentation, but leaves you to interpret financial positions. You will gain an understanding of the wider business environment, how financial control is vital to business success and how, without it, even profitable firms can fail. You will learn about the effects of economic, legal and technological change on accounting, and the social implications of accounting decisions.

An interest in business and GCSE maths will be an advantage and may be an entry requirement. You don't need a GCSE in accounting as the A/AS level can be started from scratch.

WHAT DO YOU STUDY?

The topics listed give an idea of what could be covered. The exact content of AS and A2 specifications differ according to exam boards, so you will need to check with your school or college about the exact modules available to you.

There are two main types of business accounting, both covered by A level. The first is financial accounting, which is mainly concerned with the current state of a company's accounts. Financial accountants undertake auditing (checking in detail) the financial records of companies and preparing annual accounts for HM Revenue & Customs and shareholders.

The second type is management accounting, which mainly deals with examining a company's accounts to help senior managers with forward planning and decision making. As you progress through your course, you are often put in the role of financial adviser to the managers of a business. You are asked to recommend the actions that the business should take to improve its performance or to get out of financial trouble.

The AS is a general introduction and will be useful to anybody interested in business and finance. At A level students study management accounting and company accounts.

Financial accounting

The accounting information system

- **Accounting records** – how to keep records of a company's financial activity, including double-entry bookkeeping (every credit on one account must be matched by a debit on another), how to treat debts, creditors, investments and capital. The use of ICT in accounting.

- **Formal presentation of financial information** – trial balances, cash-flow statements, balance sheets, profit-and-loss accounts and published company accounts.

- **Stock valuation** – how to organise and present information about stock held by a business organisation.

Management accounting

- **Budgeting and cash-flow forecasts** – predicting the company's financial future.

- **Break-even analysis** – assessing whether a business project can cover its costs and how much it must sell before making a profit.

> *'Try and do a placement as part of your course. You can't beat real work experience and it's something positive to put on your CV.'*
> Daniel, aged 22, trainee chartered accountant

- **Investment appraisal** – the pros and cons of investing money.

- **Overheads** – accounting for indirect costs that are not incurred in the actual product or a service (e.g. an IT system).

- **Analysing and interpreting accounts** – understanding what accounts can (and can't) tell you about the health and prospects of a business, and using ratios to analyse company performance.

- **Planning and decision making** – how decisions are made on the basis of financial information and how managers use this to plan ahead.

HOW DO YOU STUDY?

After you have learned the basic principles you will apply this to real accounting problems. This can require calculations, written analysis and management reports. You may go on visits, work experience or work shadowing. There is no coursework as the final exams are problem based.

SUBJECT COMBINATIONS

Popular A level combinations include business studies, economics, ICT, languages and law. If you are considering accountancy at degree level, mathematics A or AS level is required for some courses.

It is possible to combine all A and AS levels with other equivalent qualifications such as BTEC Nationals, OCR Nationals and they could form part of Diplomas.

Accounting A level is not a requirement for accountancy courses, and while some courses find it a useful preparation others may

not accept it. Check with higher education institutions.

GCSE maths is often required and sometimes English.

HIGHER EDUCATION OPTIONS

Degree-level study

You don't need an accountancy degree to qualify as an accountant so you could consider related subjects such as business studies, maths, economics, actuarial science or law. Quantity surveying is another option, as quantity surveyors are the accountants of the construction industry. Many accountancy employers will look at your UCAS score as well as your class of degree.

To qualify as a professional accountant after graduating (you can become an accountant without a degree – see 'Into work after A levels' overleaf), you must complete an initial stage of formal training, the 'foundation stage', followed by a three-year training contract while working and studying for professional exams. An accountancy degree exempts you from most of the foundation exams. Some degree subjects such as business economics, business information management and management science, also give exemptions. Check with professional accountancy bodies for a full list.

Many degrees are called 'accounting and finance', but have the same contents as 'accounting' or 'accountancy'. Some degrees have an international perspective, including languages and a period of study or work abroad.

Degree subject combinations

Accounting can be combined with many subjects. ICT, economics, law, marketing, business studies and psychology are popular, but if you reduce the proportion of accountancy in your degree you may not get all the professional exam exemptions.

Other higher education qualifications

There are foundation degrees available in accounting, some including business management or administration.

Accounting and related subjects such as business and management are available at HND/HNC.

Relevance to other subjects?

Your accounting A level is useful even if you don't intend to qualify as an accountant or work in business.

The understanding you gain of business and finance is useful for courses like economics, law, ICT, marketing, administration or tourism.

Important advice

If you are considering a year out between A levels and your degree, check with the institutions. Some prefer accountancy students not to take gap years, or ask that some relevant work experience be obtained during the year off. Make your plans clear on your UCAS application.

CAREER OPTIONS

Into work after A levels

Some employers recruit trainees with A levels and a minimum UCAS points score is often specified for these jobs. The Institute of Chartered Accountants in England and Wales (ICAEW) advertises these vacancies.

The ICAEW offers a training route with qualifications from the Association of Accounting Technicians (AAT). This is a fast-track route, which enables you to qualify as a chartered accountant in four years.

To qualify as a chartered accountant without a degree involves a four-year training contract with a firm of chartered accountants or with

a company finance department . During this time you would take AAT and ICAEW exams. You then join graduate entrants to the profession as you move on to the professional training stage. Note that the ICAEW recommends that you have at least 220 UCAS tariff points, whichever route you take into the profession. The route to qualification with the other professional bodies (see 'Working in accounting' below) is very similar.

You could consider qualifying as an accounting technician and may get some exemptions for the qualification because of your A level in accounting. The course is based on skills tests and simulations and training is offered by the AAT and the Association of Chartered Certified Accountants (ACCA).

If you don't plan to qualify as an accountant, there are opportunities for working in finance departments of many organisations. Such jobs involve arranging salaries, paying bills and issuing invoices. A management trainee scheme or Apprenticeship would allow you to use your accounting skills and undertake further training.

You could consider banks or building societies, or becoming a financial adviser.

Skills gained like numeracy, research and analysis, problem-solving, communication and computer skills, will be useful in many jobs.

Into work as a graduate

Working in accounting

These are the areas of accountancy open to graduates. The choice of professional body that you train with depends on the kind of work you want to do.

Chartered accountants work in private practice mainly dealing with taxation and auditing. Chartered accountancy firms mainly operate as partners, so if you become a partner, you take a share of the profits rather than a salary. Private practice accountants usually qualify with the ICAEW.

Certified accountants work as salaried employees in commerce or industry. In all but the smallest businesses, they have either a financial or management accountancy role. The professional body for this type of accountancy is the ACCA, but ICAEW and ACCA qualifications are interchangeable.

Management accountants are more firmly oriented towards business, especially financial planning and strategy, and the use of IT for management information. They qualify with the Chartered Institute of Management Accountants (CIMA).

Public finance accountants work within the Civil Service, NHS or local government. Public service has a very clear career structure but is a specialised form of accounting so it might be difficult to move into other areas. Public finance accountants qualify with the Chartered Institute of Public Finance and Accountancy (CIPFA).

Accounting technicians work alongside professionally qualified accountants collecting financial information to assist them in making business decisions. Accounting technicians usually work in a support role within an accountancy firm or in the finance department of an organisation.

Depending on the route taken to qualify for the AAT and any experience gained, accounting technicians may undertake a range of roles, which will include:

- assisting with the preparation of accounts
- preparing the payroll
- dealing with invoices needing payment
- dealing with basic bookkeeping.

At a more senior level, they may be employed in audit work, both external and internal.

Working outside accounting

Wherever you work, financial knowledge is valuable. You could consider a career in financial advice or in insurance or investment, assessing people's needs and advising them on investments. A career in business management or consultancy would require you to have a clear understanding of how finances work and you could consider a graduate training scheme. Your skills would also be useful in jobs within HM Revenue & Customs.

SOURCES OF INFORMATION

Association of Accounting Technicians (AAT)
www.aat.org.uk

Association of Chartered Certified Accountants (ACCA)
www.acca.org.uk

Chartered Institute of Management Accountants (CIMA)
www.cimaglobal.com

Chartered Institute of Public Finance and Accountancy (CIPFA)
www.cipfa.org.uk

Institute of Chartered Accountants in England and Wales (ICAEW)
www.icaew.com

Institute of Chartered Accountants in Scotland (ICAS)
www.icas.org.uk

'I loved the courses I took and it gave me such a boost in my career prospects. My choice of degree and the masters gave me a total of nine exam exemptions from my professional exams for the Chartered Institute of Management Accountants (CIMA). This meant I had an advantage over all others in my department, in the ease and speed of qualification into CIMA, and got me a higher starting salary.'
Sally, aged 25, accounting and finance degree, masters in management science now working for a large supermarket head office

Ancient history

Are you fascinated by the ancient world as portrayed in films like *Troy*, *Gladiator* and *300*? If you want to make sense of the world today, it's important to understand key events, individuals, movements and conflicts that have shaped history.

A study of ancient history covers all aspects of the classical world from Ancient Greece to the fall of the Roman Empire (from about the sixth century BC to AD 410). You look at how the political and military influence of city states and empires rose and fell and how their economy, culture and society changed. The subject involves all aspects of classical civilisation, including social factors (women, slavery and religion), artistic and literary factors (literature, sculpture and architecture), intellectual developments (philosophy and education) and economic aspects of the societies. The Roman Empire provides one example of a united Europe, something relevant today, and you will discover how these civilisations influenced the Western world and still do today.

WHAT DO YOU STUDY?

OCR is the only exam board currently offering this subject as part of its suite of classics qualifications and the official title is now classics: ancient history. OCR's classics suite offers four named pathways (Latin, classical Greek, classical civilisation and ancient history) and in addition a new subject title, classics, where units can be chosen from at least two units from the classics suite and so combine studies. The AQA classical civilisation specification offers options in ancient history.

For AS you will study the following:

- Athenian democracy in the 5th century BC
- Delian League to Athenian Empire
- Politics and society of ancient Sparta
- Cicero and political life in late Republican Rome
- Augustus and the Principate
- Britain in the Roman Empire

A2 broadens your studies:

Greek history: conflict and culture

- A study of culture and conflict in the Greek world of the 5th century BC
- Greece and Persia 499-449 BC
- Greece in conflict 460-403 BC
- The culture of Athens 449-399 BC

Roman history: the use and abuse of power

- A study of the Roman world from the late Republic to the early Empire
- The fall of the Roman Republic 81-31 BC
- The invention of Imperial Rome 31 BC - AD 96
- Ruling the Roman Empire AD 14-117

There is a GCSE in ancient history and also one in classical civilisation, which will be a useful preparation for the subject, although not essential.

Latin or Greek can provide valuable background to the ancient history A level. All texts are studied in English, so you don't need any knowledge of Latin or Greek. A good English GCSE is sometimes required for this course.

> *'It's a fascinating era which demonstrates the roots of many modern concepts from toothpaste to socio-political empire to democracy. Well worth studying –can't recommend it enough.'*
> Melissa, aged 26, degree in ancient history and archaeology

HOW DO YOU STUDY?

You study through the interpretation and evaluation of original sources and archaeological evidence (such as Hadrian's Wall and other Roman remains) and visit relevant places such as the British Museum or archaeological sites. Much of the work for this subject consists of essay writing plus a lot of background reading. Examination is by written exam.

SUBJECT COMBINATIONS

If you plan to take a degree in ancient history, an ancient history A level is the best preparation. It is unlikely that you would be required to offer any other specific A level. If you wished to offer a classics A level combining elements of the other pathways (Latin, classical Greek or classical civilisation) this would also be acceptable. The combination of A level ancient history with Greek or Latin options would open up the option of a degree in subjects like politics, English, foreign languages and archaeology.

If you are taking ancient history with an archaeology degree in mind, it would be very useful to have a science subject at A level; you would be expected to have it at GCSE level. Occasionally a GCSE in a modern language is required, but otherwise any subject that demands similar research and essay-writing techniques will be useful. This would include subjects such as history, English, and government and politics.

It is possible to combine all A and AS levels with other equivalent qualifications such as BTEC Nationals and OCR Nationals and they could form part of Diplomas.

> 'Ancient history helped to shape the world today; it's just as important as learning about the two world wars and the industrial revolution.'
> Carmel, aged 17, studying A levels in ancient history, politics and ICT

HIGHER EDUCATION OPTIONS

Degree-level study

Ancient history degrees involve a first year spent developing general background knowledge about the subject, plus the basic skills needed to analyse and interpret historical data. You are not expected to have learned an ancient language at school but most courses allow you to learn Latin, Greek or even Egyptian or Sumerian. In the second and third year, courses include a broader range of topics, but may also allow specialisation in a specific area such as Greek, Roman, Egyptian or near eastern ancient history. You may be able to go on study trips to areas or countries relevant to your chosen subject.

Degree subject combinations

Many students at university combine ancient history with a related subject such as archaeology, classical studies, Egyptology, Greek, Latin or medieval studies.

It can be combined with other history specialisms such as medieval history, the history of ideas, or modern history. Each has a unique approach to the study of past societies and provides you with a wider perspective on your studies of ancient civilisations. Ancient history can be studied as part of a combined humanities programme or modular course. Subjects that look at political, cultural, religious and economic factors in human societies work especially well with ancient history. These include religious studies, philosophy, politics, anthropology, economic and social history, history of art, and modern languages.

Other higher education qualifications

There are no ancient history foundation degrees but there are related subjects such as history, heritage and archaeology, and practical archaeology, giving you a mixture of practical and theoretical work.

There are no HND/HNC courses in ancient history. (For information on related studies see the chapter on classical civilisation.)

Relevance to other subjects?

Ancient history has a number of related areas. Archaeology can be an ideal progression from ancient history A level. Medieval history and medieval studies focus on the origins and development of societies between about AD 400 and 1500. Celtic civilisation, Welsh, Irish and Scottish history cover the languages and cultures of the peoples who have lived in the British Isles since before the arrival of the Romans and Anglo-Saxons. Classical civilisation courses are often similar to ancient history but have a specific focus on Greece and Rome, and include more study of literature, usually in translation.

Courses in classics, Latin and Greek cover similar ground, but the literary and historical sources are studied in the original so much more time is spent on language work.

Important advice

Because A level ancient history is rarely a requirement for entry to an ancient history degree, choosing to study the subject demonstrates a genuine interest. This could play an important part in whether or not you are offered a place. Evidence of such interest can come from visiting sites of historic interest whenever you have the chance, getting involved in archaeological digs as a volunteer, and reading as much as you can about the subject in your spare time.

CAREER OPTIONS

Into work after A levels

As a student of A level ancient history, you will have gained skills in evaluating different types of evidence, placing them in context, and presenting them in a clear and balanced way. These are exactly the skills you need to work in areas such as management, sales and marketing. You might also want to consider jobs as a museum or library assistant.

Into work as a graduate

Working in ancient history

It is very unlikely that a degree in ancient history will lead to a career that will use your specialist knowledge to any great extent. For example, to teach the subject in schools you would need to be able to teach another subject as well, so you would need to consider a combined degree. Ancient history is clearly related to archaeology, but again there are specialist archaeology degrees, many of which involve an element of scientific analysis. To work as an archaeologist, therefore, you should aim either for a degree in archaeology or a combined degree in ancient history and archaeology. You might also wish to consider museum or archive work.

Working outside ancient history

The skills of an ancient historian – research, analysis and reasoning – are attractive to employers in many professions. Graduates in ancient history go on to careers in a wide range of areas including business, education and the media. Your research skills could also prove valuable for a career in law as an understanding of the systems of control used within classical civilisations (in particular, that of the Romans) is helpful in understanding the origins of our present-day legal system.

SOURCES OF INFORMATION

Council for British Archaeology
www.britarch.ac.uk

Institute of Archaeology
www.ucl.ac.uk/archaeology

Website

www.besthistorysites.net

Art and design

The visual world is a key aspect in many forms of communication. This course is for anyone who appreciates the visual world as it helps you develop an understanding of all things visual. You will learn traditional drawing and painting skills, new media techniques and also theoretical terms. You will be encouraged to look at a broad range of artists and to review your own work in relation to what you have studied. You will also learn to analyse your own work as a way of improving and developing it.

WHAT DO YOU STUDY?

The topics listed give an idea of what could be covered. The exact content of AS and A2 specifications differs according to exam boards, so you will need to check with your school or college about the exact modules available to you.

Painting and drawing are the core components of art and design A level, but you also study the following:

- how and why art works as a form of communication
- the forms and styles that such communication may take
- issues relating to light, colour, form, perspective and movement.

Options could include the following:

- fine art – traditional painting and drawing in oils, watercolour and other materials
- three-dimensional design – pottery and sculpture in clay, wood, stone and similar materials
- textile design – the design and creation of fabrics and clothing
- graphic communication – two-dimensional design for business, advertising and industry (company logos, trademarks and packaging, etc), as a way of communicating information and a company's image, often using IT-based techniques
- photography – the creation and use of photographic images

- film and video – including directing and editing
- critical and historical studies – looking at a range of artists both from the past and in the contemporary art world to encourage you to develop a greater understanding of the subject and help you look more critically at your own work.

It is recommended, but not essential, to have studied GCSE art to take art A level.

HOW DO YOU STUDY?

Art and design A level work is mainly practical although written work may feature in some assignments. You learn through practice either working on your own or in a group under the guidance of the teacher.

Practising your art and design skills is time consuming and you must be prepared to spend a lot of your own time in the studio. There will be coursework – a number of pieces to be completed during your studies – and practical exams, which involve supervised working over a set period of time. You will also go on visits to a range of art galleries and exhibitions to study art first hand.

'My art teacher was really helpful in recommending a foundation course that would suit my interests. He also made sure I worked hard to prepare a killer portfolio.'
Paul, currently on an art foundation course

SUBJECT COMBINATIONS

If you want to go on to a vocational art and design course the usual route is an A level in art and design plus an **art foundation course**. For more academic higher education courses such as art history, you will need one or two more A levels. If you are considering architecture or landscape architecture, you would need to choose maths or sciences to support your application. A level art and design may not be acceptable as an academic subject for entry to unrelated degree subjects, so you should always check with universities and colleges.

It is possible to combine all A and AS levels with other equivalent qualifications such as BTEC Nationals and OCR Nationals and they could form part of Diplomas.

HIGHER EDUCATION OPTIONS

Degree-level study

The normal route to a degree in art and design is through a one-year art foundation course. This can be taken at local colleges of art, many further education colleges and several universities. The purpose of the art Foundation course is to give you the opportunity to explore a greater range of work than is usually possible in schools and to help and support you in preparing a portfolio of work to support your degree course applications. It is designed to be diagnostic – that is, enabling you to explore the breadth of your interests and abilities within art and design, helping you make decisions about your future direction within the subject. To get onto a Foundation course, you normally need to have at least one A level, preferably in art and design.

Your portfolio also needs to be of a high standard, and your A level course is the best opportunity for building that up. Your portfolio will be reviewed at interview and needs to demonstrate your ability in:

- visualisation skills (e.g. drawing, photography, 3D work)
- research and investigative skills
- creative thinking and problem solving abilities
- the use of a range of materials and processes.

It should contain between 20 and 25 pieces of your recent art and design work.

Art and design degree courses range from courses in which you continue to work in a medium that you have already used, but more intensively, to specialist areas of art and design.

Courses can be grouped into four broad areas: fine art, graphic and lens-based media, fashion and textiles, and 3D design. Under these umbrella titles each course offers particular specialisms covering such areas as jewellery and silversmithing, ceramics, animation, illustration, TV and theatre set design, interior design, industrial design, textiles and many others.

In some areas, such as furniture, jewellery, fashion or textiles, you will learn methods and use materials that are completely new to you. Alternatively, if your interest in art is on the critical and analytical side rather than the practical and creative, you could consider a degree course in history of art.

Degree subject combinations

You can combine art and design with a wide range of other subjects, although this is more common on university courses rather than art college ones. If you are interested in combining subjects, look at the modular schemes run by many universities.

Other higher education qualifications

Not to be confused with the one-year art Foundation courses that prepare you for entry to higher education, foundation degrees are available in many specialist areas such as digital art and design, fine art, graphic communication, commercial fashion , 3D design, TV and film, interior design, garden and landscape design, and furniture making. They are a mixture of work-based experience and study.

HND and HNC courses are available in broad areas like art and design, and sustainable design, as well as specialist areas like games design, furniture design, product design and web design.

Relevance to other subjects?

As art and design A level can include such a wide range of subjects, materials and techniques, you will find it a valuable qualification for many other degree courses. Degree-level study in photography, media or cultural studies, drama (including stage, costume and lighting design), advertising and architecture can benefit from the experience that you have gained through A level art and design.

Important advice

If you want to find out more about studying art and/or design at a higher level, contact your local school of art and design and ask to go to a degree show, where you can see the sort of work that students produce. Degree shows are usually held in the summer term. Some art colleges run part-time classes (often on a Saturday) for A level students, and these can help you with portfolio building.

CAREER OPTIONS

Into work after A levels

There aren't many jobs where you can use your artistic knowledge and ability straight after A level. There could be jobs as juniors in design companies, especially in multimedia design (websites, games or DVDs), and you might consider working in retail display or merchandising (which includes window dressing and designing point-of-sale materials), interior design and styling, model making and producing props for film or the stage. Working as a photographer's assistant or in printing, in art galleries, for art dealers or in specialist art shops would also be possibilities. Apprenticeships may be available.

Into work as a graduate

Working in art and design

Many art and design graduates do find work related to their degree either in the UK or abroad. It is easier for design graduates, although it depends on the specialism. Graduates have to be prepared to freelance and build up their career gradually through networking and contacts, or move into a related design discipline.

Fine art graduates who want to work as fine artists often have to supplement their earnings from art by teaching or other part-time work.

There is also the opportunity for postgraduate study to learn additional specialist skills or crafts.

Art therapists help children or adults with disabilities, or who have suffered emotional or physical harm, to overcome their problems through work on artistic projects. This type of work requires further training.

Conservation/restoration work could be anything from paintings to books to furniture. Further training may be needed for this.

Fashion and textile designers are employed by fashion companies, or work for themselves, creating fabric and clothes designs for anyone from high-street stores to international designer fashion houses.

Graphic designers work in a variety of settings, designing logos for companies or events, through to web or computer games

> 'When you go into a design job you have to learn to work to a brief. You can be creative but you have to do what the customer wants.'
> Jane, graphic designer

design. They also work in publishing, creating the covers and page layouts of books, magazines and newspapers.

Product designers use their design skills in the creation of packaging and visual appearance of products from washing-up liquid bottles to chairs and cars.

Theatre, film and television designers work creating lighting plans for the stage, costumes for period dramas on television, and complete film sets.

Teachers need to undertake postgraduate training. There are a few postgraduate art teaching courses for primary schools as they are mainly for secondary teaching.

Working outside art and design

The ability to communicate visually makes you a good candidate for a career in advertising, marketing and public relations (PR). There may be opportunities within the film or television industries, although this is a very competitive field. Another possibility is arts administration, where you might be responsible for the running of galleries, theatre companies and buildings, and other arts organisations.

SOURCES OF INFORMATION

Chartered Society of Designers
www.csd.org.uk

Design Council
www.designcouncil.org.uk

Websites

www.bbc.co.uk/blast

www.creativepool.co.uk

www.ucas.com/students/beforeyouapply/artanddesign/foundationcourses (for a list of Foundation courses)

Critical and contextual studies in art

This art A level offers the opportunity to specialise in one or more of the following: the human form, landscape and natural forms, still life and designed objects, the built environment, machine age and abstract art, and contemporary media in art. The social, political, cultural and historical influences on art and design production are studied within the specialism. Progression routes are similar to those in art and design and applied art and design A levels. Assessment for this subject will include written work as well as an art portfolio, as written as well as visual analysis will be assessed.

Art and design (Applied)

Applied art and design gives you the opportunity to experience a wide range of different art, craft and design disciplines in 2D and 3D, and will give you a broad knowledge of this sector. You will be able to use and develop your own skills in art and design. You will learn how your creative skills and ideas can relate to and influence others, as well as how the art and design industry works in practice. You will have the opportunity to develop a portfolio of work and look at the industry and opportunities available within it.

This broad-based qualification encourages you to study in a practical way. It helps you to develop a range of vocational skills that will be useful to you either for higher level study or in work and training. This A level is available as a double (twelve-unit) award, an A with AS (nine-unit) award, or as a single (six-unit) award.

WHAT DO YOU STUDY?

The topics listed give an idea of what could be covered. The exact content of AS and A2 specifications differs according to exam boards, so you will need to check with your school or college about the exact modules available to you.

- **2D and 3D visual language** – you will develop your 2D visual language skills by practising working in different art, craft and design contexts. You will learn different techniques such as drawing, painting and printmaking as well as how to plan your time, record your work, use sources and analyse your work to improve its quality. You will develop your 3D visual language skills by practising working in different art, craft and design contexts including ceramics, jewellery, crafts, interior design and product design.

- **Materials, techniques and processes** – you will look at the properties of different materials and the techniques and processes used when working with them.

- **Working to set briefs, developing your own ideas** – this will help you to understand and use the creative process to meet a set brief in art, craft or design as you would do in the commercial world. This will involve researching and developing your own ideas as well as project management skills.

- **Professional practice and progression** – you will investigate current professional practice and how this relates to the development of your own work. You will also identify possible career paths.

- **Historical, contemporary and cultural references** – you will learn about a wide range of historical and contemporary work. You will carry out research and use the results as influences in your own work; this will involve visits to art galleries and building up your own visual collection of, for example, cuttings or postcards.

- **Visual communication and meaning** – this will help you to investigate the power of visual language and to develop your ability to use this to convey meanings, messages and information. This will include studying the use of symbols and signs such as logos.

> *'Graphic design isn't one job – it includes sales, finance and marketing – business skills are very important if you want to see your designs accepted.'*
> Jane, self employed graphic designer

- **Portfolio development** – you will develop a portfolio of work throughout the course, and in some specifications this is a separate module where you will present your portfolio formally.

Other specialist options may be available, such as those listed below. You will need to check with your school or college to see what is on offer. The award is designed so that you can specialise and take a particular pathway such as:

- graphic design, photography or textiles
- fine art
- fashion and textiles
- graphic design, lens-based media and multimedia
- decorative imagery
- spatial design
- public art
- drawing and painting, or printmaking.

HOW DO YOU STUDY?

The course is unit based and assessments are made throughout the year. The work is a mixture of assessed assignments set and marked by your teacher or lecturer, and some will be prepared for external assessment. There is a mixture of practical and creative work combined with research and coursework. Visits to galleries and museums are an important part of the course.

SUBJECT COMBINATIONS

For specialist art and design courses, an A level in art and design is a requirement. You also need one other A level. For example, art and design, together with English literature, theatre studies or drama, could help with applications for theatre design courses. Design and technology could be useful if you are considering product design, and ICT will be helpful as most designers use computer-aided design as a tool in their work.

If you are considering architecture or landscape architecture you would need to choose maths or sciences to support your application. A level art and design may not be acceptable as an academic subject for entry to unrelated degree subjects, so you should always check with universities and colleges.

It is possible to combine all A and AS levels with other equivalent qualifications such as BTEC Nationals or OCR Nationals and they could form part of Diplomas.

HIGHER EDUCATION OPTIONS

Degree-level study

If you are considering an art and design-based degree, universities and colleges usually require you to complete an art and design Foundation course before entry at degree level. You may have a strong idea as to what you will specialise in and if you do an art Foundation course this may confirm this or give you the chance to experience and choose another area of specialism. You will find a wide range of art and design degrees available. There are general courses, but most students choose a particular area. Examples of courses are fine art, graphic design, 3D design, fashion and textiles, history of art, industrial design, film photography and TV and multimedia design. A teaching degree (BEd) could be another option. Some courses now include a fourth year in which you can take a Master of Design (MDes) qualification.

Degree subject combinations

It is possible to combine art and design with other courses, especially if you consider modular degree schemes. These combinations are available at universities where a more academic approach is followed than in art colleges. At art colleges, specialised vocational art and design courses are available so there is little scope to combine the study of art with an unrelated subject.

Other higher education qualifications

Not to be confused with the one-year art Foundation courses that prepare you for entry to higher education, foundation degrees are available in many specialist areas such as digital art and design, fine art, graphic communication, commercial fashion, 3D design, TV and film, interior design, garden and landscape design, and furniture making. They are a mixture of work-based experience and study.

HND and HNC courses are available in broad areas like art and design and sustainable design as well as specialist areas like games design, furniture design, product design and web design.

Relevance to other subjects?

Applied art and design can include such a wide range of subjects, materials and techniques that it will be a valuable qualification for a range of other degree courses. Degree-level study in photography, media or cultural studies, drama (including stage, costume and lighting design), advertising and architecture are all possibilities.

Important advice

As many universities and colleges prefer applicants to have completed an art Foundation course, find out if these courses are available locally. Most students will take the Foundation course locally and study for a degree elsewhere.

Your art and design teacher or lecturer will be available to advise you on an appropriate

'I feel that this course really promotes independent working and really allows you to apply your own ideas and working style.' Gary, taking applied art and design A level with business

course for your talents. For all design-based courses, a portfolio of work will be required, so building up your portfolio should be a priority and should include work done outside of your course.

CAREER OPTIONS

(see also the entry for Art and design A level)

Into work after A levels

There aren't many openings directly related to art and design at this stage so further study may greatly increase your job prospects. It might be possible to get work in art and design areas such as photography, jewellery or printing, but it could mean going in at a junior level and you could find yourself competing with design graduates later on. There may be design-related Apprenticeships available.

As you will have learned valuable transferable skills on the course you would be able to go into many areas of work including business, finance or retail.

Into work as a graduate

Working in art and design

Depending on your degree, there will be opportunities in the design field and most graduates manage to find related work. For some design areas such as product design, you may have to look for work abroad. You may also have to start off as a freelance designer or on a short-term contract. Fine art graduates who want to become self-employed and sell their work will have to build up their business slowly, so may supplement their income by teaching.

There are opportunities as artistic directors and design managers as well as in teaching and related areas such as art therapy, for which further training is required.

Working outside art and design

There are plenty of job areas where an art and design training is useful, such as advertising, museum or retail work, and graduate training schemes in other areas would be open to you.

SOURCES OF INFORMATION

Chartered Society of Designers
www.csd.org.uk

Design Council
www.design-council.org.uk

Websites

www.bbc.co.uk/blast

www.creativepool.co.uk

www.ucas.com/students/beforeyouapply/
artanddesign/foundationcourses (for a list of
Foundation courses)

'It's not an easy option, you have to be in every day, but the day goes so quickly I think it's a 9-5 job.'
Fatima, art and design applied A level with design technology and maths

Biology

Biology is the study of the structure and behaviour of all forms of life – plant, animal and human. It covers a range of topics, from cell structure and microbiology, through human anatomy and health, to environmental problems, forensic science, ecology and biodiversity. You will explore basic scientific principles and also look at how advances in science have raised other challenges for scientists, society and the economy as a whole, for example, designer babies and carbon neutral fuel.

WHAT DO YOU STUDY?

The topics listed give an idea of what could be covered. The exact content of AS and A2 specifications differs according to exam boards, so you will need to check with your school or college about the exact modules available to you.

- **The variety of living organisms** – biodiversity, taxonomy (the classification of organisms into groups and types), populations and ecosystems (how groups of organisms relate to each other and their environment).

- **Development** – tissues and organs, cell ultra-structure, protein synthesis, molecules.

- **Continuity of life** – genetics and reproduction, chromosomes, DNA (the molecule that determines an organism's characteristics), RNA, meiosis, mitosis, protein synthesis, inheritance, natural selection, evolution including environmental factors, mutations, principles of gene therapy.

- **Energy** – respiration (how energy is released from food), ATP (transports chemical energy within cells for metabolism), glycolysis, exercise and the body, photosynthesis (how plants obtain energy from sunlight, carbon dioxide and water), nutrition and metabolism.

- **Response and control** – perception of the external environment (through sense organs), interpretation (nervous system, brain), response (muscle action, control of the heart and ventilation, hormone release) adaptation to change and homeostasis (how an organism regulates its internal environment).

- **Transport and exchange** – how nutrients and waste materials are moved around animals, including the roles of the heart, blood vessels, liver, kidneys and excretion, transport of water and nutrients in plants.

- **Examination of current issues** – this could be stem cell research and its implications, the Human Genome Project, applications of genetics, the ethics of animal testing, populations and environment, global warming, or ecosystems and biochemistry.

There could also be options in human biology, forensic science, environmental biology or mammalian physiology and behaviour.

Each specification involves learning the practical, experimental and research skills needed by scientists.

A good grade in biology or a double subject science GCSE is usually required. You will need to work with data and understand the chemical processes within organisms, so good grades in GCSE mathematics and chemistry are also important.

> *'Studying biology has been so interesting. The opportunity to go on field trips in Cornwall and the Bahamas has made it an unmissable experience!'*
> Francis, BSc biology student

HOW DO YOU STUDY?

Studying biology involves class and practical lab work. Practical work is vital for understanding the topics that you are studying and teaches you vital skills, which are tested as part of the assessment. Investigative skills are also important and are assessed. All courses require some independent project work as part of your course. Field work forms a crucial part of your studies in the form of day trips or residential field courses.

SUBJECT COMBINATIONS

Many biology students take mathematics, chemistry or physics especially if they are aiming for science-based degrees. Chemistry is required for some biology degrees, so you will need to check this. It is possible to study biology without traditional science subjects and it combines well with psychology, sociology, PE, science in society, health and social care, and critical thinking.

It is possible to combine all A and AS levels with other equivalent qualifications such as BTEC Nationals or OCR Nationals and they could form part of Diplomas.

HIGHER EDUCATION OPTIONS

There is a huge range of courses in biology and related subjects like biochemistry. A level biology is required for many of these courses. It can also be required or preferred for degrees like medicine, dentistry or veterinary science.

Degree-level study

Biology is a demanding scientific subject, so an analytical mind, competence in maths, laboratory skills and a good knowledge of chemistry and biology are all important.

A typical biology degree will cover a range of topics in the first and second years, such as cell and molecular biology, microbiology, physiology and adaptation, and genes and DNA. This will build on your A level study.

You usually specialise in the third year. You might study topics such as plant biotechnology, international health and disease, evolutionary biology, conservation ecology, cancer epidemiology or bioethics.

Again field trips will be an important part of the course, giving you the opportunity to study in the UK and abroad.

Whatever the degree title, the degree format is likely to be the same; a degree in marine biology, for example, will still cover the broad range of biology topics.

There are many specialist and applied biology degrees you could consider; look at degrees in anatomical sciences, biochemistry and genome science, bioinformatics, biomedical sciences, cell and molecular biology, developmental biology, ecology, environmental biology, exercise, nutrition and health, forensic biology, genetics, microbiology, molecular biology, neuroscience, parasitology, physiology, plant science, sports biology and zoology.

Degree subject combinations

Biology is available in combination with a wide range of subjects: in principle, virtually any possible combination of subjects can be studied on the larger modular schemes. Popular combinations are subjects like biochemistry, chemistry, geography and psychology.

Other higher education qualifications

Foundation degrees are available in biology and specialist areas such as applied science and technology, biomedical studies, marine biology and coastal zone management.

There are also related courses in animal management and welfare, countryside management, life science technology and bio-manufacturing, and veterinary nursing.

Biology HND and HNC courses emphasise the practical applications of biology for a career. Applied biology, applied bioscience, chemical biology and conservation biology are possible options at HND/HNC level. Some courses are more specialised, offering training for careers such as conservation and countryside management, horticulture and animal care.

Relevance to other subjects?

Biology A level is a good preparation for many related subjects at a higher level, and in many cases is required or preferred at least to AS level. Examples include medicine, veterinary science, dentistry, nursing, physiotherapy, microbiology, biochemistry, biotechnology, pharmacy and pharmacology.

Important advice

If you are considering a biology-based degree, you will need to check that you have the right A level subject choices, as many courses will ask for another science such as chemistry. If you are looking at a specialist degree in biology such as biomedical sciences, environmental or conservation biology, and forensic biology, make sure you research the content carefully, to make sure it is right for you.

CAREER OPTIONS

Into work after A levels

An A level in biology will give you a wide range of skills. Employers will like the fact that you are numerate, a clear logical thinker and a good researcher. Most biology-related jobs at this level require further training and Apprenticeships may be available.

Jobs related to your study could be as a

> *'I want to do sports science, so biology will help me a lot with my future career.'*
> Everald, aged 17, taking biology, physical education and business

laboratory technician or assistant, which could be working anywhere from a school to a university to a commercial research laboratory. Another possibility would be a dental technician (bridges, crowns etc) a dental surgery assistant or a pharmacy technician. The study of biology is a good preparation for work in the health service, including nurse training, and with care providers. You could enter part-time or full-time training at this level and possibly progress into nursing, paramedical careers or social work if you get the right qualifications.

Your skills with numbers would be a good preparation for careers in the financial sector.

Into work as a graduate

Working in biology

Research

This can be 'pure' (not carried out with a view to its immediate use) or 'applied'. Pure research is mostly based in universities and often starts with studying for a PhD (nearly a quarter of biology graduates do further study, i.e. PhD, MSc or MRes courses). University research posts beyond PhD level are usually on short-term contracts and are quite competitive. Applied research is also carried out in universities, although much is done in the pharmaceutical, food, medical and agrochemical industries, where you would study aspects of biology related to the design and development of particular products. Further study could take you to Europe or the USA.

Medicine

It is possibly for biology graduates to take a four-year graduate course to qualify in medicine. Entry is competitive and you may be required to have taken certain science A levels, even though you are a graduate. You will also have to sit a selection test.

Teaching

Another option where you can use your enthusiasm for your subject is to teach others. This could be in a primary or secondary school, college, university or teaching adults. There is a shortage of teachers so there are incentives for training.

Other work

There are opportunities for public sector work in the scientific Civil Service, public health, medical and veterinary laboratory work, forensic science and the National Health Service (NHS). There is also environment-related work, including consultancy in the private or public sector, pollution monitoring, environmental impact assessment and conservation work.

Working outside biology

Biology graduates have skills employers value such as the ability to think logically and being numerate and IT literate. Possibilities include the Civil Service, finance, management and the IT industry.

SOURCES OF INFORMATION

Biochemical Society
www.biochemistry.org

Society of Biology
www.societyofbiology.org

Institute of Biomedical Science
www.ibms.org

Websites

www.advancedbiology.org

www.biology4all.com

Human biology

Are you interested in how the human body works? Would you like a better working knowledge of your own body and how your lifestyle affects it? What about how humans interact with the environment and the research taking place in the fields of medicine, genetics and biotechnology?

The human biology A level covers biological molecules; cells; enzymes; blood and circulation; the control of breathing and heartbeat; energy and exercise; disease-causing organisms; defence against disease; mitosis, meiosis and the cell cycle; DNA and protein synthesis; genetic engineering; heart disease and cancer; diagnosis of disease; and drugs used to control and treat disease. You then go on to genetics and variation; photosynthesis and respiration; natural selection and evolution; sexual reproduction; the development of the foetus; growth; the digestive system; diet; transport of respiratory gases; the nervous system; muscles; homeostasis; senescence; and a study of ecosystems and the environment. Practical assignments are an important part of the course.

A level human biology is useful for a wide range of careers, including healthcare, sports and leisure, and complementary therapies. The course will help you to develop essential skills and knowledge of biological principles as they relate to human beings. If you are considering a degree in medicine, veterinary medicine or biology check to see if it is accepted. Sometimes biology is preferred as it is a broader course and some biology specifications cover human biology.

Business (Applied)

Applied business gives you an introduction and understanding of business. You will look at real businesses and markets, analysing business systems, proposing improvements to business activities and products, investigating the importance of financial forecasting and producing business plans. You will develop a wide range of skills and investigate the problems and opportunities faced by businesses. You will need to be motivated, resourceful and have plenty of ideas. You will also be able to plan ahead and find out what career path you might take.

This is a broad-based qualification that encourages you to study in a practical way. The course helps you to develop a range of vocational skills that will be useful to you either for higher level study or in work and training. This A level is available as a double or a single award.

WHAT DO YOU STUDY?

The topics listed give an idea of what could be covered. The exact content of AS and A2 specifications differs according to exam boards, so you will need to check with your school or college about the exact modules available to you.

Areas covered include the following.

- **Businesses and how they work** – how the whole business environment works and the different strands that come together to make it function effectively.

- **Management** – strategy and strategic decision-making, managing change, management structures and supervisory roles.

- **People in business** – how and why people work in business and what influences them to work. You will investigate how staff are recruited, trained and developed as well as managed.

- **Marketing and promotion** – how businesses look at potential markets and decide what customers need and want. This includes marketing aims and objectives, market research, writing marketing proposals, marketing communications and how products are developed and promoted, an investigation of promotional media, constraints on promotion and assessments of campaigns.

- **Customer service and meeting customer needs** – good customer service is a key factor in maintaining a successful business and you will explore the impact of customer service and the skills, knowledge and understanding required to deliver, monitor and improve customer service.

- **Financial strategies and business planning** – how businesses manage and review their finances and construct a financial strategy. This will include business planning, managing business activities, financial management and accounting, business development, financial providers and products.

- **Business communication, ICT systems and information management** – how IT systems are used in business

> *'My degree placement was in retail, which wasn't my first choice. I wasn't disappointed because I picked up lots of transferable skills that helped me find the job I'm in now.'*
> Carla, graduate trainee with a property developer after a degree in business management

to communicate, maintain records, ensure good customer service, review performance and plan ahead.

- **E-business** – launching a business online, investigating businesses on the web, websites for business.

Other options might include:

- understanding production in business
- running an enterprise activity
- career planning
- managing information
- production in business
- business law
- managing resources
- launching a new product or service in Europe
- managing risk in the workplace.

N.B. See also A level in business studies on page 46.

HOW DO YOU STUDY?

There is a mixture of practical work and tests, set assignments, research, case study work and work experience. Practical work will include exercises such as setting up a website or a business enterprise. You will use real examples of local businesses and services to underpin your projects. There may be study visits to conferences and local and national businesses, and even visits abroad to see how businesses operate in different countries.

SUBJECT COMBINATIONS

Applied business can be combined with other A and AS levels. You could consider subjects such as sociology, languages, economics, law, maths, psychology, and communication and culture. If you combine it with economics it may not be accepted for some business degrees because of the overlap so you will need to check this. Maths may be required for degrees in management science.

It is possible to combine all A and AS levels with other equivalent qualifications such as BTEC Nationals or OCR Nationals and they could form part of Diplomas.

HIGHER EDUCATION OPTIONS

There are hundreds of business and related courses available covering many options and specialisations. Business studies is a very popular course choice. Some courses are more mathematically based and admissions tutors may be looking for evidence of this at A or GCSE level.

Degree-level study

Courses are available in business studies, business administration and business management, and also elements of business such as accounting, business law or economics, marketing, e-commerce, technology, management enterprise or human resources. There are also courses specialising in one particular business area, for example agri-business, equine business, food marketing, maritime, retail, entertainment and tourism business management.

Many will offer sandwich placements to give you valuable work experience. Courses can also have an international slant such as European business management or international business and may include a placement abroad as well as the opportunity to study languages.

Degree subject combinations

There are many combinations available on both combined and modular courses, and business can be combined with most subjects. It combines well with related subjects such as accountancy, ICT or languages but is also available with subjects as different as chemistry or astrophysics.

Other higher education qualifications

Foundation degrees are available in business and business management and in specialist management areas such as finance and law, business IT and in specialised areas such as agri-business, automotive, culinary, beauty therapy and spa, dental practice, equine, golf operations, sports, tourism, music, and wine business management.

HND and HNC business studies courses are extremely popular and course titles include business and finance, business and marketing, and business and human resources. Courses are modular and offer a wide choice of options according to the institution. There are also specialist courses available including e-business, the music industry and countryside business management.

Relevance to other subjects?

Don't just look at degrees called business studies; there are many related degrees that you could investigate. Look at financial services, logistics and supply chain management, travel and tourism, or property development. You might find that you prefer a more specialised focus for your degree.

Important advice

There are thousands of business studies and related degrees, so it is very important to start researching possible degree courses as soon as you can. Some may have particular subject requirements such as maths or a modern language. If they are sector-focused courses such as retail, rural business or hotel management, it may be useful to get some relevant work experience to support your application.

> 'I really like the way you have to find out things for yourself on this course. It shows you can work independently.'
> Anne, A levels in applied business, IT and maths

CAREER OPTIONS

Into work after A levels

You will have learned valuable transferable skills on this course such as financial and IT skills, people skills and teamworking skills, as well as gaining a good insight into the business world. There would be opportunities in administration, accountancy, building societies, banks, the Civil Service, retail management and human resource departments. Some employers offer trainee schemes.

Into work as a graduate

Working in business

You will have gained a wide variety of skills and knowledge in important business areas such as business project management, problem solving and finance, which will open up opportunities with a wide range of employers in many sectors. You could enter a company in a particular department such as marketing, purchasing, sales or as a general management trainee. Some business studies graduates go into specialised training such as accountancy or management consultancy while others go on to postgraduate study in areas such as business, law and teaching.

Working outside business

You will have gained an understanding of many aspects of business as well as excellent communication and teamwork skills and the ability to analyse information. There are many careers where this will prove useful, such as retail or hospitality management, or you could consider general administration, for example in national or local government. Your skills could prove equally useful in IT, the police and the Armed Forces.

SOURCES OF INFORMATION

Chartered Management Institute (CMI)
www.managers.org.uk

Federation of Small Businesses
www.fsb.org.uk

Websites

www.bized.co.uk

www.peoplemanagement.co.uk

Business studies

A level business studies helps you to understand all about business today, both in the UK and internationally, using examples based on real business problems. The course helps you to understand the process by which a business makes its decisions by looking at the business's aims, the information it needs and the constraints under which it operates. You may have the opportunity to research into business problems and areas in which you are particularly interested.

WHAT DO YOU STUDY?

The topics listed give an idea of what could be covered. The exact content of AS and A2 specifications differs according to exam boards, so you will need to check with your school or college about the exact modules available to you.

- **Managing a business** – recruiting and managing staff, how to make your business successful and increase your profits, how to market your business and operations management, which includes technology and how to give your customers a great service.

- **The business environment** – planning and developing your business from your first idea to starting and developing your business including financial matters.

- **Managing change** – and the impact of economic, political, cultural and technological changes on your business and working in a global economy.

- **Strategic management** – effective strategies to improve your business and profits, have great employee relations and to make your business competitive.

- **International business** – how global businesses work and marketing businesses abroad.

- **Business functions** – accounting and finance, product development, advertising, pricing, business ratios, and profits and losses.

It is not essential to have studied the subject at GCSE in order to study A level business studies.

HOW DO YOU STUDY?

You will look at case studies and examples of business organisations, how they are structured, what they do, the problems they may have and suggested solutions to those problems. You may work on starting your own business. Some of the course will involve figure work, so even though you won't need any advanced maths, GCSE maths could be useful and learning how to use a calculator is definitely important. There will be visits to local, national and even international businesses and you may undertake some work shadowing.

N.B. See also A level in applied business on page 42.

SUBJECT COMBINATIONS

Some universities may not accept economics and business studies as two separate A levels. This is because they find the areas of study are too similar. You will need to find this out before you apply whatever course you are considering. Some higher level courses

> 'I enjoy business studies because it is relevant to the world we live in. It is a challenging subject involving theory but it is also very interesting.'
> Emma, aged17, A levels in business studies, maths and law

in business may specify certain subjects at A level. An A level in maths is required for a few degree courses, especially those entitled management science. GCSE maths is usually specified for degree level study.

Apart from that, business studies can be combined with almost any other A level subject. Modern languages are a good combination as learning a language can give you a great insight into a culture and from there how business works in that country.

It is possible to combine all A and AS levels with other equivalent qualifications such as BTEC Nationals or OCR Nationals and they could form part of Diplomas.

HIGHER EDUCATION OPTIONS

An A level in business studies is not essential for the study of the subject at a higher level, although it shows you are committed to the subject. Related work experience will obviously be useful for your application.

Degree-level study

You will find there are hundreds of degree courses in business studies and in related subjects, such as marketing and human resources. Many are very popular, attracting large numbers of applicants, although entry requirements vary widely.

The first degree to consider is a general business studies degree. This is likely to be multidisciplinary covering a broad range of subjects such as accounting, banking, finance, economics, management, marketing and entrepreneurship.

There are then degrees where you would specialise in one business function such as marketing, information technology or human resources. Some of these specialist degrees can exempt you from professional exams in, for example, accountancy or marketing.

Another choice of degree would be one that focuses on one type of business or industry, such as retail, hospitality, tourism or music management.

Some courses have an international slant with links to other countries such as the USA and Australia. As trade with China increases, there are courses in international Chinese business. There are now degrees in entrepreneurship and business enterprise so you could be the next big thing!

Degree subject combinations

Business studies can be combined with almost anything, but one of the most popular subjects is a modern language as this gives you added value with employers. Important business languages are French, German, Mandarin/Cantonese, Spanish, Polish, Russian, Arabic, Portuguese, Japanese and Korean. On these courses, you are likely to spend part of your course gaining work experience with a business in another country. This might be anywhere in the world and can provide a valuable insight into the way business is conducted in that country.

Other subjects such as psychology, politics, sociology and law can complement business studies by adding to your understanding of the environment in which business must function, as well as the people it employs. You will also find business studies in many engineering degrees, or may study engineering specifically from a management perspective.

Other higher education qualifications

Foundation degrees are available in business and business management and in specialist management areas such as finance and law, business IT and in specialised areas such as agri-business, automotive, culinary, beauty therapy and spa, dental practice, equine, golf operations, sports, tourism, music and wine business management.

HND and HNC business studies courses are extremely popular and course titles include business and finance, business and marketing, and business and human resources. Courses are modular and offer a wide choice of options according to the institution. There are also specialist courses available including e-business, the music industry and countryside business management.

Relevance to other subjects?

The business studies A level provides a good starting point for a degree in accountancy, financial services or management. Even if you do not wish to go on to take a business-related course you will have a good understanding of the business world, which could well prove useful to you in the future, especially if you go on to study subjects such as economics, law, media studies or politics.

Important advice

It is important to look closely at the contents of each business studies course that you are considering. You will find that some courses require a higher level of maths than others. Some courses are very competitive. To give yourself the edge over other applicants you should try to get as much relevant work experience as you can. This can range from a weekend retail job to working during your holidays in an office. This experience can help you to make good contacts, which could be useful later on if you wanted, for example, work experience on your degree course.

CAREER OPTIONS

Into work after A levels

A level business studies gives you a good idea of the careers available in business and shows employers that you have some relevant knowledge and interest. You could consider jobs in administration, accounts or trainee management. Retail companies such as supermarkets and department stores often recruit A level trainees or apprentices, as do some banks, building societies, insurance, IT, law and finance companies. As a trainee or apprentice, you could go on to get professional qualifications or even study for a degree later on.

Into work as a graduate

Working in business

Business studies graduates can go into a wide range of jobs, depending on the emphasis of their degree.

Administration – within a public or private organisation. This could include buying business IT and other equipment, creating a good working environment through facilities management, administering staff salaries, car fleets or business travel. In a small business you could well be doing all of this and more.

Advertising – working on behalf of clients to develop advertising campaigns for products from toothpaste to banking services.

Financial services – assessing the needs of individuals or companies in terms of investment, insurance, savings plans and pensions. You may be self-employed as a financial adviser or work for an organisation such as a bank, building society or investment company. You could also train to be an accountant. About 25% of business studies graduates go into a financial role.

Human resources – recruiting and training staff.

Management – this could be in general management or in a particular sector such as retail, or hotel and catering.

Marketing – identifying the potential market for a product or service and devising the most effective way of selling it.

Teaching or lecturing – in schools or colleges. With the increasing popularity of business studies A level and higher courses, there is an increasing demand for good teachers. However, you will need to gain practical business experience before you can teach it to others.

Working outside business

A business or management degree is very useful in almost any area of work, as you learn how organisations work and grow. Areas such as health, education and charities all value people with business skills and experience, and there is a wide range of opportunities available.

SOURCES OF INFORMATION

Economics and Business Education Association (EBEA)
www.ebea.org.uk

Website

www.thetimes100.co.uk

Economics and business

Economics and business A level combines elements of economics and business and is designed so that you will develop an understanding of economic and business theories and be able to apply them to a range of real-world issues. You will also learn how to make decisions using economic and business information, and how to appreciate economic and business issues from the perspectives of everybody involved including customers, managers, creditors, shareholders and employees. You learn how to analyse, explain and evaluate the strengths and weaknesses of the market economy in a wider context, including in international business. There is also an emphasis on enterprise and entrepreneurship.

'Business has opened my eyes to the financial world and, increasingly, I have become interested in reading newspapers and tracking the business world.'
Joseph, aged18, A levels in business studies, German and politics

Chemistry

Why does a mixture of hydrogen and oxygen explode and form water when you pass a spark through it? Why does copper sulphate change from white to blue when you add water? Why is mercury a liquid at room temperature? Chemistry will help you answer these questions and more. The answers come in the form of theories, which can be used to make predictions about other reactions. The predictions can be tested by experiment to find out whether the theory stands up.

Chemistry is everywhere in our lives . It encompasses the environment, with pollution control, recycling and the development of biodiesel. In industry you will find it in the development of new foodstuffs, synthetic materials and medicines.

In fact anyone studying chemistry has a difficult career choice because there are now so many possibilities.

WHAT DO YOU STUDY?

The topics listed give an idea of what could be covered. The exact content of AS and A2 specifications differs according to exam boards, so you will need to check with your school or college about the exact modules available to you.

- **Structure and bonding** – the structure of the atom, how atoms are joined together to make molecules, the periodic table, what happens when the bonds break and reform.

- **Physical chemistry** – what determines whether a possible chemical reaction actually takes place (energetics) and how quickly it happens (kinetics), the properties of gases, liquids and solids, and electrochemistry.

- **Organic chemistry** – the chemistry of carbon compounds, the variety and complexity that has allowed life to evolve (it is this connection with the chemistry of living organisms that gives this branch of chemistry its name).

- **Inorganic chemistry** – the chemistry of all the other elements and the ways that their properties are related to their position in the periodic table.

At A level you relate the chemistry you learn to industrial and medical applications and consider the environmental and social impact of chemistry.

There may also be options to study, for example, biochemistry, environmental chemistry or materials chemistry. Some courses have an emphasis on applied chemistry and how it is used in everyday life.

To survive into the next century we need to develop imaginative new sustainable technologies including new sources of energy, new efficient materials, recyclable devices and clever new molecular-based medical solutions. Legions of humanitarian contributions to society have come from the chemistry-based sciences from penicillin to sewage treatment, from shampoo to anaesthetics and from paints to liquid crystal displays. There can thus be little doubt that they will in the future make similarly revolutionary and beneficial contributions to the way we shall live. If the future is in anyone's hands it is in the hands of the next generation of ingenious young chemists.'
Professor Sir Harry Kroto, Nobel Laureate in chemistry

A level chemistry builds on and develops what you learned at GCSE, so you should have chemistry or combined science at grade C or above before starting the course. You will need to be confident in handling numbers, as chemistry uses many quantitative methods, so you should have GCSE mathematics at grade C or higher.

HOW DO YOU STUDY?

Chemistry is a practical subject so you will carry out your own experiments. The practicals give you real-life experience of what you are studying and teach you essential skills. You will also be involved in investigations that allow you to get into a topic in more detail than is possible in the usual laboratory work, and the investigative skills you learn doing this will be assessed. Most class work takes the form of information and notes presented by the teacher, discussion and examples to work through. This will be supported by presentations showing industrial processes and computer programs simulating experiments and processes that cannot be carried out in the school or college laboratory. You may go on industrial visits to see how chemistry is used in practice.

SUBJECT COMBINATIONS

Chemistry is an essential subject for some degree courses such as chemistry, chemical engineering, biochemistry, medicine, dentistry, pharmacy, pharmacology and veterinary science where it will need to be combined with maths or other science subjects. Combined with biology, it is very useful for any biological-related courses.

Studying chemistry can provide valuable support for a wide range of other subjects including physics, geology, environmental science and geography. It is a well-respected academic subject, regarded well by universities, so there is no reason why you couldn't combine chemistry with subjects such as economics, business studies, languages or any other. You would have to check that the combination is acceptable for the courses or careers you're aiming for.

It is possible to combine all A and AS levels with other equivalent qualifications such as BTEC Nationals or OCR Nationals and they could form part of Diplomas.

HIGHER EDUCATION OPTIONS

A good pass in A level chemistry (grades A*-C) is usually required to study chemistry at degree level.

Degree-level study

As well as courses simply called chemistry, there are many other closely related courses with titles such as chemical science, analytical chemistry, forensic chemistry, medicinal chemistry, applied chemistry, industrial chemistry, environmental chemistry and marine chemistry.

You might wish to look at subjects that don't have chemistry in the title such as cosmetic science, design and colour technology or molecular medicine.

Many chemistry courses provide an opportunity for a high degree of specialisation. You will find courses linked to universities in places such as Australia, Japan, Europe and the USA, offering a period of study overseas. Try to find out as much as you possibly can about the courses that interest you, and make sure you understand exactly what you'll be letting yourself in for.

Degree subject combinations

If you do not want to specialise in chemistry alone, you can combine it with other science subjects such as environmental science, nanotechnology, molecular medicine, pharmacology or forensic science. There are also specially designed degree programmes combining chemistry with non-science subjects, for example, modern languages, IT, law and business. Languages will be important if you will be studying or working in a non-English speaking country as part of your course.

Other higher education qualifications

Foundation degrees are available in applied chemistry, forensic science and chemical and pharmaceutical science. These are linked to degree courses if you wish to continue studying after the initial foundation degree.

HNC and HND courses in chemistry-related subjects are available. You could consider applied chemistry, forensic science, chemical and pharmaceutical science and related programmes, for example: chemical biology, agriculture, animal science, countryside management, environmental hazards or medicinal horticulture or horticulture. In institutions also offering degree courses, you can often transfer to the second or third year of the degree course after completing an HND.

Relevance to other subjects?

A related subject to investigate is chemical engineering. This looks at the development, design and operation of industrial chemical processes, such as the manufacture of synthetic fabrics, plastics and metal alloys. You would need to be taking maths and physics with chemistry to study this.

Pharmacy is another option and A levels should include chemistry and two others from biology, maths or physics.

Important advice

Chemistry is such a huge subject that no degree course can cover it all.

If you aren't sure which type of chemistry you want to specialise in then take a straight chemistry course to get a good grounding of the subject. You can then specialise later on, either in the later stages of a degree or at masters level. This allows you to keep your options open.

A number of companies are willing to sponsor students through degree courses in chemistry and chemical engineering. University chemistry departments will have details of these companies.

CAREER OPTIONS

Into work after A levels

The chemistry A level is highly regarded by employers and the knowledge and skills you will have gained will help you in virtually any career. However, if you wish to work within professional chemistry you will need to obtain some extra qualifications first, or your options may be limited. Other possibilities that would use your knowledge of chemistry include working as a laboratory assistant or technician, pharmacy technician, a dental or veterinary assistant, or a nurse, but you will need further training for these as well. Don't forget that Apprenticeships are a real option at this stage, offering the chance to work and study. They can lead to degree-level study.

Into work as a graduate

Working in chemistry

Most chemistry graduates work as professional chemists when they leave university. However, chemistry is a very large and highly developed subject, so you can only cover a small part of it in a degree course. This is why about 25% of chemistry graduates stay on after their degree to do further academic study or research for higher level qualifications.

There are many career options for the professional chemist, including the following:

- **research and development** – chemists work to develop processes for making new products such as plastics, drugs, fuel, pesticides, fertilisers, dyes and foods

- **production** – chemists are involved in planning the manufacture of products and in monitoring quality

- **support** – some chemists are employed to support research and production activities by searching technical papers for information and in writing patent specifications. They may also be involved in the selling and marketing of chemical products and in advising customers

- **technical writing and journalism** – there are opportunities in writing technical articles for scientific publications and journals, editing science books or websites, or writing more popular scientific articles for newspapers and magazines

- **Civil Service and local government** – chemists employed by government bodies monitor and advise on the safety of foodstuffs, water and environmental pollution, and chemical safety

- **forensic science** – chemists are employed by forensic science laboratories examining evidence relating to crimes

- **teaching** – chemistry is a shortage subject and there are incentives to train.

Working outside chemistry

A degree in chemistry is useful in many jobs not directly related to chemistry because chemistry graduates are numerate, have problem-solving, investigative and analytical skills, and good IT and communication skills, which will have been developed during the course of the degree.

Finance is a popular area and approximate 10% of chemistry graduates go into this type of work.

Chemistry graduates are also employed by local government, the Civil Service and in many areas of industry and business including marketing, sales and advertising; arts, design and sport; and social and welfare professions.

SOURCES OF INFORMATION

Chemical Industry Education Centre
www.ciec.org.uk

Royal Society of Chemistry
www.rsc.org

Websites

www.vega.org.uk

www.whynotchemeng.com

> *'Chemistry is a challenging A level but you learn so much. The range of techniques you have to be proficient in is enormous. One minute you are carrying out experiments in a lab, the next you are using computer software to design molecules with particular characteristics.'*
> Peter, aged 18, taking A levels in chemistry, maths and geography

Citizenship studies

What is a good citizen? How does our national identity develop? Why do so many people not vote? What rights do you have if you are stopped and searched by the police? How can you become involved and make a difference in your local community? If you have an interest in society, politics, community and equality then you'll enjoy citizenship studies. You study subjects such as justice, power, and law and order. Citizenship studies draws on aspects of geography, history and religious education and includes elements of economics and politics.

Being a good and active citizen involves responsibilities as well as rights and the course looks at these rights and responsibilities, how society works, and how to participate in the democratic process. You will be asked to look at issues from different points of view, learn how to advocate, negotiate, plan, make decisions and take action on citizenship issues. You will learn how to work with others as well as using problem-solving and critical approaches to the issues. A central theme running through the subject will be how individuals can influence the decision-making process at a local and national level. You may already have studied some aspects of citizenship, as it is a National Curriculum subject, so you will have some idea as to what is involved in this subject.

WHAT DO YOU STUDY?

AQA is currently the only exam board offering this specification at AS/A level.

- **What is the definition of a citizen?** What does it mean to be a British citizen in a diverse society? Prejudice and stereotyping; discrimination and disadvantage – how can government policy influence these?

- **Rights and responsibilities**. How they work in society, including information about the Human Rights Act, the Data Protection Act and the Freedom of Information Act.

- **Who can make a difference?** What is power and who holds it in the UK? How

> *'I think it is important to participate in society and this course helps you become more socially and politically aware. This is important for the future of UK politics.'*
> Sandi, aged 18, taking A levels in English, politics and citizenship

is the power of the media controlled? The different types of government, European, national and local, and how they have an impact on our lives. What is the democratic process and how can citizens bring about change both individually and together? How can citizens successfully campaign and how does this impact on political decision making.

- **Active citizenship**. You will be required to become an active citizen yourself and take part in a range of citizenship activities to demonstrate your knowledge and how you can bring about change while working alone or with others. You will complete an active citizenship profile as part of your course.

- **Crime, justice and punishment**. How crime is defined and how the criminal justice system works, including the role of the police and the courts. What is justice? Who makes decisions? How a jury works and what happens in miscarriages of justice. Sentences and the types of sentences available, and how they relate to different age groups.

- **Politics, power and participation**. Who speaks on our behalf? How we choose who represents us, how they are held to account and how they represent us.

- **How is the UK governed?** The power of Parliament, political parties and the prime minister. The impact of the EU and other international organisations, such as the UN and NATO. The global village and how citizens can have an impact.

- **Human rights**. How they are protected in the UK. Universal human rights, human rights abuses and what citizens can do to change things.

- **Global issues**. Conflict and how it can be resolved.

- **Trade and environmental issues**. The world economic system, globalisation, fair trade, poverty and industrialisation. How can citizens make a difference?

You don't need citizenship studies GCSE to take the AS/A level.

HOW DO YOU STUDY?

The subject is taught by a mixture of lessons, reading, essay writing and class discussion. You will study topical material from newspapers, the web, radio and TV. There will be visits to relevant places, which might include visiting your local council meetings or other local forums, magistrates and county courts or Parliament. You might organise or participate in a citizenship day at your school or college or help run a mock election. All examinations are by written papers, although you will prepare an active citizenship profile, which is taken into the exam. You will use the information in your citizenship profile to analyse and evaluate your own evidence and experience in response to the questions set.

SUBJECT COMBINATIONS

Citizenship studies combines well with government and politics, sociology, law, philosophy, business studies and economics. It will help you in any subject where you have to present or analyse reasoned arguments. World development could also be a good choice if you have an interest in global citizenship.

It is possible to combine all A and AS levels with other equivalent qualifications such as BTEC Nationals or OCR Nationals and they could form part of Diplomas.

HIGHER EDUCATION OPTIONS

Degree-level study

There are no single honours degrees in citizenship studies but you will find it covered in other courses like care, community and citizenship; community engagement and governance; community leadership; human rights; religion; culture and society; and social policy. There are also some combined degrees in law and citizenship and film and citizenship.

The emphasis of these courses varies, but all emphasise the importance of getting involved in your community and how every citizen should be empowered so they are able to make a difference locally and nationally.

Care, community and citizenship aims to give understanding of social welfare, exclusion and disadvantage. It provides an insight into the concept of citizenship together with knowledge of key statutory and voluntary welfare services for children and adults. A key part of the course is getting involved through placements and exchanges both in the UK and abroad.

Community engagement and governance develops skills, knowledge and confidence for working with local communities. The aim is to promote sustainable communities and effective governance and service delivery, responding to local needs through citizen empowerment and partnership working.

Human rights courses introduce students to debates over the nature, range, purpose and limits of human rights. They examine the recognition, revision and enforcement of human rights at domestic, European and international levels. All aspects of human rights are considered including the philosophical, sociological, political and legal aspects.

As citizenship is now part of the National Curriculum, there is a degree available in primary education (citizenship) and a PGCE in citizenship in secondary education.

Degree subject combinations

There are combinations available with law and film and you will also find combined honours and modular courses.

Other higher education qualifications

There are no foundation degrees with the title citizenship but you will find it included in foundation degrees in community engagement and governance, individual and community empowerment, police and community studies, community development and community governance and enterprise.

There are no related HNDs.

Relevance to other subjects?

You could look at courses in politics, sociology, police community studies, youth and community development, public administration, social welfare and politics.

Important advice

You will need to show some involvement in aspects of citizenship to prove you have an understanding of what these courses involve. This could mean getting involved with the school council, attending meetings on local issues, voluntary work, or sitting in the public gallery at council meetings. If you have already become involved and made a difference to your community then make sure this is included in your personal statement.

Make sure you check the degree course content to make sure that it covers what you want to study as the subject matter is so wide ranging.

CAREER OPTIONS

Into work after A levels

You might consider any sort of work in your local community, which could include the local authority or paid work with voluntary organisations. You will have an understanding of how courts work so could look at opportunities there as well as with organisations such as the police, Civil Service or the National Health Service.

Into work as a graduate

Courses with an emphasis on citizenship could lead to careers in the public and volunteering sectors, including community and youth work, outreach and advocacy, charities, local or national government. You might also wish to pursue a career in law, working for campaigning organisations, social movements or in political lobbying.

There is a PGCE in citizenship education. This is part of the secondary curriculum, so there is a demand for specialist citizenship teachers. Citizenship is also included in primary level teaching training.

You will have developed skills to communicate and articulate different views, advocate, negotiate, plan and make decisions. You will have been taught to select, interpret, analyse and evaluate information, to construct reasoned and coherent arguments, propose alternative solutions and form conclusions. In addition you will be able to work with others, using problem-solving and critical approaches to the issues, problems and events.

You could consider postgraduate study to become a social worker or in law. With all these skills you will have a wide range of options including human resources and marketing.

SOURCES OF INFORMATION

The Citizenship Foundation
www.citizenshipfoundation.org.uk

Citizen X
www.bbc.co.uk/schools/citizenx

'Citizenship has given me an insight into the justice system, politics and so on. I now have an increased knowledge and confidence to talk or debate about these things and other current affairs.'
Omar, aged 18, taking A levels in business, law and citizenship

Classical civilisation

The classical civilisation A level is designed for students with an interest in classical studies, but who do not necessarily want to learn Latin or ancient/classical Greek. The period covered is Greek and Roman civilisation, from about 1500 BC to about AD 450. The specification covers all aspects of classical civilisation and allows for specialisation in different areas. You have the opportunity to study architecture, archaeology, art, history, politics, literature and philosophy.

WHAT DO YOU STUDY?

The topics listed give an idea of what could be covered. The exact content of AS and A2 specifications differs according to exam boards, so you will need to check with your school or college about the exact modules available to you.

OCR offers this subject as part of its suite of classics qualifications and the official title is now classics: classical civilisation. OCR's classics suite offers four named pathways (Latin, classical Greek, classical civilisation and ancient history) and in addition a classics AS/A level, where units can be chosen from at least two units from the classics suite and so combine studies. AQA also offers classical civilisation.

The examination boards offer the opportunity to study topics such as:

- **the Homeric epics** – the Iliad and the Odyssey
- **Greek tragedy** – plays dramatising the frailty of human success and its dependence on fortune by Aeschylus, Sophocles, Euripides; Greek comedy such as Aristophanes and Menander

> *'Knowledge of our classical heritage is invaluable to anyone trying to understand culture in the 21st century.'*
> Gregory, taking a degree in history with A levels in classical civilisation, government and politics and history

- **Roman society and history** – through a study of Roman literature (Pliny's Letters and examples of satire from Horace, Petronius and Juvenal Virgil's Aeneid) and its context
- **ancient philosophy** – values and politics, especially Plato's Republic
- **archaeology** – looking at important sites and what they tell us about the civilisation
- **archaeological methodology** – the principles and practices
- **Roman architecture and town planning**
- **Greek architecture and sculpture**
- **Greek historians** – historical texts by Thucydides, Herodotus and Plutarch
- **city life in Roman Italy** – the cities of Pompeii, Herculaneum and Ostia in their social, cultural, political and historical contexts
- **Athenian democracy**
- **Athenian vase painting**
- **Athenian imperialism**
- **Socrates and Athens**
- **Aristophanes and Athens**
- **the life and times of Cicero**
- **the Persian wars**
- **Augustus and the foundation of the Principate**
- **Alexander**
- **Tiberius and Claudius**

- **The Second Punic War**
- **Mycenaean civilisation**.

You might also study themes such as women in Athens and Rome. You will be encouraged to make comparisons between the classical world and the world of today. The exact subjects you study will be chosen by your institution. You do not need any previous experience of studying the ancient world or its languages in order to study classical civilisation A level.

You do not need classical civilisation GCSE to study the subject at A level.

HOW DO YOU STUDY?

You study translations of the literature of ancient Greece and Rome and descriptive works on topics such as art and architecture. Most of the work is essay based, and you will need to do additional reading beyond the prescribed lists. You might visit relevant places such as Bath, the Ashmolean Museum in Oxford and the British Museum in London or go to see some classical plays. There may be the opportunity to go on a study trip to Greece or Rome.

Knowledge of ancient Greek and Latin is not required but some students become interested in these languages and some schools and colleges may be able to offer the languages from scratch. The OCR classics specification offers this language option if available within your institution.

SUBJECT COMBINATIONS

Some classics degrees require an A level in Latin or ancient Greek, and others will accept a modern language as evidence of your language skills and learning ability. Classical civilisation can be combined with most other A level subjects, particularly those where essay writing and textual analysis are involved. Examples of these are English, communication and culture, theatre studies,

history of art, media studies, religious studies and philosophy. It is a useful A level for archaeology degrees (although may need to be combined with a science subject at A level for some courses). Art, government and politics, and history are also popular combinations.

If you want to study classical civilisation with ancient history, check with universities for their entrance requirements. They may not be accepted together because of the possible overlap in content.

It is possible to combine all A and AS levels with other equivalent qualifications such as BTEC Nationals or OCR Nationals and they could form part of Diplomas.

HIGHER EDUCATION OPTIONS

Degree-level study

At degree level, you may have the option of starting a classical language if you have not done so already. Some degrees with the title classical civilisation or classical studies require you to spend some time on language work, while on others it is an option or available as a minor. Many of these degrees are open to students who have not taken classical civilisation or any classics subject at A level. However, an A level in a classical subject does demonstrate an interest in and commitment to the subject. In contrast, degrees called classics, Latin or ancient Greek all involve the study of one or both languages. You may be able to start one of the languages (although not usually both) from scratch at university.

Degrees in classical civilisation cover a broad range of topics (look also for classical studies, classical past, or ancient world studies courses). They include the philosophy, art, literature, religion, history, drama, science and archaeology of ancient Greece and Rome.

The classical civilisation A level would be a good preparation for a degree in archaeology (some courses concentrate on classical

'After seeing the film 'Gladiator' I became really interested in Roman history. It was really fascinating to be able to study it and see how it influences us today.'
Jack, aged 18, taking A levels in maths, business studies and classical civilisation

archaeology) or related courses, like classical archaeology .

Classical civilisation is often a preferred A level for ancient history degrees.

(For information on degrees in classics, Latin and ancient Greek, see the entry for Greek (classical)/Latin.)

Degree subject combinations

Classical civilisation or classical studies form a part of many combined degree and modular degree programmes, which may include related subjects such as ancient history, classical languages, Greek and Roman civilisation, Byzantine studies, classical literature and archaeology. You will also find combinations with a wide range of related humanities or social science subjects, which require similar techniques of research and analysis of evidence. Possibilities include modern history, English, religious studies, philosophy, politics and history of art.

Other higher education qualifications

There are no foundation degrees in classical civilisation, but related subjects available include history, heritage and archaeology, and practical archaeology. There are no HND or HNC courses in classical civilisation.

Relevance to other subjects?

A level classical civilisation is worth considering, even if you are not thinking of continuing it beyond A level. The ancient world has helped to shape the culture and civilisation of Europe, its languages, literature,

history, art and political structures. Classical civilisation is a good introduction to that world, and so is a useful A level qualification for many humanities degrees. Subjects such as English, history, history of art, drama, religious studies, modern languages and philosophy all greatly benefit from a knowledge and understanding of classical civilisations.

Important advice

Your chances of being accepted onto a higher education course in classical civilisation or a related subject will be improved if you can get some first-hand knowledge of the subject. You can get this by visiting museums and sites of historical importance, going on archaeological digs or excavations, reading related material in your spare time and generally being as active in your interest as you possibly can. Remember that you may have to pay something towards going on an archaeological dig.

CAREER OPTIONS

Into work after A levels

An A level in classical civilisation would provide you with a respected qualification for a wide range of careers. Even if there are few jobs that could immediately make use of what you have learned, the skills developed while studying the subject will be useful to you. These skills would include the ability to do research, analyse what you have found, reach an understanding about the people and society that you are studying, and argue your point, both in writing and verbally.

Into work as a graduate

Working in classical civilisation

It is unlikely that a degree in classical civilisation will lead to a career that will use your special knowledge to any great extent, unless you decide to become a teacher or lecturer. Classical civilisation is related to archaeology but remember that there are specialist archaeology degrees, many of which involve an element of scientific analysis, so to become an archaeologist you should aim for a degree in archaeology. Some opportunities may be available in museum work, exhibition design, library or archive work, but you will be in competition with graduates in ancient history or archaeology. Postgraduate study in a subject like museum information or archive studies might be worth considering to make you more marketable.

Working outside classical civilisation

Don't let the limited opportunities for using classical knowledge put you off a degree in classical civilisation. Remember that a large proportion of graduate jobs are open to graduates in any subject. For example, you will be as well placed as any graduate to work in local government, administration in business or the public sector, management, insurance and financial services. You can consider entering training and further study to become a lawyer or an accountant or consider jobs in the media or IT.

SOURCES OF INFORMATION

Council for British Archaeology
www.britarch.ac.uk

Website

www.classicspage.com

Communication and culture

Communication and culture is all about how we communicate in today's world and you start by looking at your own forms of communication within your culture.

Have you got a mobile phone or MP3 player? Are they important to you and why? Do these cultural objects tell us anything about ourselves and the way we relate to others? Do people communicate in a different way using Facebook or Bebo, texting and twittering? Does this alter our behaviour? Does our spoken and body language change according to which group of people we are with? All these are forms of communication and shape our lives and our identities. Through this course you will develop your own communication skills and a sense of your own identity in the world. You will also look at our modern culture and topics like the cult of celebrity and body modification.

WHAT DO YOU STUDY?

AQA is the only exam board currently offering communication and culture.

What do we mean by communication? You look at how you communicate and how this gives you a sense of who you are.

In looking at how you communicate, you investigate the importance of non-verbal communication: the impact that your body language can have in conveying information about yourself and how you can use this to your advantage.

This links closely with group identity: how do we change ourselves to fit into various groups in society, how do we manipulate group situations and develop leadership skills, and how is this significant in shaping our identity?

Identity is a key word throughout the course and links closely with an examination of the nature of culture. What is it that defines us, not just as an individual but as a member of a particular cultural group?

You will examine the differences between high and popular culture and the reasons why different values are placed on different cultural products and practices; for example: is skateboarding better than rugby?

You then develop understanding of these ideas by preparing a portfolio of investigations, explorations and a presentation with a choice of topics.

Examples of topics are:

- **clothes make the person**: to what extent are we what we wear?

- **speak that I might see you**: the relationship between personal language use (idiolect) and personal identity

- **good taste/bad taste**: in what ways are we defined by what we like?

- **in my room**: personal places and their wider cultural significance

- **'don't forget the songs that saved your life'**: popular music as cultural communication

- **retail therapy?** explore the meanings of shopping.

In A2 you will investigate and discuss theories such as feminism, Marxism, post-colonialism,

> *'You start to look at how we are influenced by culture and you really start to examine what you say and how you behave. It's got a lot of psychology in it.'*
> Jo, aged 18, studying A levels in communication studies, ICT, French and business applied

post-structuralism, queer theory and post-modernism. This helps you to analyse how society's values and beliefs help define our identities and sense of self.

You will undertake a close study of a modern cultural topic in order to explore and apply theoretical approaches and key concepts of communication and culture.

Examples are:

- **spaces and places** – the constructed environment of town and cityscapes, the countryside, shopping malls and holiday destinations. The property market and the association of desirable 'lifestyles' with particular buildings or places, think of *Location, Location, Location*

- **fictions** – the 'stories' that make up our culture in the form of plays, novels, films, exhibitions, displays, computer games, cyberspace and virtual worlds like 'second life'. The association of desirable identities with objects in advertising and promotion. Product placement, 'spin-offs' and merchandising based on fictional texts

- **objects of desire** – the products that we may covet or cherish, such as particular brands of mobile phones or MP3 players, and that symbolise important aspects of different cultures. This is the study of how culture invests things with meanings.

You will then look at communication and culture in practice.

You will work on an independent project, consisting of a case study and a presentation.

Examples of topics for the case study are:

- body modification
- celebrity
- cinema-going
- holiday.

Your presentation must be a web-based presentation. This will be in the form of a website, multimedia, PowerPoint style presentation or a podcast.

'My degree was so vocational. It teaches you all about different forms of communication and how to get your message across. It has set me up for my current job and future career.'
Brendan, press officer with a degree in communication studies

HOW DO YOU STUDY?

There is a mixture of exams, practical coursework and group discussions. There could be field trips to contemporary shows linked to the course content and also study visits to places like the Tate Modern and other contemporary galleries.

You may get the opportunity to attend additional practical skills classes in presentations, web design and film making to support your work. This could lead to additional qualifications.

SUBJECT COMBINATIONS

Since communication is so central to our everyday lives, the course naturally links with aspects of other subjects like English language, English literature, media, film studies, languages, psychology, art, photography, health and social care, ICT, business studies, government and politics, sociology or theatre studies.

It is possible to combine all A and AS levels with other equivalent qualifications such as BTEC Nationals or OCR Nationals and they could form part of Diplomas.

HIGHER EDUCATION OPTIONS

The content of communication studies degrees can vary, covering a wide range of disciplines including psychology, linguistics, sociology, new media and media studies. Some degrees include placements in the communications industry. You could also consider courses such as cultural and media studies.

Degree-level study

Communications degrees are usually broad-based academic degree programmes aimed at those who are interested in communications or the media, but who don't want to specialise yet. You will find many degrees in media communications and culture, and also cultural studies.

Degree subject combinations

Communication studies combines with many subjects and you could look at closely related areas such as journalism, media studies and new media. You could also consider combining with languages, business, sociology, information technology or psychology.

Other higher education qualifications

There are foundation degrees in communication and cultural studies and also many in related areas such as broadcast media, interactive media, multimedia design, TV and film production, media production and digital media arts.

HNDs and HNCs could include media and communication, journalism and media, and communication.

Relevance to other subjects?

Communication studies courses contain some aspects of media studies, cultural studies, psychology, sociology and English language, so have a look at these courses and compare their contents.

Important advice

Think about which aspect of communications studies interests you and examine the courses carefully. Think about what you want out of a course.

If you are considering a career in the media/communications industry, any relevant work experience can help you to build up a portfolio that could prove useful in the future.

CAREER OPTIONS

Into work after A levels

The communication and culture A level will give you skills in communication and the ability to examine and analyse issues. These skills could help you in a wide range of careers such as business, administration, media, sales, retail and ICT.

Into work as a graduate

Working in communications

A communication studies degree can open up career opportunities in areas such as public relations, advertising, marketing, arts administration, broadcast and print journalism, broadcasting, communications consultancy, internet communications, media production, publishing, arts management, advertising, new media technologies and communication therapy. For some of these careers additional study and training are required. (See also career options after English and media courses.)

Working outside communications

You will have gained presentation, communication and analytical skills, which can be useful in whichever field you are aiming for, so you could look at careers in management and administration in a wide range of business areas. Your communication skills could be useful in jobs such as personnel or human resources, social work, counselling and teaching. Careers such as librarianship and information management are also possibilities.

SOURCES OF INFORMATION

Skillset
www.skillset.org

Websites

www.communicationandculture.co.uk

www.aber.ac.uk/media (the media and communication studies site)

Computing

Computers are an essential feature of 21st century life, controlling daily activities such as transport, medicine, banking and retailing. This course aims to encourage you to develop an understanding of the main principles of solving problems using computers – programming in a range of languages – and of the range of applications of computers and the effects of their use. You will develop an understanding of the organisation of computer systems, including software, data, hardware, communications and networks. You will also acquire the skills necessary to apply this understanding to developing computer-based solutions to problems.

See also ICT and ICT (Applied) A levels, which are concerned with the applied use of software and applications. The computing A level is more concerned with computer science.

WHAT DO YOU STUDY?

The topics listed give an idea of what could be covered. The exact content of AS and A2 specifications differs according to exam boards, so you will need to check with your school or college about the exact modules available to you.

- **Hardware** – the computer and its peripherals.

- **Software and systems** – the software 'life-cycle', from identification of requirements and problem analysis, through design and implementation, to improvement and eventually obsolescence; hardware use and design.

- **Operating systems and programming** – why operating systems are necessary and how they work.

- **Software engineering** – different types of programs available for different purposes. Designing solutions to particular problems, how procedural programs are structured, the types of data and data structures, the common facilities of procedural languages, how to write maintainable programs, and how to test and run solutions. Programming languages such as Pascal, PHP, VB, C#, Java, Python or C.

- **Data** – the presentation, structure and management of data, files and processing; database design, data security, SQL.

- **Communication and networking** – communication methods, serial data transmission, parallel data transmission, handshaking, protocol, baseband, broadband, local area networks (LAN), wide area networks (WAN), which include the web, wireless networking, Wi-Fi and Bluetooth.

- **Implications** – the impact of computing on individuals, organisations, the economy and society.

There are also software development and testing exercises and projects.

You do not need a GCSE in computing or IT to study computing at A level, but if you do this will help you with your studies.

You would be expected to have some experience and interest in using computers. You don't have to be a brilliant mathematician for this course but success in GCSE maths can show an aptitude for the more technical side of computing. English will also be very useful.

> 'My degree had a placement year, which was a fantastic opportunity to get a taste of the business world. I found it a very rewarding experience and would recommend it. The year out reinforced the skills I'd learned on my course.'
> Dee, BSc software engineering

HOW DO YOU STUDY?

You will learn by analysing case studies and developing IT-based solutions for them. There will also be practical projects based on real-life problems where you will document a design to solve a problem along with the analysis, design, construction, testing, training and maintenance of a programmed solution. You may also visit companies to see how their computer systems work, for example a travel company to see booking systems or a theme park to see how control systems are used in the management of the rides.

Some specifications include 'on-screen' exams – so no paper and pencils required!

SUBJECT COMBINATIONS

A level mathematics and sometimes further maths is a requirement for some computer science degrees, and physics is an essential preparation for some of the more hardware-orientated courses, so you may want to consider these.

Even if you do not plan to go into a computing degree, you will find that computing is a valuable A level in combination with many others. It could be taken alongside A levels suitable for careers in medicine, law, business, politics or any type of science. Your ability to manipulate and manage information in a logical manner will prove invaluable when it comes to project work, note taking, essay writing and revision in any other subject.

It is possible to combine all A and AS levels with other equivalent qualifications such as BTEC Nationals or OCR Nationals and they could form part of Diplomas.

HIGHER EDUCATION OPTIONS

Computing A level is not essential for entry to computer-related courses at a higher level, although mathematics and science subjects are sometimes required.

Degree-level study

There is a huge variety of computer-related degree courses. You should never read too much into a course title without checking but, in general, courses called computer science are more likely to have a theoretical bias. You may find yourself looking into the formal and mathematical foundations of computing, as well as learning how to design and write complex programs in high-level and low-level languages. Courses called computer studies are more likely to focus on the applications of computing. Courses simply called computing can fall into either category. Course titles are changing all the time as the industry develops, and you will find courses in computer science (games) and internet computing. There is also an intriguing new course in digital forensics.

In addition, there are engineering-focused courses dealing with, for example, robotics and cybertronics, computer systems engineering and network engineering. There are also specialised degrees in artificial intelligence. In this field, computers are used to do the complex things normally associated with human intelligence, such as planning, making decisions, understanding language, and recognising places and people. Many degrees are sandwich courses, in which you spend some time in industry, with placements abroad often available.

Degree subject combinations

Many students combine computing with business studies or management, either as separate subjects or on a course specially designed to bring the two together (as in degrees called business computing, or business information systems, for example). Computing is included in most combined studies programmes, allowing you to combine it with almost any other subject. Mathematics is the most widely available combination, closely followed by statistics, business studies/accounting, psychology, physics and languages.

Other higher education qualifications

Foundation degrees are available in computing, applied computing and in related areas such as computer networking, system support, information systems design, interactive computing, internet technologies, business computing, computer aided design, software applications development, multimedia and computer games design.

HND and HNC courses are available with different specialisations. They prepare students to be able to design and implement a wide range of computer applications in a variety of business and industrial environments. The focus is on the technical and personal skills required for a career in computing. Practical work is in the form of projects linked to industrial and commercial problems and includes work experience.

The HND courses available include: computer science, computing, computing systems security, computing technology, software engineering, mobile computing and network management, and security and computer networking.

Relevance to other subjects?

You will find your understanding of computing useful whatever you study, and in some subjects it will be extremely relevant. It is especially important for business courses and all science and engineering courses which involve computers for control, data collection and statistical analysis of results.

Important advice

Some prospectuses give quite detailed information on the computing facilities provided, but it is also a good idea to attend open days, to find out first hand what is available. It is also useful to find out what happens to graduates from courses in which you are interested, so that you can see if this is the direction you want to take.

CAREER OPTIONS

Into work after A levels

Having studied computing at A level, you will be a valuable asset to any employer. There will be some Apprenticeships and trainee jobs available in the computing industry but your skills and knowledge could prove useful in many business, financial and technical careers.

Into work as a graduate

Working in computing

Depending on your area of specialisation at degree level, you will find a great deal of choice in potential careers. However, many will require some further training and some graduates progress onto masters courses.

The main areas of work open to a graduate are as follows:

- **account manager** – acts as the interface between ICT and the users or customer, advising on the best solutions for different types of application
- **software engineer** – specifies, develops, documents and maintains computer software programs in order to meet client or employer needs
- **database administrator** – responsible for the usage, accuracy, efficiency,

security, maintenance and development of computerised databases

- **applications developer** – writes and modifies programs to enable a computer to carry out specific tasks, such as stock control or payroll, typically for technical, commercial and business users

- **systems operator (technical support)** – takes the specification for the requirements of a computer system and designs the system including hardware, software, communications, installation, testing and maintenance

- **systems developer** – sets up the computer operating systems and standard software services essential to the operation of any computer

- **information technology consultant** – gives independent and objective advice on how best to use information technology to solve business problems. The work includes analysing problems, making recommendations and implementing new systems

- **computer virus expert** – works in a virus lab, identifying, unravelling and fixing computer viruses. A thorough knowledge of programming and applications is required for this

- **network engineer** – responsible for the management of a computer network. This will include software installation and configuration, upgrades, diagnostics and troubleshooting.

Working outside computing

Computing graduates working outside the computing industry or specialist IT departments can put their skills and knowledge to work in business, administration or finance. All businesses need a good knowledge and understanding of computers among their general management staff. As a computing graduate you could consider management training schemes in many different organisations.

SOURCES OF INFORMATION

BCS, The Chartered Institute for IT
www.bcs.org

e-skills UK
www.e-skills.com

'I have enjoyed my course so far, it's exactly what I thought it would be. Make sure your course is accredited by BCS, The Chartered Institute for IT, as it gives you a bit more street cred.'
Matthew, on BSc computer science

Critical thinking

Do you believe everything you see on TV or find on the web? Do you think that all politicians are telling the whole truth? What are the arguments for and against euthanasia? Can you argue your point of view calmly, sensibly and logically? Or do you get all emotional and start shouting instead?

Critical thinking is different from other subjects at A level because it is less about learning material and more about developing and applying explanatory, analytical and evaluative skills. It goes very well with other A level subjects because the skills you develop in critical thinking can help you to do well in those too.

You learn to analyse and evaluate ideas and arguments and how to construct clear, logical and coherent lines of reasoning. A good critical thinking student will have an interest in developing skills for devising logical, coherent arguments and will want to improve their analytical skills – useful in subjects as diverse as English literature, history, psychology and chemistry. You should want to make your mind up about the plausibility of various styles of argument and enjoy engaging in reasoned discussion. The course will help you to develop your communication skills and you will be able to influence people with sound reasoning, but at the same time listen to and value their views. It will help you to use and analyse information from different sources and become a problem solver who can make reasoned decisions, based on evidence.

WHAT DO YOU STUDY?

The topics listed give an idea of what could be covered. The exact content of AS and A2 specifications differs according to exam boards, so you will need to check with your school or college about the exact modules available to you.

You start with an introduction to the concepts, principles and techniques that underlie critical thinking, and then expand their application to a range of contexts. You need to be able to identity the difference between argument and explanation, the different types of reasoning used to construct an argument and how conclusions are drawn. You may learn how to use statistics to back up your arguments.

You will learn how to recognise the language of reasoning, be able to analyse other people's arguments, spot the assumptions and flaws in their reasoning, and evaluate the strength and effectiveness of reasoned arguments. You will discuss and debate topical issues,

construct your own arguments with logic and clarity, and learn transferable thinking skills that will help you with your other subjects.

You then go on to apply your critical skills to the evaluation of beliefs, knowledge claims and hypotheses, and develop skills of logic and decision making.

At the end of the course you should be able to express your opinions about the things that are important to you; question, consider and argue against views that oppose your own; and learn how to use calm, persuasive argument to express those views clearly.

HOW DO YOU STUDY?

The course is mainly skills based, and you will undertake a range of class-based activities. You will look at various sources including books, newspapers, magazines, radio, television, advertising materials and the web. You may look at other data such as statistics and the way that they are interpreted and used. You will take part in debates and discuss a wide range of topical issues, which could be national, international or local issues, such as speed cameras, building on the green belt or extending airports.

The course encourages you to reflect on things. It teaches you how to observe your feelings on a subject (are you being emotional or logical?) and to try and understand the feelings of others, even if you don't necessarily agree with them. It's about argument, but reasoned argument – so you don't start shouting and getting emotional!

SUBJECT COMBINATIONS

Critical thinking is a suitable option alongside many A levels or vocational qualifications. It can go with science subjects equally as well as with humanities or arts subjects. It can also form part of the AQA Baccalaureate.

It is possible to combine all A and AS levels with other equivalent qualifications such as BTEC Nationals or OCR Nationals and they could form part of Diplomas.

HIGHER EDUCATION OPTIONS

Degree-level study, foundation degrees and Higher National qualifications.

Critical thinking skills are of great benefit for a wide range of degrees and HND/HNC courses including law, social science, journalism, medicine, business, accounting and engineering. Critical thinking is taught in many courses as an essential skill. Many university and college departments recognise that students who have studied critical thinking possess the reasoning skills necessary to succeed in higher education.

University courses that involve analysis and evaluation of data or arguments particularly value A level critical thinking. However, when researching courses you will need to check with higher education institutions to see if critical thinking A/AS level will be counted as

part of any offers made. Some universities will accept it as a useful fourth A level, whereas others will include it as part of their main offer.

Don't forget that many universities now set entrance tests that assess your critical thinking skills, so taking the AS or A could help you with these.

Relevance to other subjects?

Critical thinking skills will be extremely useful to you whatever subject you study and will go on being useful throughout your career.

Important advice

Get involved in a debating group or start studying the ways that the same news story is reported by different types of newspapers, TV channels or on the web.

CAREER OPTIONS

Into work after A levels

Critical thinking skills will be useful for many careers including business and finance, management, retail and IT – in fact, any jobs where you need to analyse information, make reasoned decisions or influence people.

Into work as a graduate

Critical thinking will teach you how to evaluate and analyse information, weigh up evidence and communicate complex ideas effectively. Graduate recruiters often test critical thinking skills in their selection procedures. Critical thinking can provide an excellent foundation for a number of popular careers whatever your degree subject, including business, marketing, human resource management, law, public administration, teaching, uniformed services, journalism and the media. To be able to apply advanced critical thinking skills in the workplace is an advantage in any career or profession that involves difficult decision making or the resolution of dilemmas.

Dance

Dance A level is designed to meet the needs of students who wish to study dance in depth. On this course you will gain experience of choreography and performance, and you will be encouraged to think critically about dance. The course promotes progression in the depth and complexity of study through AS and A level examinations.

You don't have to be a wonderful dancer but you do need to be motivated and fairly fit. The course encourages participation and the developing of skills in order to choreograph, rehearse and perform your own work. You don't need any prior qualifications to take dance A level and your experience of dance need not have taken place at school.

WHAT DO YOU STUDY?

The topics listed give an idea of what could be covered. The exact content of AS and A2 specifications differs according to exam boards, so you will need to check with your school or college about the exact modules available to you. Dance A level is offered by the AQA board.

For AS you will study the dancer as a performer, the process and craft of choreography, and the significance of dances. You will create a solo choreography and perform in a duet or a trio.

For A2 you will study a chosen area of dance from modern dance, ballet or jazz dance, and one set work in depth. You will create a group dance (in which you do not perform) and perform a solo related to what you have studied.

- **Performance** – how to create and perform your own solo dances as well as performing from notated scores. You will use your skills in choreography when creating your own pieces. For the A2 you

will gain the knowledge and skills required to choreograph for a group and you will prepare and present a group work for performance.

- **Choreography** – how dances are written down (notation) and the different types of notation used. You will be required to study only one form of notation, which you will use throughout the course in performance and appreciation. You will also study important choreographers and their work.

- **Dance analysis and appreciation** – how to analyse, for example, how a dance is created and look at it critically to increase your enjoyment of what you see. You look at how professional dance works and study professional dancers.

- **Basic anatomy and physiology** – in relation to dancing; this includes safeguarding your own health when dancing.

Throughout the course you will be analysing and evaluating your dance.

In order to follow this course you may be required to have GCSE dance or experience in dance outside of school.

'When I graduate I want to go into venue management. The course is preparing me for this by developing my communication and team-working skills.'
Luciana, aged 22, on a dance degree course

HOW DO YOU STUDY?

You will participate in practical dance and choreography classes. Theoretical study will involve watching professional works and discussing them. Notation lessons will involve both practical and theory work.

You will take part in workshops including dance technique, choreography, anatomy, dance notation and dance analysis. Your course may include visits to local and national dance performances, and workshops with visiting dance companies.

You will be assessed through a combination of performance and choreography, coursework and exams. Much of the theory is taught through practice – even the anatomy and physiology of dance.

SUBJECT COMBINATIONS

Drama and music are obvious choices, but you could consider media studies, film studies or other subjects such as English language, literature, psychology, biology, human biology and sports science. Some people take AS level dance as a contrast to more classroom-based subjects. Some dance degrees prefer A levels offering writing skills, such as English or history, if there is an academic element to the course.

It is possible to combine all A and AS levels with other equivalent qualifications such as BTEC Nationals or OCR Nationals and they could form part of Diplomas.

FURTHER EDUCATION OPTIONS

Some further education colleges run dance foundation courses. The course content for these courses varies considerably but usually includes an emphasis on dance technique with some choreography and dance appreciation. They may include GCSEs, A levels or BTEC performing arts courses.

It is also worth remembering that many vocational dance courses take students from the age of 16.

HIGHER EDUCATION OPTIONS

Degree-level study

If you want to become a professional dancer, the most common route is to undertake training at a specialist dance school or college. Entrance requirements vary and competition for places is very strong. Most of the courses last three years and some lead to a degree, although they are mostly Diplomas. You do not necessarily need a degree to become a dancer so it is worth considering all your options.

Some colleges of higher education and universities also offer degrees in dance. These vary in their content and course titles include dance, dance studies and dance performance. Besides practical dance tutoring, these courses have an academic content, covering areas such as the physiology of movement, dance analysis, dance history and the sociology of dance. Some are not intended as courses for professional performers but more of a general education for those who want to be dance teachers, company administrators, education officers or to work in a related area. You will need to look at the content carefully to find out which course is suitable for you. You might want to consider a performing arts course or a specialist dance area, for example contemporary dance, dance theatre performance, urban dance, choreography or community dance. Your choice will depend on how much further dance training or performing you want to do.

Degree subject combinations

Apart from the more obvious combinations such as music, drama or movement studies, you could combine with law, education, maths, archaeology and even waste management.

Other higher education qualifications

Foundation degrees are available in dance, performing arts, theatre, contemporary dance practice, performance, contemporary circus and physical performance, festival, site specific and street arts, musical theatre and performance, and events production.

There are also some HNDs and HNCs in dance, performing arts and professional stage dance. Some of the course elements concentrating on performance skills may enable you to transfer onto a performing degree course after completion of the HND.

There are Diplomas of Higher Education (DipHEs) combining dance with related subjects such as performing arts, choreography and media production. There is a specialist DipHE in street arts.

There are also some postgraduate courses specialising in dance including performance, dance science, dance notation, movement therapy, choreography and teaching.

Relevance to other subjects?

Depending on your A level choice you could consider degrees in arts and entertainment management, theatre studies, community arts, teaching, stage and technical theatre management, PE, English literature, media studies, communication studies and music.

Important advice

Make sure you do your research into the right type of degree for you. How much performing do you want? Do you want to study other subjects? What facilities are there? It is important to make the right choice of degree in this area.

You might think it won't happen to you – but dancers are prone to injury. So if you are considering a career in dance or the performing arts it is always worth choosing

some academic subjects at A level, just in case you ever need to retrain or if you need to work between dance jobs.

CAREER OPTIONS

Into work after A levels

It will be difficult to get a dance-related job after A levels, but you will have knowledge of the performing arts, anatomy and physiology as well as study and team-working skills. You could work in the health and fitness or leisure sector, either in administration or as a leisure centre assistant, or train to become a personal trainer. You might find work within the performing arts sector, such as front-of-house or box-office work.

Into work as a graduate

Working in dance

If you don't become a professional dancer, there is related work in the fields of choreography, dance therapy, dance teaching and arts administration.

For some of these careers you will need to undertake further training, such as a PGCE in dance for teaching in state schools, and postgraduate courses for dance therapy and dance movement therapy.

Working outside dance

If you have studied an academic dance degree, you will be able to compete with graduates for jobs where graduates are accepted with any subject. This could include anything from the Armed Forces to jobs in business, IT, finance and administration. You could consider jobs connected with the performing arts in some way, such as arts administration, marketing, theatre management or community arts work. As you will have some knowledge of health and fitness, you may wish to consider jobs in fitness centres, gyms, personal training or working in health promotion in jobs such as a healthy lifestyles officer. You might consider also working in paramedical or complementary medicine by becoming a physiotherapist, osteopath, Alexander Technique teacher or reflexologist, although you would have to be prepared to undertake further training for all of these.

SOURCES OF INFORMATION

Conservatoire for Dance and Drama
www.cdd.ac.uk

Council for Dance Education and Training
www.cdet.org.uk

Dance UK
www.danceuk.org

National Association of Teachers of Dancing
www.natd.org.uk

National Resource Centre for Dance
www.surrey.ac.uk/NRCD

Websites

www.young-dancers.org

www.dancing-times.co.uk

'If dance is what you really want to do, go for it, so you won't regret it later. Remember that dancing is 95% mental so a positive mindset is a must.'
Jess, studying A level dance with English and ICT

Design and technology (food technology)

Do you understand how and why food is labelled? What's in a ready meal? What are smart foods? What is a BMI and what constitutes a healthy diet? What are the health benefits of free-range versus factory-farmed chickens? Design and technology (food technology) will help you to answer these questions and find out more about this topical subject.

WHAT DO YOU STUDY?

The topics listed give an idea of what could be covered. The exact content of AS and A2 specifications differs according to exam boards, so you will need to check with your school or college about the exact modules available to you.

You will find out about the use of food technology in all aspects of food production, from small one-off organic products through to mass-produced items. You will study a variety of food issues including production techniques, sampling, testing, marketing and the design of new food products. The course covers the social, scientific, economic and technological facts, principles and experience in industrial food production; and the impact and effect of market forces on consumers, manufacturers, producers and suppliers.

The topics studied include:

- **understanding food science** – the properties of the main food components and the effect of processing on them. How products are manipulated and combined in manufacture and processing, including food additives

- **design and market influences** – the food industry, consideration of environmental, technological and socio-economic factors in the development of new food products. Trends in new food production, concept development, market research, prototype designs, packaging, testing, launching and evaluating new products

- **the relationship between diet and health** – dietary planning, BMI, health promotion, lifestyle and how it is influenced by social, cultural and economic factors

- **environmental factors influencing food choices** – organic food and sources of energy

- **food hygiene and safety legislation** – including food labelling.

HOW DO YOU STUDY?

Practical work is expected in the form of investigations, product analysis and coursework. You will need to be able to plan appropriate schemes of work together with the technological processes necessary to achieve them, and to have the ability to develop and produce solutions to any problems encountered. There is a mixture of written and project work including studies of products. There will also be design-and-make exercises where you will be able to demonstrate your skills. You will be encouraged to establish links with food manufacturing companies and visit them to see the production processes. This will provide

> *'After graduating I had a choice of jobs. You have the choice of working in this country or abroad.'*
> Sarah, HND food technology, junior trainee

the opportunity to develop skills and extend background knowledge, which will help your coursework as well as your understanding of the industry.

SUBJECT COMBINATIONS

If you are considering higher education in food technology, food science, food manufacture, nutrition or dietetics, one or more sciences are usually required, so chemistry and/or biology are recommended. For courses geared more towards the manufacturing process and engineering, you will need maths and physics or engineering A levels or equivalent. For careers in catering and hospitality management, or travel and tourism, business studies or modern languages would be helpful.

It is possible to combine all A and AS levels with other equivalent qualifications such as BTEC Nationals or OCR Nationals and they could form part of Diplomas.

HIGHER EDUCATION OPTIONS

Degree-level study

There is a wide variety of courses available including food technology, food science, food and consumer management, food and consumer health, food product design, diet, nutrition and health, food marketing and sustainable food management. There are also specialised courses such as food and nutrition, food microbiology, and food production and supply management. Many courses have a sandwich period involving work experience in the UK or abroad. There is currently a shortage of suitably qualified food technology graduates.

If you want to become a registered dietitian or nutritionist you will need to study for a degree in nutrition and dietetics. This will mean at least two sciences at A level. You will also find public health nutrition degrees, which might be worth considering for a more community-focused career.

Degree subject combinations

Many food technology courses can be studied in combination with subjects like hospitality, management and bio-processing.

Other higher education qualifications

There are a number of foundation degrees available including food manufacture, food studies, food and consumer management, food science manufacturing and technology, primary food production and environment, hospitality and food management, baking technology management, and sustainable food management. This reflects the shortage status of this subject.

HND and HNC courses are available in food and nutrition, human nutrition, food management, food technology, food marketing, hospitality and food management, and food technology, and will give a mixture of practical experience and theory.

Relevance to other subjects?

You could consider related areas such as hospitality and catering, or travel and tourism. In addition, you will have gained a good knowledge of manufacturing and business so could consider business and marketing-related courses.

Important advice

Many food technology and nutrition courses will ask for sciences at A level so check that you have the right subjects to progress in your chosen course. There is such a wide variety of food science/technology courses available that you will need to research the content thoroughly to make sure you are choosing the right course.

CAREER OPTIONS

Into work after A levels

With A level food technology you would be able to work for food manufacturers, in hospitality and catering, or in food retail such as supermarket management. You will have good problem-solving skills and knowledge of how business works so you could consider a wide range of jobs in business and administration. Your scientific skills could be used in investigative and analytical work, for example, in laboratories in the food industry, hospitals or in public health. Your knowledge of consumers could prove useful in consumer advice or other jobs working with the public.

Into work as a graduate

Working in food technology

A degree in food science and technology almost guarantees graduates a well-paid and interesting job and you could progress to a wide range of careers in food manufacturing, food packaging, manufacture, retail food distribution, food service, food legislation, food science, research and development, quality control, hygiene, packaging, food microbiology and food analysis, environmental health or food research. In addition, there could be related jobs in food writing or journalism as well as marketing, sales and management. You could also consider teaching, training or lecturing. Food technology is being widely promoted for all ages so there is currently a demand for teachers in this area.

Working outside food technology

You will have a good insight into industry from a business and scientific point of view as well as good problem-solving and teamwork skills. There are related jobs such as the food retail industry, and hospitality and catering. Your knowledge of the manufacturing process could be equally useful in careers in business and management.

SOURCES OF INFORMATION

British Dietetic Association
www.bda.uk.com

Institute of Food Science & Technology
www.ifst.org
www.foodtechcareers.org

British Nutrition Foundation
www.nutrition.org.uk

Nutrition Society
www.nutritionsociety.org

Improve (food and drink sector skills council)
www.improveltd.co.uk

Website

www.careersinfoodanddrink.co.uk

Home economics (food, nutrition and health)

This A level overlaps with many topics from the food technology A level. You will study properties of food; design, development and production of food; advances in the food industry; consumer studies and consumer

> *'It's made me want to read the labels on everything I eat. Now I know how food is manufactured, I really want to know what is in it!'*
> Bess, taking A levels in food technology, biology and chemistry

protection. Topics include nutrition and diet, health and lifestyle, and the management of resources such as food, finances and energy to meet individual and family needs. You will also gain a thorough knowledge of resources, food provision, selection and purchase of food and household goods, food preparation and cooking equipment, food safety and hygiene.

Design and technology (product design)

Everything that has been made has been designed. You will learn what makes for good design and how design affects society and the environment. Central to the subject is the design process, which will teach you how to tackle real-life problems in a practical way. You will get involved in the design and manufacture of your own products as well as learning about how this process operates in industry.

You must be able to communicate your ideas and will have the opportunity to use a wide range of graphic techniques, from traditional drawing methods to computer aided design (CAD). You will learn to consider the materials and manufacture of a product in its design and will work with wood, metals, paper, card, plastics and some textiles, using your imagination and creativity to produce quality products. You will learn to evaluate your own work and the work of others.

WHAT DO YOU STUDY?

The topics listed give an idea of what could be covered. The exact content of AS and A2 specifications differs according to exam boards, so you will need to check with your school or college about the exact modules available to you.

In the first year, you learn and develop skills in design and production, gaining an understanding of the properties of a broad range of materials. You will carry out coursework assignments, evaluate existing products and assess how they could be improved. You will consider broader issues such as the environmental sustainability of products and their manufacture, as well as health and safety issues. You will look at how CAD and computer aided manufacture (CAM) have influenced the production process and about other factors such as ergonomics and anthropometrics (different sizes of people), inclusive design and consumer safety. An important consideration will be the lifecycle of products, their manufacture, use and final disposal.

In the second year, your knowledge of materials, manufacture and design is developed further. You will complete a design project as coursework, and in

some specifications carry out a marketing presentation to assess the commercial potential of your product. You will need to be able to plan appropriate schemes of work together with the processes necessary to achieve them. An important aspect of your work will be how to produce solutions to design problems. Again there are broader issues to take into consideration, such as health and safety as an element of design activity. You will also look at the use of natural resources, materials utilisation, conservation, waste disposal pollution, recycling and the moral, economic, social and environmental responsibilities of the designer.

HOW DO YOU STUDY?

You'll work on projects that will help you to develop the range of skills you will need. These are all related to designing, communicating, making and manufacturing, production, testing, evaluating and marketing your product. The practical coursework for

> *'It gives you a chance to be creative. It's going to help me become a product designer.'*
> Kevin, aged 18, A levels in maths, physics and design technology (product design)

each year of study usually involves a design portfolio and 3D modelling, which must be to a high professional standard of design and manufacture. One specification has an innovation challenge where you have to design and model a product and then reflect on the design concept. Marks are awarded for innovation and originality.

Coursework will be assessed as part of the final grade plus written exams. You will be expected to undertake personal research in groups and present findings to other students. You will need to support your studies with your own background reading. Coursework will cover a range of researching, reading, design portfolio work and writing. You will be expected to use your private study time for this, to supplement your work in the classroom and workshop.

SUBJECT COMBINATIONS

Design and technology (product design) combines well with other subjects. If you are interested in engineering, it would be a good idea to consider A levels in maths and physics. For architecture and product design courses, a 'creative and analytical mix' is often considered desirable, such as a combination with maths, physics, ICT or art. It could be combined also with engineering A level, BTEC Nationals or Advanced Diplomas in manufacturing or engineering, although you would have to check that there is no major overlap with your school or college's specification for these subjects.

HIGHER EDUCATION OPTIONS

Degree-level study

When combined with other related AS or A level subjects, design and technology (product design) can lead to a wide range of higher education courses.

Popular courses include industrial product design, sustainable design, 3D design and product design technology. Most of these courses have strong links with industry and will include a sandwich placement. The design-focused courses will ask for a portfolio of practical work.

Product design degrees have different focuses and specialisms. Examples include: engineering product design, automotive product design, medical product design and sports product design.

In addition you might consider degrees in architecture or architectural design technology. You must check with institutions for their exact entry requirements.

Degree subject combinations

Product design tends to be offered in combination with related subjects such as management, business and innovation.

Other higher education qualifications

Foundation degrees are available in product design, and product design and development plus an interesting course in product design for special effects. There are also more engineering-focused degrees such as electrical or electronic manufacturing engineering, engineering design and development, and engineering design.

There are HNDs and HNCs available in design technologies and product design. You might also want to consider engineering courses such sustainable design and innovation, manufacturing engineering or automotive engineering.

Relevance to other subjects?

Combined with relevant subjects, design and technology (product design) can lead to engineering, architecture, design and art courses.

Important advice

You will find a wide range of product-design related courses available so you will need to spend some time investigating them. You will be developing a portfolio as part of your course, but don't forget that any work you do outside your coursework may be a useful addition to your portfolio when you apply.

CAREER OPTIONS

Into work after A levels

It may be possible to go into an Apprenticeship in design, engineering, construction or manufacturing. There could be technician-level jobs in CAD or engineering. You would have to undertake part-time study for many jobs to gain the necessary technical skills.

Into work as a graduate

Working in product design

Product designers work in many business areas including consumer electronics, sports equipment, medical products and the automotive industry. Many product designers work directly for large and small businesses while others work for independent consultancies both in the UK and abroad. The skills learned in a product design degree make many other careers a possibility, and of course you could start your own business. Teaching is another option, as design and technology is a shortage area. You would need to undertake a PGCE for this and there may be financial incentives to study.

Working outside product design

Good problem-solving, creative and analytical skills can lead into many other careers such as management, and business and finance.

SOURCES OF INFORMATION

Chartered Institute of Architectural Technologists
www.ciat.org.uk

Creative choices
www.creative-choices.co.uk

Design Council
www.designcouncil.org.uk

Websites

www.careersinarchitecture.net

www.design-technology.info

www.ieee-virtual-museum.org

'One of the first lessons we learned was about health and safety in the workshop. Our teacher had worked in industry and told us some horror stories about what could happen in factories. It's really made me careful and it will stay with me when I get a job.'
John, taking engineering, maths and design technology A levels

Design and technology (systems and control)

This course is about designing and making things using electrical, mechanical and electronic systems.

Think about how cars are now manufactured by robots and other automated systems. What about other manufacturing processes? How about how heating, air conditioning and security systems? All these control systems have become an essential part of our lives.

You will learn about the processes of how products are designed and manufactured. During the course you will investigate, analyse and evaluate a broad range of products to create your own original solutions and then design and manufacture models, prototypes, products and systems.
Electronics and computers play a large part in the control of many systems and this forms a significant part of the course. It will include robotics and control systems (including electronics, computer control and a range of other technical areas such as structural and mechanical systems).You will design and make a system that does a job for you; this could be anything from a system that regulates the temperature or humidity in a greenhouse to something that might make life easier for a disabled person, like a keyboard that will control gadgets around their house.

WHAT DO YOU STUDY?

The topics listed give an idea of what could be covered. The exact content of AS and A2 specifications differs according to exam boards, so you will need to check with your school or college about the exact modules available to you.

At AS you will have the opportunity to learn through practical activities while producing solutions to control- and systems-based problems. You will learn the basics about the control-system process. You will study the materials and components and how they are used, and how cost and availability can influence your work. You will then demonstrate your ability to design, make, test and evaluate products by producing your own products.

At A2 level you will go on to see how industrial processes work and how engineers

and designers overcome problems within commercial constraints.

The specification gives you the opportunity to study the subject in more detail including, for example, computer simulation and its use to replicate an environment, product or system; industrial production; methods of harnessing alternative energy sources, energy transmission and storage. You will then manufacture a single prototype, system or product involving substantial designing and making.

The whole specification gives you the chance to apply all the skills you have learned. You

'It's not just knowing about engineering systems, it's being able to work commercially as well. That was the beauty of my degree.'
Joel, MEng in systems engineering, working for BAE

learn principles of design, research techniques and problem-solving strategies, and learn how you can think creatively and originally to get your designs to work for you.

It would be helpful to have studied a design technology subject at GCSE but this is not essential. You would be expected to have good GCSEs in maths and English and possibly a science.

HOW DO YOU STUDY?

Lessons are a mixture of designing and modelling, theory and practical work on projects. You will be expected to undertake personal research in groups and present findings to other students. You will need to support your studies with your own background reading. The subject is examined by written papers and coursework where you will design and manufacture a product and show proof of how you carried this out by means of a design folder. Examples of projects for systems and control could include a car alarm system, a roving robot, a foot-operated keyboard for the disabled, a wheelchair lift or rainfall meter.

You will visit trade shows and companies using systems and control technology processes, such as automated warehouses or car manufacturers.

SUBJECT COMBINATIONS

Systems and control technology combines well with many subjects. If you are interested in engineering, it would be a good idea to consider A levels in maths and physics. For architecture and product design courses, a 'creative and analytical mix' is often considered desirable, such as a combination with maths, physics, ICT or art. It could be combined with engineering A level or BTEC National qualifications in manufacturing or engineering, although you would have to check that there is no major overlap with your school or college's specification for these subjects.

It is possible to combine all A and AS levels with other equivalent qualifications such as BTEC Nationals or OCR Nationals and they could form part of Diplomas.

HIGHER EDUCATION OPTIONS

Degree-level study

When combined with other related AS or A level subjects, systems and control technology can lead to a wide range of higher education courses. You could consider courses in systems engineering (specialising in robotics, sustainability or instrumentation) and more specialist areas such as medical systems, and chemical and biosystems. You could also consider electronic engineering courses, which will include systems and control work. Software engineering courses could include systems and control elements, as could the more traditional engineering degrees of engineering or mechanical engineering. Product design courses would be another possibility. Many courses are likely to include a sandwich placement; the design-focused courses will ask for a portfolio of practical work. Courses tend to be either BSc, BEng or MEng. You must check with institutions for their exact entry requirements. Some degrees may offer a foundation year for those without the exact required qualifications.

Degree subject combinations

Systems engineering degrees are usually combined with electronics and other engineering subjects. You will find combinations with business management on some courses.

Other higher education qualifications

There are no foundation degrees entitled design and technology (systems and control), but plenty that are relevant to the subject. Look at engineering systems, engineering

> *'This course is evolving all the time as the technology evolves. It will give me a future-proof career.'*
> Jerry, aged 20, studying for a BEng in electronic, control and systems engineering

electrical systems, refrigeration systems management, and engineering manufacture, as well as electrical and mechanical engineering, production engineering, engineering design, and product design and development.

Related HNDs and HNCs are available in engineering systems, electronic and computer engineering and product design.

Relevance to other subjects?

Combined with relevant subjects, the study of systems and control can lead to a wide range of engineering, manufacturing and design courses.

Important advice

If you are considering future study in systems and control technology, such as systems engineering, you must make sure that you make the right choice of A levels. Some courses will require maths, physics or science in addition to your design and technology (systems and control) A level.

Don't forget that in control work there is a big emphasis on software engineering because of the embedded system nature of controllers so you must be interested and prepared to study this.

There is such a wide range of design and engineering courses available that you will need to spend some time investigating them. You will be developing a portfolio as part of your course, but don't forget that the work you do outside your coursework may be a useful addition to your portfolio when you apply.

CAREER OPTIONS

Into work after A levels

Depending on your subject choices it may be possible to enter an Apprenticeship in engineering, construction or manufacturing. There could be technician-level jobs in manufacturing processes or engineering. This would involve part-time study, which could eventually earn you a degree.

Into work as a graduate

Working in systems and control technology

Systems and control technology is a discipline at the core of many traditional and modern engineering disciplines. These include electrical, mechanical, aerospace, and chemical process engineering, manufacturing, automation and robotics. A degree in systems and control technology or a related subject will provide a sound foundation if you wish to pursue a career in designing, building and operating large-scale engineering systems, including those for railways, power generation and distribution, air traffic control, and oil and gas exploration and production. There will be opportunities to travel abroad on short- or long-term projects. With a thorough knowledge of engineering systems and processes you could also consider careers in management or sales within the industry.

Teaching is another option, as design and technology is a shortage area. You would need to undertake a specialist PGCE for this and there may be financial incentives to study.

Working outside systems and control technology

Good problem-solving, creative and analytical skills can lead into many other careers such as management and business and finance.

SOURCES OF INFORMATION

Institute of Measurement and Control
www.instmc.org.uk

Institution of Engineering and Technology
www.theiet.org (go to the 'control' section)

Websites

www.apprentices.co.uk (details of engineering Apprenticeships)

www.design-technology.info

www.ieee-virtual-museum.org

Drama and theatre studies

If you enjoy or participate in the performing arts then this course is for you.

The skills gained from this course are a good preparation for the performing arts as well as being transferable to other areas of work. As well as the practical part of the course, you study the origins, aims and techniques of theatre, and gain an ability to view performances with a critical eye.

WHAT DO YOU STUDY?

The topics listed give an idea of what could be covered. The exact content of AS and A2 specifications differs according to exam boards, so you will need to check with your school or college about the exact modules available to you.

Exam boards vary in the amount of performing involved but all courses contain elements of the following:

- **live performance** – how to devise your own performance with other students, which will give everyone the opportunity to try all aspects of organising and producing a piece of theatre

- **theatre texts** – (as pieces meant for performance) how they are translated into a stage performance; how creative opportunities are presented by this process; how effectively they communicate the feelings and ideas that they contain

- **set and costume design** – how these may be used to communicate ideas and add to the overall effectiveness of the performance

- **stage lighting and sound** – lighting and sound management skills; their importance in the creation of mood and atmosphere, use of special effects

'It's hard work and really makes you think.'
Chloe, taking A levels in drama and theatre studies, psychology and history

- **masks and puppets** – the skills behind their use in theatre directing

- **theatre practitioners** – includes playwrights, directors, designers and theatre companies: playwrights from Shakespeare, Aristophanes to Marlowe to more contemporary playwrights like Ibsen, Buchner, O'Casey, Littlewood and April De Angelis; directors such as Steven Berkoff, John Godber, Peter Hall and Deborah Warner; designers such as Edward Gordon Craig, Ralph Koltai and Anthony Ward; theatre companies such as Complicité, Forced Entertainment, Frantic Assembly, Kneehigh and Shared Experience.

It is not essential to have studied the subject at GCSE in order to take the A level but you do need good grades in English and a genuine interest in the theatre.

There is also an A level available in performing arts, which includes options in dance, drama and music in its specifications.

HOW DO YOU STUDY?

Depending on the specifications, you are encouraged to experience and gain skills in a number of areas, including direction, performance, design (set, lighting, costume, props and sound) and rehearsal. In addition there may be small group projects and some individual research for assignments. You will see live theatre performances, which will give you a means of comparison between theatre styles, playwrights, companies and periods. You create original drama presentations in which your theatre studies group is entirely responsible for all aspects – developing an original idea, producing, designing and performing it.

SUBJECT COMBINATIONS

English and drama and theatre studies is a popular combination. Some theatre studies courses at a higher level require A level in English in addition to, or instead of, a performance-based one. You mustn't make the mistake of assuming that the work you do on set texts in A level drama and theatre studies is exactly the same as that done on set texts in English or modern languages. In drama and theatre studies, you study the texts as a starting point and foundation for producing a performance rather than as literature. Drama and theatre studies is a subject in its own right, and not a variant of English literature. Other popular combinations are sociology, history, media studies, psychology and religious studies.

It is possible to combine all A and AS levels with other equivalent qualifications such as BTEC Nationals or OCR Nationals and they could form part of Diplomas.

HIGHER EDUCATION OPTIONS

An A level in drama and theatre studies is not essential to study at a higher level.

Degree-level study

Theatre and drama-related degree courses come in many forms with different titles. Your choice of course will depend on your areas of interest. For example, how much practical work do you want in comparison to theory? Do you want technical training in lighting, sound, stage management and set design?

Drama or theatre arts courses tend to provide the most general grounding in all aspects of theatre skills and theory. You have the

opportunity to choose options in later years in areas such as playwriting, design and physical theatre.

You might want to specialise and choose a course focusing on a particular aspect of theatre, for example technical theatre or stage management.

Many traditional drama schools offer BA courses as well as Diplomas so you must research your choice of course carefully. Auditions will be an essential part of the selection process, especially for courses at drama schools. You have to be persistent and it may be worth reapplying if you are turned down the first time. You may be accepted later on, so waiting and getting more experience may pay dividends.

Degree subject combinations

You can combine a theatre or drama course with related subjects such as English, music, media studies and modern languages. There are some modular courses that give you flexibility in your studies. For example, you could study a module in new theatre writing, followed by performance practice, followed by directing, while being assessed on each as you go.

Other higher education qualifications

There are a number of foundation degrees leading to degree-level study or employment:

- acting
- artistic make up and special effects
- circus and physical performance
- costume construction for stage and screen
- festival, site specific and street arts
- lighting and sound design
- live music and theatre production
- make up for media and performance

- performance and event management
- performing arts: music theatre
- specialist make-up design
- technical theatre
- theatre arts (costume design and realisation)
- theatre arts (dance)
- touring and community theatre.

Examples of HNDs and HNCs available include:

- performing arts
- technical theatre
- theatre
- theatrical media make-up and costume.

Relevance to other subjects

Theatre is a form of communication and expression that looks at human beings and how they behave in different situations. You will find a broad range of related subjects for which the drama and theatre studies A level will provide a good background. These include psychology, history, sociology, politics and classical civilisation. Your ability to analyse and extract information from the written word would be a valuable skill in the study of any subject that requires work on texts, such as English, modern languages, cultural studies, media studies and philosophy.

Important advice

Courses involving practical performance or direction work will require an audition, where you may have to act, sing, direct or dance. In addition you will be judged according to how much performance experience you have and how much live theatre you have seen.

You should try to gain as much practical experience as possible, by taking part in productions at school or college and joining local drama groups. For courses that involve a large design or technical element, you

may be required to show evidence of your practical experience. This can be in the form of photographs or drawings of productions for which you have designed sets, lighting, costumes, etc.

CAREER OPTIONS

Into work after A levels

An A level in drama and theatre studies will not automatically get you a career in the theatre but then neither will a degree course, although the degree route into the profession is becoming more common. Acting is a competitive and crowded profession. It is virtually impossible to perform without an Equity membership card (Equity being the union responsible for professional actors and performers), yet it is almost impossible to get an Equity card without having been offered professional work as a performer. You can get round this in two ways. First, gaining further training at one of the accredited drama schools and thereby getting a provisional (temporary and basic level) Equity card. Second, getting involved in a semi-professional or amateur production, and persuading a director or agent to come along. If they are impressed with you, they may be able to help you get work.

You could gain relevant experience and training in theatre-related careers by working in a theatre as a box-office assistant or usher, or volunteer working on community, youth or amateur theatre projects.

Into work as a graduate

Working in drama and theatre

The professional theatre is full of people looking for their next employment opportunity, and it can be difficult to get work. If you have determination and a realistic understanding of the difficulties involved, it is possible to break into the industry.

- **Actor** – usually self-employed but may have an agent to search out and negotiate contracts. Actors move between the various media, theatre, film, television and radio, and can often make the most money by doing commercials, voiceovers and training films.

- **Costume designer or costume and wardrobe** – this involves the design and creation or hiring and buying of costumes for a play, and keeping tabs on a theatre's stock of costumes.

- **Designer** – some work on sets, others on sets and costumes and even lighting designs. Most have further training in the design field and are freelance.

- **Director** – responsible for choosing the actors; with the designer and lighting designer, working out the look of the piece. In rehearsals, the director works on the overall shape of the scenes, as well as perfecting the actors' performances.

- **Drama therapist** – a rewarding career where you use drama to help the recovery of people with emotional or behavioural problems. Specialist training is required in addition to your drama qualification.

- **Education officer** – employed by many theatres to work with schools and colleges and arrange educational trips to the theatre.

- **Marketing manager** – finds a way to get 'bums on seats'. May work with a press manager to deal with publicity.

- **Sound or lighting technician** – often employed by a theatre on a full-time basis. Works with visiting designers and directors on the aural and visual environment of a play.

> *'The subject gives you confidence, whatever you decide to do later on.'*
> Judith, taking A levels in drama and theatre studies, English literature and business

- **Stage carpenter** – makes and paints scenery and sets.

- **Stage manager** – responsible for running the production in rehearsal and performance. Tasks range from photocopying the script to managing the stage crew, and telling actors and lighting technicians when they are to 'go on' or 'switch on'.

Working outside drama and theatre

Any career that demands confident verbal and physical communication skills is one that a graduate of a performance-based degree would enjoy. A good example is sales and marketing. Your skills could also be used in HR work, conference organising (including lighting, sound and direction), museum and other exhibition work, and advertising, where an awareness of the importance of visual image and design in the communication of an idea is vital.

SOURCES OF INFORMATION

Equity
www.equity.org.uk

Get into theatre
www.getintotheatre.org

National Association of Youth Theatres
www.nayt.org.uk

National Council for Drama Training
www.ncdt.co.uk

Economics

Economists are interested in all aspects of life, not only in the more obvious issues such as consumer spending, inflation, house prices, unemployment, wages and international trade but also in environmental pollution, how firms compete, living standards, how we behave as consumers, taxation, poverty, health, education and much more. All aspects of economic theory are applied to the real world – to what determines growth, unemployment, inflation, the balance of payments, the gap between wealth and poverty, and society.

The study of economics will broaden your understanding of the business world and encourage you to evaluate the consequences of business and government decisions. Economics is useful to anyone wanting to go into business and finance since it is included as a core subject in the examinations of all the professional bodies including law, banking, marketing and accountancy.

N.B. There is also an A level in economics and business, described at the end of the business studies A level entry.

WHAT DO YOU STUDY?

The topics listed give an idea of the range of issues that are covered in an A level economics course. The exact content of AS and A2 specifications differs according to exam boards, so you will need to check with your school or college about the exact modules available to you.

The four-module AS/A2 course concentrates on: the workings of the market economy, the causes of breakdown in the market economy (such as mismanagement, crime, pollution and waste), threats to consumers from monopoly power etc, and the national and international economy.

For the AS you cover both microeconomics and macroeconomics.

> *'Get some work experience; it will really help you. You learn more about the work and whether it would suit you. You'll find out about the organisation and they will find out about you; it can be a great foot in the door!'*
> Parmjit, economics graduate, working in banking

At A2 there are extended courses that analyse the UK and international economy, transport economics, the economics of work and leisure, and the wider economy on a global scale.

In most A level courses, you study the main issues of the day and then use your knowledge and applied skills to investigate and understand the underlying causes, explanations and consequences. The topics covered range from those dealing with the economy as a whole (macroeconomics) to those dealing with individual parts of the economy (microeconomics):

- **inflation** – why does the Government have an inflation rate target and how does it affect us?

- **pensions** – can a future government afford to pay them?

- **the environment** – can pollution effectively be controlled?

- **the international situation** – why is there a gulf between rich and poor nations?

- **house prices** – why do house prices rise and fall?
- **the Euro debate** – should Britain join?
- **competition between companies** – why is this good for customers?
- **wages** – what affects students' wages in part-time employment?
- **privatisation** – is a service better if it is privatised?
- **the low-cost airline revolution** – has it benefited consumers?
- **supermarkets** – are they cheats?
- **the new millionaires** – who are they?
- **unemployment** – the big debate; how to reduce it?
- **globalisation** – how are we affected by the Chinese and Indian economies?

It is not essential to have studied economics at GCSE in order to take the A level. You need to have a good understanding of maths, as GCSE maths at grade A*-C is usually preferred.

HOW DO YOU STUDY?

If you want to study or work in economics, you need to be good with numbers and able to put your ideas across. You must be able to interpret data, use graphs, calculate accurately and write intelligent, well-structured analyses. You are taught through case studies, multimedia presentations, visits, fieldwork and note-taking. You must take an interest in current affairs, read a quality newspaper and get involved in discussion and argument. You will be required to carry out research on your own, and need to be able to evaluate the merits of alternative arguments.

SUBJECT COMBINATIONS

Economics combines well with a wide variety of other A level subjects and popular subjects are maths, English, history, government and politics, geography, philosophy and modern languages. If you have chosen business studies as one of your A levels it may overlap with economics, and some higher education institutions may not accept it. If you want to study economics at degree level, think about combining it with A level mathematics as this is requested or preferred by some universities. This could really help your application as economics is such a popular course and will also help you on your degree. You should check this with the universities you are interested in.

It is possible to combine all A and AS levels with other equivalent qualifications such as BTEC Nationals or OCR Nationals and they could form part of Diplomas.

HIGHER EDUCATION OPTIONS

No previous study of economics is required for most university courses although it is preferred by some. Economics is a popular degree and so the grades required are high.

Degree-level study

Economics courses typically begin with a broad-based first year when you study economics along with other social sciences. In this first year mathematics and/or statistics are often compulsory subjects, especially for students who have not done them at A level. IT and languages may also be available at this stage. In the later years of the course, you can specialise through your choice of options, which could include forecasting and planning, public finance, or monetary theory, although some topics such as econometrics (mathematical economics), international trade, and labour economics are sometimes compulsory. You may also get the opportunity to study abroad.

Universities often specialise in very different aspects of economics, so you should look at course outlines very carefully to decide exactly which areas you would like to study.

Related courses include financial economics, applied economics, international economics and business economics.

Degree subject combinations

You may choose to specialise in economics and there are related combinations available in finance, econometrics, economic history, international business, management, banking and statistics. However, there is also a whole range of other subjects available such as politics, accounting, geography, international development, sociology and modern languages.

Many universities offer modular programmes allowing a wide choice of options. If you are keen on maths, you may be able to broaden your studies through a modular scheme.

Economics can be studied as a branch of applied mathematics, and there are courses in econometrics.

Other higher education qualifications

There are no pure economics foundation degrees but there are a few using applied knowledge: these include enterprise development, and business and finance. You could also consider business studies courses, which could include some elements of economics.

Economics topics feature in many HND and HNC courses such as business studies, accounting and marketing and there are also options in economic development.

Relevance to other subjects?

Many students decide on a degree course in a related subject area such as business studies, finance, marketing, management science and international relations. In all these courses the study of economics is included, so your A level in economics would prove helpful.

The development of your analytical skills also makes economics a good A level for law degrees.

Important advice

Some degrees in economics and business studies are run as sandwich courses, where part of the course is spent on a work placement. When you apply for these courses you may be considered on your suitability for employment as well as your academic ability. Try to get some work experience in a related area such as banking, finance or accountancy. As well as improving your chances, you will be able to find out what you might be letting yourself in for.

CAREER OPTIONS

Into work after A levels

An economics A level is useful for a lot of jobs after A levels. You will possess a lot of transferable skills in research, analysis and evaluation of written and numerical economic data, communication and working with others.

You could consider the Civil Service or retail and business companies' training or Apprenticeship schemes. It is also useful in the financial world and is a good entry qualification for jobs in the City or banking.

Into work as a graduate

Working in economics

The majority of graduates get employment in banking and finance, business management or computing. A numerate degree with problem-solving skills is very marketable to employers.

There are not many jobs for pure economists, but if you are considering this you will need to go on to postgraduate study.

However, there are many types of work in which you can use and apply your degree.

- **Government Economic Service** – advising government departments on economic policy.

- **Economic analysis and advice** – relating to share, currency or bond markets or the profiling of industries or different economies. The most prominent jobs are in the City, but more economists work for large companies, advising on their products and markets.

- **International work** – for example, for multinational companies or institutions such as the European Union or International Monetary Fund.

- **Economics or financial journalism**.

- **Teaching or lecturing** – in school and colleges. You will need a PGCE.

Working outside economics

Knowledge of the economy and the logical, numerical and analytical skills that you gain through studying economics are valuable for many careers, such as banking, finance or accountancy. There are management training opportunities in large companies and organisations, including the Civil Service, and some openings in the financial departments of companies and local authorities. Careers in buying, marketing and selling, law and insurance are also popular.

SOURCES OF INFORMATION

Government Economic Service
www.civilservice.gov.uk

Websites

www.whystudyeconomics.ac.uk

www.economist.com

> '*There is a lot of theory and you have to learn how it works in the real world. It does affect our daily lives although you might not think so.*'
> Brian, taking A levels in economics, maths and business studies

Engineering

Engineering is all about practical problem solving and creativity. This course will help you to understand engineering principles and their applications, and gain skills and knowledge of the industry and the many routes available into careers and education. You will be able to apply your understanding of engineering and its practical and technological aspects through project-based study of engineering design, production, commissioning and maintenance.

WHAT DO YOU STUDY?

This exam is only available as a single AS or A level (three or six units) and is currently offered only by the Edexcel examination board.

Engineering materials, processes and techniques – engineers need to be familiar with a wide range of materials. You will examine the structure, properties and behaviour of materials currently used in engineering. You will learn how materials are selected for their properties and performance according to the product required.

The role of the engineer – investigating the role of a professional engineer responsible for the design or manufacture of an engineered product or service. This will include how new technologies, time and cost constraints, legislation and standards, and health and safety legislation influence the engineering decisions made during the design and/or manufacture of an engineered product or service. You will pick an engineered product and service and look at the role of the engineer responsible for it.

Principles of design, planning and prototyping – producing a design solution to a client brief, planning the project and developing a prototype. You will report back to the other students about how you did this.

Applied engineering systems – looking at ways in which engineering techniques and principles are applied in some important systems and how a systems approach can be used to solve engineering problems. The range you will cover includes static structures, pneumatic systems and the electrical lighting and power systems used in homes, offices and public buildings. You will also look at elements of the electromechanical and electronic systems found in everyday life and the means by which they are controlled.

The engineering environment – investigating a different engineered product or service to the one studied previously. You will extend your studies to learn how laws, regulations and codes of practice are used to ensure that developments are safe. You will explore how procedures and paperwork systems are used to control engineering practice and product quality. You will also learn about the different ways in which the environment is protected by the way products are designed and manufactured. You will explore how new techniques and scientific advances are used to improve the way that products work, and how to create new products and services.

Applied design, planning and prototyping – using your engineering expertise to design, develop and manufacture an engineering solution to a given client brief, you will:

- carry out appropriate research into the requirements of the given client brief

'You have to be able to get on with people. You have to be able to get your ideas across clearly and simply.'
John, civil engineer

- develop a technical design specification, negotiated and agreed with your client, which contains measurable points

- generate alternative design ideas and their development into a final design solution

- discuss your design solutions with other students to evaluate progress and make modifications if necessary

- plan for production – identify tasks, time constraints, quality control points and budgetary constraints

- consider recording and explaining the use of appropriate regulations, standards and documentation during the manufacture of the engineered product

- produce a prototype of the engineered product that fully meets the specification requirements

- evaluate your final outcome against all the measurable points of the specification and suggest modifications to improve the performance of the product.

The course helps you to develop a range of skills that will be useful to you either for higher level study or in work and training. You will design and manufacture engineering products that will be assessed in both AS and A2 units. You will be assessed externally in A2 on your work for three practical engineering activities.

For details of A level electronics see the end of this section.

HOW DO YOU STUDY?

The course is a mixture of assignments, tests, set assignments, projects and case studies assessed both internally and externally. You will go on industrial study visits and to museums and trade shows.

> 'If you want to travel, then the sky's the limit.'
> Peter, chartered engineer

SUBJECT COMBINATIONS

It is possible to combine this with AS and A levels, but for entry to higher education a minimum of 12 units may be required in certain subject areas. Mathematics or physics A level would go well and be useful for applications for engineering courses; design and technology would be helpful for courses such as product design or design engineering.

It is possible to combine all A and AS levels with other equivalent qualifications such as BTEC Nationals or OCR Nationals and they could form part of Diplomas.

HIGHER EDUCATION OPTIONS

Degree-level study

You could study a broad area such as engineering science, electrical or mechanical engineering, or go into a more specialised area such as aeronautical engineering or renewable energy. There are BSc, BEng and MEng courses available. MEng courses are for the most able students who want to go into fast-track management. Many courses have the opportunity for a sandwich year or industrial placement in the UK and sometimes abroad.

Degree subject combinations

Engineering can be combined with subjects such as IT, economics, languages, communications and management and also with pure sciences such as physics and biology. If you are doing a general engineering course then combining can be easier than specialising. It is possible to take totally different subjects such as sociology, drama, politics or tourism, which are often available as part of modular degree courses.

Other higher education qualifications

There is a wide range of engineering foundation degrees available covering areas such as electronics, mechanical, automotive, sound/broadcast and telecommunications, and more specialist areas such as aircraft or motorsport engineering. These run in partnership with industry, providing a good route into further study while working.

There are many HND and HNC courses you could progress to that will give you training and skills in a specialised area combined with work experience. Subjects include: electrical and electronic engineering, software engineering, aerospace engineering, automotive engineering and civil engineering. It is possible to progress on to the second year of a degree course after completing your HND.

Relevance to other subjects?

Engineering A level gives you useful transferable skills so you could consider many other courses. You will need to check that you have the right A level subject combination for entry – maths may be required, for example. Possible degree subjects might include, cybernetics, mechatronics and robotic systems, disaster management, fire safety engineering, horology, interactive computer systems, media technology, multimedia technology, naval architecture and special effects.

Important advice

Check the facilities offered by schools and colleges when you are investigating courses to make sure that you can follow the pathway of your choice. There are so many different branches of engineering that it makes sense to do some research and find out which one is for you.

If you are considering sponsorship for a degree, you must find out about this early on as many companies have early closing dates. You will have to undergo company selection tests and interviews as if you were applying for a job. Try to arrange some work shadowing or work experience to find out if engineering is for you.

CAREER OPTIONS

Into work after A levels

Many engineering students progress to further study but there may be the opportunity to do an Apprenticeship that can lead to the opportunity to study up to HNC, HND or degree level.

The kinds of jobs you could enter as a trainee are:

- **draftsperson/CAD operator** – drafting plans and documents, using computer technology
- **estimator** – working out how much it will cost to design and make a product
- **quality assurance technician** – making sure that the product is just right
- **inspector** – making sure that everything is running as it should
- **planner** – scheduling everyone else's work
- **laboratory technician** – helping with research and testing, sometimes at supervisory level
- **technician** – helping to develop new ideas and working with other departments in your organisation.

Into work as a graduate

Working in engineering

Most engineering graduates will be recruited onto graduate trainee schemes with companies. These are the areas of work you could consider:

- **design, development and research engineering**

> 'It takes a lot of nerve to get up in front of the class and do a presentation, but you get used to it.'
> Josh, studying engineering with design technology and maths

- production engineering
- control engineering
- quality assurance engineering
- sales and marketing positions
- management.

Once in employment as a trainee, you will undertake professional training towards registration as an incorporated or a chartered engineer.

Many companies offer sponsorship for engineering degrees so you would be working for them all the time you are studying, including during vacations.

Working outside engineering

Your degree will provide you with good problem-solving skills as well as a good scientific and maths grounding, so you could consider trainee schemes in many areas including accountancy, banking and retail.

SOURCES OF INFORMATION

Engineering Careers Information Service (ECIS)
www.enginuity.org.uk

The Institution of Engineering and Technology
www.theiet.org

Institution of Mechanical Engineers
www.imeche.org.uk

Website

www.howstuffworks.com

Electronics

Electronics touches every part of our lives. At AS you study all the key components that go into electronic design such as capacitors, diodes, transducers, logic gates, amplifiers etc. These are all part of the toolkit used by electronics designers and engineers. You'll also have a first-year project to design and make an electronic solution to a real-life problem. At A2 you'll step up a level to topics like microprocessors, robotics and communications systems. This will help you to decide which area of electronics really interests you. Again you'll have a practical project so you can get to grips with a solution that you can see really working.

Please note that A level maths and often A level physics (or equivalent) are required for electronics degree courses, although some institutions offer foundation courses in these subjects.

English language

The study of English language at A level gives you the skills to analyse and evaluate written and spoken English and will improve your communication skills. Language is essential to our daily lives: it helps us to understand who we are, and what others might think of us; it is also a way to express thoughts and feelings; it even shapes our view of the world. If you study English language at A level, you develop your knowledge and understanding of the ways in which the English language can help us to communicate, how and why it is used differently by different speakers – and by the same speaker in different situations – and how it has changed over time and is still changing today. Think about the new words or phrases that didn't exist a few years ago such as twitter, staycation and credit crunch.

WHAT DO YOU STUDY?

The topics listed give an idea of what could be covered. The exact content of AS and A2 specifications differs according to exam boards, so you will need to check with your school or college about the exact modules available to you.

English language looks at the following:

- **detailed study of the language** – grammar, sentence and word structure, phonology (the sound of words and how they are formed), and typography (studying, for example, the layout and typeface of newspapers)

- **parsing** – how to unpick a sentence into basic constituents; language development, variation and change through the ages from early-modern English (Middle Ages) to the present day

- **the different theories whose research underpins attitudes** – for example, there are three different theories as to how children acquire a language and you will have a chance to see how these theories fit in with the latest thinking

- **the social aspects of language** – dialects and the difference between male and female language use

- **the difference between speech and writing** – the theories behind this; you will study various types of media including newspapers and adverts

- **language variation** – how language has changed over time, how individuals speak English differently, through accent and dialect, and how we all vary the language we use according to the situation that we are in or who we are talking to

- **the future of English** – does *Eastenders* improve the quality of English throughout the UK? What is estuary English? How is language evolving with the introduction of new words? Has English been affected by different immigrant communities in the UK?

- **language and representation** – the philosophy of language, e.g. gender and politics. This will cover political correctness, including slang, jargon and taboo language, and occupational usage such as in teaching, building or journalism

'You usually speak without thinking much about it, but this course helps you to listen and really understand what different people are saying and to really understand what they mean.'
Elaine, taking A levels in English language, law and business

- **writing for specific genres, audiences and purposes** – you will demonstrate your skill in writing and explore the techniques of a variety of genres in order to produce effective texts for specific genres, audiences and purposes.

Most students who take English language A level will have done both English language and literature at GCSE. Good grades are necessary in order to study at A level.

N.B. There is also an A level in English language and literature (see the end of this entry for more details).

HOW DO YOU STUDY?

You must read widely beyond the textbooks and develop a keen ear for eavesdropping on other people's conversations or listening intently to conversations that you have. This latter skill is particularly useful in the part of the course that deals with the spoken word. You will look at newspapers, advertisements, pamphlets and other marketing material, as well as conventional literature such as poetry, plays and novels. There will be transcripts of interviews, conversations of all sorts (especially everyday transactions), which will be used for close study. You will get the opportunity to write your own texts. The coursework options are wide ranging, giving you the chance to focus on a topic of particular interest. An example could be looking at obituaries from local or national newspapers or an unfolding news story, or carrying out your own fieldwork in an aspect of language that interests you.

SUBJECT COMBINATIONS

If you are thinking of going on to study English language at a higher level, a modern language would be a good subject to combine with A level English. It means that you have a basis for comparison of what you read. If you are thinking of studying linguistics, a modern or classical language (or even two)

> *'I really liked the course and realised that some of my classmates speak in a different language with one another and in normal English to adults.'*
> Jaycinth, taking A levels in English language, history and drama

is almost essential. Subjects that combine well with and support English include history, philosophy, sociology, psychology and media studies.

It is possible to combine all A and AS levels with other equivalent qualifications such as BTEC Nationals or OCR Nationals and they could form part of Diplomas.

HIGHER EDUCATION OPTIONS

An A level in English language is often (although not always) required for degree courses in the subject.

Degree-level study

In practice, an English language degree is often a degree in English language and linguistics. This means that you study linguistics in general and the linguistics of English in particular. The topics that you study include those found in the English language A level, but cover much else besides. They range from quite technical descriptions of the structures of language, through the acquisition of language by children and second-language learners, to the history of English and the status of English as a world language. There are degrees available combining English language and literature and specialising in creative writing. Both English language and literature can be studied for a BEd degree, in which you study education and gain a teaching qualification alongside your English work. There are also courses and options on degrees in teaching English as a foreign language (TEFL) or teaching English as a second language (TESOL). If you are considering an English literature degree, you should look at English language and literature A level or English literature at A level, as English language A level alone may not be accepted.

Degree subject combinations

English language can be combined with many subjects. A combination with English is useful for any subject that requires an ability to understand how language can be used to communicate images, thoughts, emotions and a sense of the society in which the text was written. The most widely available combinations are communication, history, modern languages and sociology. A degree in international business English offers the opportunity to study business English with another language.

Other higher education qualifications

There are some foundation degrees where English language could be useful including journalism, printing and publishing production, media, and creative writing.

There are HND and HNC courses available in journalism combining practical experience with skills training. There are also pre-entry courses for journalism, which require good A levels or equivalent and sitting the National Council for the Training of Journalists (NCTJ) entrance test.

Relevance to other subjects?

The study of English at A level develops skills that will help you in subjects at a higher level. Among these are history, media studies, film studies, drama and linguistics. More applied courses such as teaching and journalism are worth investigating.

Important advice

Start taking an interest in English language in its written and spoken form. Look closely at newspaper headlines in different newspapers. Start listening more closely to conversations to hear how people really communicate. Think about the way that you communicate with your friends. How much slang do you use? Do you talk in text speak?

CAREER OPTIONS

Into work after A levels

Studying for A level English gives you plenty of practice in communicating in both speech and writing, which is an essential skill valued by many employers. You could consider a wide range of administration jobs. It might be useful to gain extra skills in administration, IT or secretarial studies and you could consider taking a full- or part-time course at college. You will find that some companies offer training schemes and Apprenticeships. Other possible job areas include retail, marketing and sales.

Into work as a graduate

Working in English language

Studying English language and linguistics equips you with skills that are relevant to a wide range of careers. There are many professions that require specific linguistic expertise, for example, publishing, journalism, public relations, advertising copywriting and technical authorship. You could also consider teaching in the UK and abroad, although you might have to do some further training. The ability to 'think linguistically' is of great value to computer programmers and communications experts. English language and linguistics graduates are seen by employers as literate, numerate and articulate; studying English fosters skills in analysing and summarising data, arguing effectively and with supporting evidence, thinking logically, strategically and critically, working both independently and as part of a team, meeting deadlines and using computer technology. (See also the entry on English literature.)

Working outside English language

You will have learned excellent communication skills on your course and a good understanding of the way that different people communicate. These skills can be useful in many types of work and you could consider careers in sales, the media, law, IT, accountancy and finance, management, personnel, retail and administration. For some of these careers there are postgraduate diplomas available such as publishing, information science, management and marketing.

SOURCES OF INFORMATION

Websites

www.literaturetraining.com

www.ppa.co.uk

www.bl.uk/soundsfamiliar

English language and literature

In A level English language and literature, there is a strong emphasis on language and how it is used in different communicative situations. You learn to study systematically both written and spoken language by analysing different sorts of texts and transcripts, and by writing your own text and commentaries on the language with which you have created them. You will learn the skills of summarising, editing and recasting written material for practical purposes, and coursework will provide an opportunity for creative writing. In addition, you will study literature from various periods in the form of plays, short stories, novels or collections of poems. You will analyse the text and look at the representation of speech as well as exploring the stylistic and thematic issues. You will learn to write fluently and coherently.

(For details of higher education, careers and further information see the English language and English literature entries.)

English literature

You need to love reading to study this course but it's not just reading for the sake of it. This course develops your ability to discuss ideas, argue points of view and understand how literature affects and reflects our lives.

You will usually study a range of works of literature written at any time between the end of the 14th century and the present day.

You will study prose, poetry and drama and examine the techniques writers use to build characters, create atmosphere, drama or tension, and develop themes and ideas. You will learn to read in a way that will help you to evaluate not just the set texts but any piece of writing, learning how to communicate your own response to the texts in the form of essays. You will learn to develop and express your own opinions. You'll be able to read types of literature you've never read before or look at familiar pieces in a new, more analytical way.

WHAT DO YOU STUDY?

The exact content of AS and A2 specifications differs according to exam boards, so you will need to check with your school or college about the exact modules available to you.

You will study some set works, which could be from any period from Chaucer (14th century), through Shakespeare, Victorian novels to the present day. Recent contemporary set books have been by authors like Maya Angelou, Carol Ann Duffy, Sebastian Faulks and Owen Sheers. You must study at least some Shakespeare. Some specifications allow you to study on the basis of periods, such as 'World War I literature' or 'poetry and prose 1800–1945' or covering a whole genre such as a study of tragedy. You might also study thematically, which will enable you to compare works written from a similar perspective at very different periods, so for 'love through the ages', for example, you would look at the consequences of love in

> 'Be prepared to read a lot! We started out by reading Ulysses, and just kept going for challenging literary experiences from all over the world.'
> Alicia, on BA degree in English literature

Shakespeare's *Romeo and Juliet*, Browning's *Dramatic Monologues* (19th century) and *Enduring Love* by Ian McEwan (late 20th century).

Most students who take English literature A level will have done both English language and literature at GCSE. Good GCSE grades are necessary in order to study the subject at A level.

HOW DO YOU STUDY?

A level English literature involves a lot of reading. This could be set texts and, in some specifications, extracts from texts. You will need to know the texts inside out if you are to do well. You should 'read around your texts', i.e. read other texts that are related in some way to those you are studying, whether in terms of the themes covered, when they were written or because they were written by the same author. When you study plays for English literature, it is important to remember that they were originally meant to be performed so that must be taken into account in your reading and interpretation.

You will usually take part in readings of the texts you are studying in class. Sometimes you are assessed on how much and how well you take part in this. You must take every opportunity to go to the theatre and to watch films and plays of literature on TV, at the cinema or on DVD. Don't wait for a trip to be organised, try and see as many productions and performances as you can (and not just of your set plays!). Some of your course will consist of coursework, which is usually a folder of work containing, for example, criticisms of some of your set texts. There is also the option of an extended essay.

SUBJECT COMBINATIONS

English literature combines well with most subjects and popular combinations include history, philosophy, media studies, sociology, psychology, religious studies, drama and theatre studies, and modern languages. If you are thinking of studying linguistics, a modern or classical language is very useful. Don't forget there is a need for literate scientists so English literature could go well with sciences.

It is possible to combine all A and AS levels with other equivalent qualifications such as BTEC Nationals or OCR Nationals and they could form part of Diplomas.

HIGHER EDUCATION OPTIONS

An A level in English literature is often (although not always) required for degree courses in the subject.

Degree-level study

English literature degrees are flexible and wide ranging. They cover not only traditional areas (like Shakespeare or Dickens) but broader fields such as American literature, creative writing, postcolonial literature and developments in literary theory. Courses could include topics such as crime fiction, literature and addiction, women writers, writing in multicultural Britain, the literature of food or children's literature. Some courses include popular fiction, song lyrics or film.

Some degrees will include the study of Old English language and literature (also known as Anglo-Saxon). This is very different from modern English and is learned as a foreign language. Other courses have a particular emphasis and can include, for example, study in North America, creative writing or English literature with English language. Both English language and literature can be studied for a BEd degree or as a BA with qualified teacher status (QTS), where you study education and gain a teaching qualification alongside your English work.

Degree subject combinations

English literature combines with related subjects, like journalism and media studies, and specialisms within English literature, such as American literature.

Other popular combinations are history, modern and classical languages, and sociology, as well as more unusual ones including law, biology and IT. Subjects can be combined equally in a joint honours degree (two subjects) or a number of subjects studied on a modular course.

Other higher education qualifications

There are no pure English literature foundation degrees but there are related degrees like English and history, applied literary studies, creative advertising, and journalism.

There are no English literature HNDs or HNCs but look at courses like media and communication and journalism. There are pre-entry journalism courses, run by the National Council for the Training of Journalists (NCTJ), which require good A levels or equivalent.

Relevance to other subjects?

The English literature A level develops skills that make a good background for many subjects at a higher level including history, sociology, religious studies, media studies, film studies, drama and linguistics. Consider courses in American, cultural or communication studies.

Important advice

If you apply for an English literature degree one of the most common interview questions is: 'What have you read apart from your set texts?' You should try to get into the habit of reading as much as possible in your spare time. Sunday newspapers contain book review sections, which will help you keep in touch with new books and writers. You could also read the *Times Literary Supplement* or *London Review of Books* – available online or in your local library.

CAREER OPTIONS

Into work after A levels

A level English literature gives communication skills in both speech and writing, which are valuable in the job market. You could consider sales, marketing, and HR or administration jobs. If you want to work with books and literature look at library or bookshop work or you could work in admin for a publisher. For all these jobs you will be in competition with graduates, so you should look for opportunities for further training or take an office or business course to help you get in.

Into work as a graduate

Working in English

English graduates have a wide range of careers open to them.

- **Train to teach in schools, colleges or as a TEFL teacher** (teaching English as a foreign language) – English is part of the National Curriculum, which means that every school must teach it at both primary and secondary levels. Postgraduate training is necessary for this.

- **Publishing** – be prepared to take any job in publishing and work your way up. Opportunities include copy-editing (checking a manuscript for accuracy, consistency and conformity with the publisher's 'house style') or working as a researcher for non-fiction publications. Don't forget that there are now opportunities in digital publishing and e-books. Selling and marketing in publishing can provide good opportunities as can the legal site and publishing rights. There are opportunities in bookselling both in real shops and online.

- **Advertising, marketing and PR** – jobs such as copywriter, media planner or buyer, marketing assistant or PR officer. Entry could be via graduate training schemes or by working your way up from a junior job. There are postgraduate courses available in these areas, which could give you an advantage.

- **Journalism** – there are opportunities in printed, digital and broadcast journalism. Consider a postgraduate course to give you an advantage. It is essential that you gain experience and can demonstrate your commitment by, for example, working for a student newspaper or radio station, or a hospital radio service. You need to build up a good portfolio of experience and work to help you get in and progress.

- **Other writing** – the number of people who make their living from 'creative' writing (novels, short stories and drama) is very small. Don't be put off, but remember that you will probably have to do your writing in your spare time to start off with. It may never earn you any money, but if you want to write you will do it anyway. If you are happy to pursue other forms of writing, you might want to consider technical or non-fiction writing.

Working outside English

Apart from those entering teaching, most English graduates do not use their knowledge of English literature professionally. However, you will have learned to propose ideas and theories and to think creatively. This can be useful in many careers including law and business (especially sales and marketing). For many of these careers, further qualifications or training either in or outside of work will be necessary.

SOURCES OF INFORMATION

National Council for the Training of Journalists (NCTJ)
www.nctj.com

Publishers Association
www.publishers.org.uk

London Review of Books
www.lrb.co.uk

Website

www.whystudyenglish.ac.uk

'The sheer discipline of it, the amount of reading you do, I think it makes you quite confident. You can tackle anything, really.' Shona, taking a degree in English literature with philosophy

Environmental studies

Studying environmental studies will give you the knowledge, understanding and skills to make informed judgements on current environmental issues. It is the study of the environment and the place of human beings within it. You learn the principles that are used to decide how to manage the environment and promote sustainability. You cover not only the scientific concepts that provide a basic understanding of the environment but also the social, economic and political aspects of environmental management. You investigate how humans affect the world in which they live, and you will learn objective and critical approaches to environmental politics. Issues explored on the course include climate change, nuclear power, acid rain, air and water pollution, land use, ecosystem and habitat loss, endangered species, genetically modified (GM) foods, over-fishing, and organic versus chemical farming.

WHAT DO YOU STUDY?

AQA is the only exam board currently offering environmental studies. It replaces the environmental science specification.

At AS you acquire a broad understanding of the environment and how it works and at A2 you expand your studies to gain a greater understanding of important environmental issues, develop your skills further and learn more about science and how it relates to the environment.

The living environment:

- an introduction to the biodiversity of life on Earth
- reasons why the conservation of life on Earth is important
- methods that may be used to achieve effective conservation
- conservation in the UK, coral reefs, Antarctica and tropical rainforests
- 'Life processes in the biosphere' explores the ecological relationships between organisms and their abiotic and biotic environment (the six major abiotic factors are water, sunlight, oxygen, temperature, soil and climate; biotic means relating to, produced by, or caused by living organisms) in order to understand conservation problems further and how these may be managed.

The physical environment:

- atmospheric gases, water and mineral nutrients and how they are essential for life on Earth
- human exploitation and management of physical resources to provide higher material living standards
- unsustainable natural resources.

Energy resources and environmental pollution:

- future problems of energy supply and how these may be resolved; looking at alternative sources of energy
- properties of pollutants to explain why some materials or forms of energy cause environmental damage; the study of atmospheric, aquatic and terrestrial pollutants

'I did some local conservation work, helping tidy up the local canal. It's something positive to put on my personal statement.' Thomas, aged 17, taking environmental studies with chemistry and biology

- minimising releases, treating effluents and managing the damage caused by pollutants.

Biological resources and sustainability:

- factors controlling human population growth in relation to the demands placed upon the planet's resources and life-support systems
- food production and forestry systems and environmental problems caused by them, how these problems can be tackled
- study of the sustainability of human lifestyles.

In addition, you will develop skills in mathematical and statistical analysis.

Although environmental science (not studies) is available at GCSE level, many people start the A level with GCSE biology, geography or combined science.

HOW DO YOU STUDY?

Environmental studies involves classroom work, essay writing, discussions, research and class presentations. You spend time on laboratory experiments, fieldwork, surveys, role-play sessions, environmental impact assessments, cost–benefit analysis, computer modelling and energy audits. An example could be analysing the water in a local river using various tests to determine the pollution level. You visit relevant sites, which could be a nuclear reactor or nature reserve. You are encouraged to do as much reading around the subject as you can, especially about issues currently in the news.

SUBJECT COMBINATIONS

Environmental studies combines well with biology, geography, geology and chemistry. If you want to study environmental studies at a higher level, biology and geography may be required or preferred, and, in some cases,

chemistry. Maths or statistics could be useful as data analysis can be an important part of environment degrees. Some environmental science or studies degrees are more issue based, so you might consider A levels in economics, government and politics, or law.

It is possible to combine all A and AS levels with other equivalent qualifications such as BTEC Nationals or OCR Nationals and they could form part of Diplomas.

HIGHER EDUCATION OPTIONS

Degree-level study

There are many degrees with the word 'environmental' in their title. The most widely offered are environmental science and environmental studies. These include the topics you will have already studied for A level environmental studies, although in much greater breadth and depth. They vary in the emphasis they give to basic scientific principles so you must check the course content carefully.

Other environment degrees available include climate change, environmental biogeochemistry, environmental chemistry, environmental conservation, environmental planning, environmental forensics, environmental geography, environmental geoscience, environmental sustainability, conservation science and marine environmental science.

Degree titles are not always a reliable guide to content, so you should check carefully before you decide which courses to apply for.

> 'It's important to build up your contacts and keep networking during your degree. You never know when a contact might help you later on.'
> Ben, graduate in environmental sciences, working for a climate change company advising the public on reducing their carbon footprint

Environmental engineering is another option (you will usually need A level mathematics and physics for entry). This is concerned with engineering techniques for solving environmental problems, such as water resource management, pollution, waste management and land reclamation. It is often available combined with civil engineering. A related degree is disaster management.

Some environmental degrees offer a study year abroad or a sandwich placement.

Degree subject combinations

Environmental science and environmental studies are available in combination with related subjects. Examples are environment and planning, environmental earth science with education, environmental studies and geographical information systems, and environment and business.

Other higher education qualifications

You can study foundation degrees in related areas including rural environmental management, managing environments, environmental conservation and countryside management, green space management, renewable and sustainable energy, civil and environmental engineering, sustainable land management, sustainable engineering, ecology and conservation management.

There are also foundation degrees available in environmental health and occupational health and safety management.

There are environmental science Diploma courses leading to the HNC or HND, most of them designed as vocational training. Examples include environmental management, conservation biology and green technology.

Relevance to other subjects?

The environmental studies A level is concerned with the interaction between people and their environment, so it has a social science element that would be relevant to subjects such as sociology, history, politics, psychology, economics or law. It is also acceptable for courses such as countryside or land management or business administration.

Important advice

If you are taking biology, geography, physics or science in society, there may be some slight overlap (depending on the options taken) so check the course content carefully if you are studying environmental studies with any of these subjects.

Try and get as much experience as you can if you are planning a career in the environment. Try voluntary work with a local environmental or conservation group.

CAREER OPTIONS

Into work after A levels

Many companies now operate in a more sustainable and environmental way and there has been a rise in 'green collar jobs', which are jobs concerned with the environment.

You will usually need further training to make direct use of your environmental studies knowledge in a job. However, you may be able to work for one of the many groups and organisations concerned with environmental issues, especially if you have some experience of business or administration work. Your technical knowledge may be helpful in the preparation of publicity, or in local group activities and education programmes. Experience as a volunteer may help you to obtain paid work later. The study of environmental studies will have given you the ability to take a logical approach to problems as well as developing good problem-solving skills, which could help you in careers in business administration, banking or finance.

Into work as a graduate

Working in environmental studies

- **Environmental scientist** – working in a university or large commercial company in research or consultancy, a postgraduate qualification will be useful for this type or work.

- **Environmental health** – local government employs environmental health officers, whose responsibilities include noise control and food safety inspection (although here you would be in competition with graduates in food science).

- **Housing management, surveying and town planning** – you will need additional specialist qualifications.

- **Waste management** – organisations such as local authorities and private companies employ environmental scientists as recycling or waste management professionals.

- **Government agencies** – there could be opportunities with the Environment Agency or DEFRA as well as the Health and Safety Executive (HSE).

- **Nature conservation officer** – working for local authorities or national organisations.

- **Environmental organisations** – for example Natural England, the Royal Society for the Protection of Birds and the National Parks. These organisations recruit environmental scientists, as do environmental pressure groups such as Friends of the Earth. There is a lot of competition for jobs in these organisations and factors other than academic qualifications are important. You must be able to demonstrate enthusiasm for the work and a good portfolio of voluntary experience.

- **Domestic energy assessor or installer** – assessing how green houses are or installing green energy technologies in houses and businesses, for example solar panels or water reclamation systems; further training will be required.

Working outside environmental studies

The general scientific education you will receive as part of an environmental science degree helps you to develop strong observation, data-recording, interpretation and IT skills, as well as the ability to write high-quality reports on your findings. These skills could help you in many careers such as business and finance, advertising and marketing.

SOURCES OF INFORMATION

Chartered Institute of Environmental Health
www.cieh.org

Department for Environment, Food and Rural Affairs (DEFRA)
www.defra.gov.uk

Environment Agency
www.environment-agency.gov.uk

Natural Environment Research Council
www.nerc.ac.uk

Websites

www.environmentalcareers.org.uk

www.letsrecycle.com

www.wwf.org.uk

'The best thing about studying environmental science is the extra knowledge you get by taking course units from other areas such as geology, town planning, chemistry, biology and geography.' David, second year BSc environmental science

Film studies

Film studies will increase your understanding and enjoyment of film, the major art form of the 20th century and still developing today. You will learn to understand and appreciate how films communicate meaning and entertain us, their social context and the industry that produces them. The course covers the study of British and US films, and world cinema, and gives you the opportunity to make your own films and write storyboards and screenplays.

WHAT DO YOU STUDY?

WJEC is the only board offering film studies at A level. An A level in moving image arts is offered by the CCEA examination board.

The topics covered are:

- **film form** – how the micro-features of a film work and produce meaning. Micro-features are elements of the film such as cinematography, editing, sound, performance and mise en scène (sets, props, costumes etc)

- **British and American film** – how the British and American film industries work. Who are the film audiences in the UK and how is film viewed, for example cinema, home cinema and the web. Topics in British film include: What makes a film a British film and what genres exist? (e.g. horror and comedy). What are the characteristics of British film stars? (e.g. Ewan Macgregor or Julie Christie). British production companies like Ealing Studios or Working Title. How are films influenced by their cultural period? (e.g. the 'swinging sixties' or 'Thatcher's Britain'). What about the social and political contents of film, such as those involving the crime culture? (e.g. *Bullet Boy* or *Get Carter*). How have other cultures arriving in Britain contributed to the British identity in film? (e.g. *Yasmin, Ghost, and Gypo*). You will also study aspects of finance, organisation, production, distribution and marketing within the film industry

- **US film** – you will study and compare two films from a specific genre or dealing with a specific theme. For example, two films dealing with personal identity: *Imitation of Life* and *Boys Don't Cry;* you could also consider remakes such as *King Kong* (1933 and 2005) or *The Invasion of the Body Snatchers* (1956 and 1978).

In A2 you will develop your understanding of all of the work you've been introduced to in AS with new topics. You'll be studying world cinema such as Bollywood, Iranian, Japanese or Mexican cinema or international film styles such as German and/or Soviet cinema of the 1920s, surrealism and neo-realism and new waves. There are specialist studies in urban environments or the empowerment of women. There are topics covering early cinema, documentaries, experimental film and video, popular film and emotional response (e.g. what makes a weepie). You will write a critical study of one film from a prescribed list. You will also undertake a film project and make your own short film or write a screenplay.

There is a film studies GCSE available but you don't need this to take the A level.

> *'It's the old chestnut, but it is a really hard slog. Nearly the entire industry is freelance now and when you haven't worked for two months you begin to doubt why you got started in the first place. Just make yourself indispensable.'*
> Jenny, assistant director, with a degree in film and video

HOW DO YOU STUDY?

Lessons include film screenings and close analysis of sequences from different films, followed by essays, criticism and case studies. You will have the opportunity to produce work in the form of a screenplay, storyboard, film criticism, film or DVD either in a group or alone. You will be expected to take an active interest in film outside the classroom and be able to talk about it knowledgeably and critically.

SUBJECT COMBINATIONS

If you are considering a degree course in professional film production and direction you will need a portfolio, which can be prepared by taking film studies A level. You could consider taking art and design or photography with film studies, as they will increase your understanding of how visual images are put together and how they can communicate different ideas.

Some art and design courses allow you to use film and video as part of the practical work. English literature helps you to express your ideas on paper and offer clear criticism of others' work, using evidence from texts to back up your ideas. Communication and culture, media studies, history or modern languages also combine well.

It is possible to combine all A and AS levels with other equivalent qualifications such as BTEC Nationals or OCR Nationals and they could form part of Diplomas.

Skillset has created a network of Screen Academies that are recognised as centres of excellence in film education in the UK,

> 'It is really hard work, long hours - a big shock after college. You must learn to fit in with all sorts of people, if you don't, you don't work.'
> Damien, working as a runner, after a film studies degree

including a film business academy. Courses at these academies are at further education, degree and postgraduate level, as well as short technical courses.

HIGHER EDUCATION OPTIONS

A level film studies is not necessary for film degrees. Note that for some of the more practical courses based at colleges of art and design, an art Foundation course may be helpful to gain entry.

Degree-level study

Film studies courses take a variety of forms: some focus more on the critical and historical study of film, others on the practical skills involved in film making. However, most courses include elements of both and aim to find their own balance between them. As film studies A level is not offered by every school or college, most degree courses start from scratch. You can then often decide on the direction that your own course will take through your choice of options, which cover specialised areas such as theoretical and analytical studies, camera techniques (using both film and video), scriptwriting and technical production.

Look out for titles such as film production, film and video studies, and moving image. You will also find more focused courses like computer visualisation and animation, scriptwriting for film and television, animation production, 3D computer animation, animation (CGI) and virtual reality design.

Degree subject combinations

Film studies can be combined with many subjects, for example, English or a language. Many film studies degrees are already 'combined' degrees, as you study video, television, radio or digital media from a practical and/or theoretical viewpoint. If you are interested in the production side of film making you might combine film with business or management.

Other higher education qualifications

Foundation degrees are available in film and TV production; media practice (film and video); creative digital video; digital film production creative industries (film and video); film and video production; film production; post-production technology for film, TV and CGI; media production; hair and make up for film and TV; and moving image. Courses can link into degrees or professional practice courses and some will require a portfolio of work.

There are some HND and HNC courses specifically geared towards film and media. Course titles include applied multimedia, media moving image, and digital film making.

Postgraduate courses are available in film and all aspects of film making.

Relevance to other subjects?

Film studies A level encourages you to develop observational, critical, written and practical skills. It helps you to look at creative products in detail in the context of the society or culture in which they were made. Film studies can lead to degrees in communication studies, English, American studies, sociology, psychology, and philosophy. It could also help you on drama or performing arts courses.

Important advice

If you are considering a degree in film studies or a related area, start by investigating the exact contact and entry requirements of each course as they can vary a great deal. Try to find out where their graduates went.

CAREER OPTIONS

Into work after A levels

The film industry is competitive so you might get in at a junior level. There may be administration jobs or you might get in as a 'runner' for a film or television company. Runners help everything to run smoothly and provide a range of support in every area of film production. There are also Apprenticeships available at, for example, Pinewood Studios (see Skillset website).

You might wish to work in an area related to film, such as advertising, distribution (getting films to cinemas around the country) or marketing. Roles available are likely to be as an administrator or general assistant, and if you are good at networking and making useful contacts you may be able to get work from there.

Into work as a graduate

Working in film or television

You should be prepared to get further training or to start in a junior position and work your way up. Postgraduate study could be an option to enhance your skills.

Most people earn a low wage, work extremely long and unsociable hours and are on short-term freelance contracts. If you are serious about a career in film you must be prepared to network and make contacts at every opportunity as you really have to build your career yourself. You must be prepared to work as a freelance and self-employed.

Here are some examples of the types of jobs available to you:

- **production runners or assistants** – help run the producers' and directors' offices, involved in films from planning to post-production. Tasks include booking crews, organising the shipping of equipment and arranging timetables. Could lead to production roles such as script supervisor

- **assistant directors** – work with the production manager to carry out many of the practical jobs needed during the production of the film. There are different levels of assistant director: first assistants have the most responsibility and help to maintain the shooting schedule; second, third and fourth assistants work with the first assistant and have decreasing levels of responsibility, carrying out tasks such as calling actors and delivering scripts and messages. This work can lead to the role of director, who takes full responsibility for the production

- **camera operators** – carry out the director's instructions regarding shot composition and development. Start as trainees

- **designers** – work in film, television or video and use technical and artistic skills. Work in this area can range from costume and set design to designing the continuity sequences used on screen between programmes. To enter this area, you need additional specialised training, which can often involve a postgraduate course or an Apprenticeship

- **script writers** – work freelance and are commissioned by film or television companies. Writing for the screen is very different from writing a book and a good understanding of film terminology and techniques is needed.

For details of other jobs, visit the Skillset website.

Working outside film or television

Film studies graduates could enter advertising and marketing, journalism, publishing, research, and arts administration. They can also get into careers for graduates in any discipline such as business and finance or retail and management training.

SOURCES OF INFORMATION

British Film Institute
www.bfi.org.uk/education

Film Education
www.filmeducation.org

Skillset
www.skillset.org/careers

London Film School
www.lfs.org.uk

National Film and Television School
www.nftsfilm-tv.ac.uk

Websites

www.bbc.co.uk/jobs

www.ukfilmcouncil.org.uk

'Working as a freelancer is hard as you are always wondering where your next job is coming from .You are also expected to keep up with the trade press so you know what you are talking about.'
Jools, assistant director, with a degree in English literature

General studies

General studies focuses on the contemporary issues that affect our lives. The subject is very broad so different types of teaching styles and approaches are used. These include discussions, debates, written and investigative work. As well as developing important thinking and communication skills, the course gives you the opportunity to broaden your general knowledge about a range of world issues and current affairs, e.g. human cloning, media censorship, the impact of globalisation, contemporary art, religious conflict and environmentalism. An interest in current affairs is vital for success in general studies.

The specifications are very wide. To give you an idea, here are the module titles from different exam boards:

- challenges for society
- the individual in society
- change and progress
- beliefs, values and responsibilities
- the social domain
- culture, arts and humanities
- science maths and technology
- culture and society
- science and society.

Within these modules you will find themes on a wide range of issues covering everything from human rights, the role of the media, religion, psychology, technology, business, maths and statistics. You will also be taught thinking and analytical skills.

Here are some examples:

- the origins of the universe, natural forces and sources and forms of energy
- explanation and evaluation of human behaviour
- commerce and industry and the impact of political and economic issues on science, society and the environment
- mathematics in science and society
- the moral responsibility of scientists
- the social, ethical and environmental

implications of scientific discoveries and technological development

- the contribution of science and technology to lifestyles in different societies
- space exploration
- climate change
- the energy debate
- medicine and health
- ethical responsibilities of scientists
- the role of religious and value systems, beliefs and values, tolerance and moral issues
- the individual and society; tolerance and intolerance
- freedoms, rights and responsibilities

'This is a good course because I looked at things I didn't cover in any of my other subjects, and it can get you into your first choice university! I got an A in general studies in my AS year, so the pressure was off a little for the second year. My second choice of uni accepted general studies, meaning I only had to get 2 out of my other 3 subjects to go to my second choice. Knowing I had that back up helped me not to worry for the whole of upper sixth. I actually got into my first choice.'
Peter, A levels in geography, history, politics and general studies, now studying a BA in war studies

- evaluating the media and recognising bias
- the impact of advertising
- large corporations; free trade, fair trade
- the British political system and the role of the monarchy
- the role and responsibility of artists
- the power of language and images to transmit, persuade or distort; 'spin' and propaganda
- heritage conservation
- trends in consumerism
- economic growth
- migration of people; urban and rural distribution of power
- equal opportunities; law enforcement.

You will be expected to read newspapers, watch TV and generally 'get informed' about current issues that affect all of us in our daily lives.

General studies is an excellent additional subject and will combine with a whole range of A level subjects. Some of the topics covered are similar to those in the science in society, and citizenship A levels, so you should check to make sure these don't overlap.

It can be taken as a contrasting subject (for example, with specific science subjects) to give a varied and enhanced curriculum, or as a complementary subject (for example, with social science subjects) to give a thorough grounding in one field of knowledge. General studies A level is a useful course for anyone wanting to show that they have studied a broad curriculum and can think critically and flexibly in examination conditions, rather than memorising information in a specialised area. It is sometimes not accepted as a third subject for university entrance. However, as a fourth subject it can be very useful to convince university admissions tutors of your general academic ability. Some students find that general studies helps their university applications as it teaches critical and thinking

skills as well as giving you a broad outlook on a wide range of subjects. It can prove useful on a personal statement for university entry.

Please note that general studies may not always count towards UCAS point offers. You will need to check with each individual institution.

> 'It sets you apart from students who have similar grades in other subjects but can't offer general studies. I always find that students who have taken general studies interview very well.'
> HE admissions tutor

Geography

Are you interested in the world around you? The world we live in is constantly changing. Think about natural and man-made catastrophes in the news such as flooding, earthquakes and war. Geography allows you to see why and how the world changes. It is multidisciplinary, offering the opportunity to develop a range of skills including investigative, IT, graphical, cartographical and statistical, numerical and research. You study a range of topics covering current major global concerns looking at issues like population growth and globalisation as well as tsunamis and volcanoes. The course will enhance your understanding of the environment and help you understand some of the pressing environmental, economic and social problems facing the world today.

WHAT DO YOU STUDY?

The topics listed give an idea of what could be covered. The exact content of AS and A2 specifications differs according to exam boards, so you will need to check with your school or college about the exact modules available to you.

The study of geography is divided between two branches.

Physical geography is concerned with the Earth, its physical structure and the processes that take place on its surface, as well as physical hazards such as tornadoes, earthquakes and flooding.

Human geography looks at the activities of human beings in their physical settings; it addresses current issues, such as food shortages, war, immigration, population and sustainability.

A core theme at A level is the study of how the two branches of geography interact: the effect that the human and physical worlds have on each other. Contemporary concerns such as climate change and global warming are included in the specifications.

The topics covered include:

Physical geography

Biogeography – ecosystems (communities of organisms and their environment), vegetation (why particular species of plant grow in particular parts of the world) and soils.

Geomorphology – the shaping of the Earth's surface by the environment (wind, the oceans, glaciers, etc) through the processes of glacier formation, weathering, erosion and desertification, and plate tectonics.

Hydrology – water on and just above the Earth's surface: how it goes through a cycle by evaporation, rainfall and the return of water via rivers to the sea; how these processes can be managed by applied hydrology (dams, irrigation, hydroelectric power, flood prevention, etc) for our benefit.

'Project work means you are often working to deadlines, which is an important skill. The projects are always varied and involve a more rounded approach, instead of just writing essays. The A level course has taught me lots about the world we live in and you learn much more about other societies. It inspired me to travel around east Africa in my gap year!'
Peter, aged 20, studying for a degree in war studies after A levels in geography, history, politics and general studies

Atmospheric systems – climate and weather, atmospheric pollution and global warming, the implications for human life.

Coastal studies – the processes that shape coastlines and their reaction to the impact of human culture.

Human geography

Economic geography – the distribution of the world's economic resources including agriculture, food, health, industry, economic development, tourism, energy and transportation.

Population – global population change, migration and resources.

Settlement – where and how people settle in different parts of the world: the location, character and structure of villages, towns and cities and how they grow, change and decline.

Management – of human geographical processes through planning systems.

GCSE geography is not always essential for A level study but most schools and colleges will assume some background knowledge.

HOW DO YOU STUDY?

Apart from formal lessons, you will take part in classroom discussions and debates .You will learn how to obtain, record, represent, classify and interpret data of different types from both primary and secondary sources. This will include using software to manipulate geographical data.

Fieldwork is an important part of the course and you may be examined on this. It involves measuring and collecting data, and conducting surveys using questionnaires and interviews. It might be in your local area or further afield, giving you the opportunity to observe and record in a variety of settings and landscapes.

SUBJECT COMBINATIONS

Geography is a subject that falls neatly between the arts and the sciences and combines well with many AS and A level subjects. The scientific nature of geography, especially physical geography, means that there is a useful overlap with biology, physics, environmental studies and geology. Some universities might not count geography as a whole A level if you also offer environmental studies. If you want to study environmental science at degree level you may need a science at A level. You should check this if you have a particular degree course in mind. The human, economic and social aspects of geography go well with subjects such as history, economics, politics, sociology and world development.

t is possible to combine all A and AS levels with other equivalent qualifications such as BTEC Nationals or OCR Nationals and they could form part of Diplomas.

HIGHER EDUCATION OPTIONS

Geography is a popular degree and a good grade in A level geography is needed for entry.

Degree-level study

Geography can be studied for either a BA or BSc degree. The BA concentrates more on human geography and the BSc more on the physical aspects of the subject. A BA might include topics such as population studies, settlement, and distribution of wealth and resources. A BSc course is more likely to involve topics such as geoscience (the scientific study of the structure of the Earth and issues relating to natural resources) and hydrology and geomorphology. However, many universities allow for flexibility in choosing topics from both types of degree.

Fieldwork is an essential part of geography degrees and may include overseas trips. Your first year on a geography course will cover some of the topics you began at A level. However, its scope will extend to urban and rural studies, biogeography, and economic geography and development studies. There will then be specialised options such as medical geography (the characteristics of illness and disease in relation to where they occur), cartography and environmental monitoring, and impact assessment. There are specialised degrees in related subjects such as geographical information systems, human geography, natural hazards and sustainable development. Geography can be taken as a BEd degree, qualifying you to teach the subject in state schools.

Degree subject combinations

Geography can be combined with one or more of many other subjects. Popular choices include economics, English, history, languages, mathematics and sociology. Biology, IT and environmental studies are also possibilities.

Other higher education qualifications

There are foundation degrees available in development geography as well as some related courses in ecology, eco-technology and conservation management.

HND and HNC courses are available in geography-related courses in environmental hazards, environmental management and geology.

Relevance to other subjects?

Geography A level can be used as a foundation for a wide range of other subjects, like law, politics, economics, architecture, business studies and anthropology. It is useful for land-based industry courses. It would also be valuable preparation for degrees in environmental science, ecology, surveying, conservation, geology, travel and tourism, and any course that has an international dimension to it like European studies. Landscape architecture, meteorology, oceanography and planning are other possibilities.

Important advice

You will need to examine course content carefully to find out which courses will be suitable for you. A geography degree can be useful for getting into environmental and conservation work. If considering this, it is important to build up a portfolio of voluntary and work experience in conservation. This could be anything from helping to clean up a park at weekends through to a gap year spent in conservation work abroad or in the UK.

CAREER OPTIONS

Into work after A levels

The skills you will have learned on your course, like data handling, team working and IT plus an interest in the world around you, will be useful in all sorts of jobs such as business administration, insurance, retail, finance, media, and travel and tourism.

Into work as a graduate

Working in geography

Your geography degree gives you many useful skills such as the ability to undertake research and analysis and to interpret data of all types. You will also be numerate with a good knowledge of global issues and the environment.

There is a wide range of careers you could consider, although some will need extra study or training.

- **Environment and sustainability** – environmental campaigners, recycling officers, cycle route planners or environmental impact officers.

- **Planning** – surveying, town planning, landscape architecture working for local or national government or in industry.
- **Mapping** – geographical information systems (GIS), cartography, aerial surveying and remote sensing.
- **Science and conservation** – hazard prediction and management, coastal engineer, flood protection officer, pollution analyst.
- **Travel and tourism** – travel agent, expedition leader, eco-tour guide.
- **Development** – aid worker, policy adviser.

Working outside geography

Geography gives you many skills that could be applied to lots of different careers. There are opportunities in local government such as leisure, recreation and housing management. Having a numerate degree could get you into finance and banking, management training, marketing, advertising and the Civil Service; teaching is also a possibility.

SOURCES OF INFORMATION

Ordnance Survey
www.ordnancesurvey.co.uk

Royal Geographical Society
www.rgs.org

Websites

www.geography-site.co.uk

www.geographyinthenews.rgs.org

> 'Geography is not only up to date and relevant; it is one of the most exciting, adventurous and valuable subjects to study today. So many of the world's current problems boil down to geography, and need the geographers of the future to help us understand them.'
> Michael Palin, broadcaster

Geology

Geology is a branch of science concerned with the structure, evolution and dynamics of the Earth, and with the exploitation of the mineral and energy resources that it contains. If you have a science or geographical background, or just an interest in the planet Earth, geology offers a wide range of topical subjects.

Earthquakes and volcanoes are always in the news. Asteroid impact is now seen as a very real threat to the planet. Earthquakes, volcanoes and asteroid impact are all topics in geology A level, which offers exciting ways of understanding how the inner parts of the planet work.

There will be fieldwork at home or abroad, and the internet keeps you up to date with the latest geological events around the globe.

Geology combines well with A level geography and other science subjects like environmental studies, physics, chemistry or biology. Science GCSEs can be helpful and GCSE maths is sometimes required.

Geology could lead to a career in the environment, prospecting for natural resources, climate studies, engineering, surveying, or monitoring volcanoes, earthquakes and other natural hazards.

Government and politics

Where does the real power lie in this country? Why do people choose not to vote? Although these matters may seem remote to many of us, they are important and need to be understood if we are to play a full role as a citizen in our democracy.

Government and politics is about much more than who is going to win the next general election. As a student of A level government and politics you will explore how political power is gained and used, and learn about how governments and other political institutions and systems work both in the UK and the USA. You look at political structures, such as the voting system and Parliament, and the case for and against changing those structures; the definitions and the functions of concepts such as democracy, justice and rights; and recent developments in the world of politics. You will also examine political ideas and concepts including other political ideologies.

WHAT DO YOU STUDY?

The topics listed give an idea of what could be covered. The exact content of AS and A2 specifications differs according to exam boards, so you will need to check with your school or college about the exact modules available to you.

At AS you gain a broad understanding of the UK political system, including the role of elections, political parties and pressure groups and how policy is made.

You cover the central ideas of citizenship, democracy and participation and how the representative processes work in the UK. What is democracy and how does it differ from dictatorship? Voting and electoral behaviour; how the voting system works; what influences how people vote? Do elections guarantee democracy? What is the role of political parties? How important are pressure groups? The major institutions of contemporary UK government: their relationships with one another and their effectiveness. How adequate is the UK constitution? The UK does not have a written constitution but does have a constantly evolving collection of laws and principles, according to which the country is governed. What is the role and significance

of Parliament? How powerful is the prime minister? Do judges deliver justice and defend freedom?

At A2 the specification includes a number of optional units and you might specialise in US politics or look at issues that are central to the study of modern politics, such as the environment, ideologies, globalisation, power, devolution and the European Union (EU).

The representative processes of the US political system and their adequacy in terms of popular participation and full democracy. The institutional framework of the US government and the interrelationships between its legislature (Congress), executive (President) and judiciary (Supreme Court) and their role within the US Constitution – the oldest constitution in the world.

We learned about not just British politics but also political theory, e.g. communism, fascism etc. A level politics opens your eyes to how our country is run and governed, and is unique because there are no other subjects where you learn about how and why Britain is like it is today, from a political point of view.'
Peter, with A levels in geography, history, government and politics and general studies, now taking a BA in war studies

Elections and voting, political parties, pressure groups, and racial and ethnic politics; political ideas and ideologies such as socialism, liberalism, conservatism, fascism, feminism and nationalism; power in modern society; Britain in Europe.

Issues such as: ethnicity and gender, the environment, education, the economy, perspectives on modern politics participation and representation, globalisation, change and continuity, territorial politics, rights in practice and power in practice.

All of these are studied in the context of current and recent issues, arguments and events. A GCSE in the subject is not required for study at A level but you must be enthusiastic about politics and have a good grasp of English.

HOW DO YOU STUDY?

You study through lessons, discussions, research tasks and may take part in mock elections or 'Question Time' sessions. You may listen to invited speakers, visit political organisations, the House of Commons or even Washington DC. Outside class, you must be prepared to do a lot of extra reading. You need to read a quality newspaper and monitor the media to keep up to date with issues and events.

SUBJECT COMBINATIONS

Universities do not ask for any specific A levels for entry to degrees in government, politics or related subjects. Appropriate A levels include history, philosophy, citizenship, English, economics, law and sociology.

It is possible to combine all A and AS levels with other equivalent qualifications such as BTEC Nationals or OCR Nationals and they could form part of Diplomas.

HIGHER EDUCATION OPTIONS

Degree-level study

There is a wide range of politics degrees and each has its own specialism although these are generally the main areas of study.

- **British politics** – constitutional reforms and the devolution of Scotland, Wales and Northern Ireland. Britain's membership of the EU, the possibility of the euro and the sovereignty debate.

- **The EU and Europe** – comparing them with British and other political systems. Many universities offer courses focusing on the politics of various countries such as the USA, the Middle East, Latin America, Asia, Africa or Australasia.

- **Political theory** – where you consider key questions about the nature of freedom and the strengths and limitations of democracy. Other topics include the relationship between government and society, the right of dissent and the limits of toleration, and questions of social justice and equality.

- **Elections** – and how they can change the course of a country. Studying elections can be about predicting results, trying to work out why people vote as they do, or even why they don't vote at all. Party campaigns, what policies are put forward and how parties select candidates.

- **International relations** – covers topics such as the role of international organisations (such as the United Nations), the strategies of various characters on the international political stage, the role of international non-governmental actors (for example large corporations) and vital international policy areas like the environment. It addresses questions such as why wars occur, how peace is negotiated and maintained, and what is international justice.

On many courses you can spend some time on fieldwork and this might involve working with a political party or pressure group, or you may even go abroad, observing the work of the European Parliament, European Commission or NATO.

You will also find there are specialist degrees in politics such as European politics and international politics, political economy, globalisation and governance, and political science. You could also consider international relations.

Degree subject combinations

Government and politics is available in combination with economics, history, philosophy, sociology, law and languages. There are also combinations with subjects like human rights and international relations, peace studies or social policy.

Other higher education qualifications

There are no foundation degrees available in government and politics but there are some in related topics, such as community regeneration and community governance, public administration and trade union studies.

There are no HNDs or HNCs available in government and politics but you might want to look at related courses in public administration and legal studies. These are more vocational than degree courses and aim to prepare you for careers in local/national government or as a legal executive. (For more information, see the entry for law.)

Relevance to other subjects?

The government and politics A level gives you skills in how to develop ideas and arguments backed up with reliable evidence. This will be useful in many other subjects, especially economics, philosophy, law and history.

Important advice

You must get into the habit of reading a quality newspaper regularly and keeping in touch with current events and issues. Applying what you learn to real-world events will make your studies far more interesting and give you a head start over other students, especially if you decide to apply for government and politics courses at degree level.

CAREER OPTIONS

Into work after A levels

It may be possible to get into jobs in national or local government. The study of government and politics increases your awareness of what is going on in the world and develops your skills of argument and discussion (both written and spoken), which can be used in many areas. Politics affects the work of the police and customs services, so an appreciation of issues such as immigration, civil liberties, and protest and pressure groups would be helpful in these careers.

Into work as a graduate

Working in government and politics

- **Elected politicians** – you usually start off by working unpaid for a political party, whether at a local or national level, and are then selected by the party to stand at an election for a council seat or parliamentary constituency.

- **Agents and researchers** – some people enter politics by becoming an agent for an MP (they are usually in the political party first) and there are opportunities to become researchers or assistants to MPs.

- **Political consultants and lobbyists** – employed by companies or other groups that want to see a particular issue raised and examined in Parliament.

- **Local government officers** – work at a local level in areas such as housing, roads and other public facilities.

- **Civil servants** – if you reach the senior grades in Whitehall, you will be advising government ministers on how policy should be put into practice. Recruitment to the senior Civil Service is through intensive selection tests, after which you are assigned to a particular department such as health, defence or education. Civil servants also work for the European Commission and a modern language up to A level standard is required for fast-stream recruitment.

- **Other related jobs** – trade union work, political party organiser, academic teaching and research, and political journalism.

Working outside government and politics

A degree in politics is accepted for a wide range of careers. As a politics graduate you will be able to express yourself clearly in speech and writing. This makes you an ideal candidate for work in business, the media, journalism, management or the law.

SOURCES OF INFORMATION

The Political Studies Association
www.psa.ac.uk

Civil Service careers (including EU fast-stream recruitment)
www.civilservice.gov.uk/jobs

Political parties:

Conservative Party
www.conservatives.com

Labour Party
www.labour.org.uk

Liberal Democrats
www.libdems.org.uk

Websites

www.parliament.uk

www.w4mp.org

www.politicsresources.net

www.studypolitics.org

> *'We went to Strasbourg to see how the EU works. I particularly enjoyed the visit to the Court of Human rights where we got to talk to a human rights lawyer. I now understand how the EU works. There's nothing like seeing it at first hand.'*
> Elinor, taking A levels in politics, history, English language and literature

Greek (classical)/Latin

Also known as classics: classical Greek; and classics: Latin.

These subjects give you the opportunity to learn the ancient Greek and Latin languages (ancient Greek is known as classical Greek) and to study a selection of Greek and Roman literature. The cultures of ancient Greece and Rome are fascinating to study in themselves, but they are also the foundation of modern Western civilisations and cultures. By studying Greek or Latin, you begin to appreciate the language and literature, history and society of the classical world and begin to understand how it has influenced our own. Studying classical languages also trains you in logical and analytical skills as well as providing a foundation for studying a modern language and writing English.

WHAT DO YOU STUDY?

OCR is the only board offering ancient Greek and Latin.

This part of their classics suite, which offers four named pathways (Latin, classical Greek, classical civilisation and ancient history). There is a fifth pathway leading to a classics A/AS level, which offers combinations of units chosen from Greek, Latin and classical civilisation.

- **Knowledge and understanding of the language** – translating passages taken from the set texts as well as 'unseen' passages of Greek or Latin into English. You carry out comprehension exercises similar to those you are used to in modern languages, and sometimes translate into Latin or Greek (this is known as 'prose composition'). There is an option of translating English into Latin or Greek.

- **Literary knowledge and understanding** – looking at how characters, thoughts, actions and situations are presented in Greek or Latin texts, how meanings are conveyed, whether directly or indirectly, and how the texts can be understood in their social, cultural and historical settings.

- **Literary criticism and personal response** – considering the choice and arrangement of words, their rhythm and how the moods they convey are exploited in Greek and Latin literature, how to think about and explain your own response to the text. The texts studied could include those written by Homer, Lysias, Xenophon, Plato, Aristophanes, Euripides, Sophocles, Herodotus or Thucydides (for Greek) or Cicero, Ovid, Catullus, Propertius, Livy, Sallust, Virgil or Tacitus (for Latin). Most people taking A level Latin will already have taken it at GCSE, but many take A level classical Greek as beginners.

HOW DO YOU STUDY?

Latin and ancient Greek stopped being everyday languages long ago. You cannot learn to speak them, or listen to the spoken language, as you do with a modern language. Instead, you work through reading and writing. You will study literature in translation and translate 'unseen' texts from Latin or classical Greek into English and (optionally) from English into Latin or classical Greek.

> *'When I went on holiday to Spain, I realised that my knowledge of Latin helped me to understand the language.'*
> Doug, IT consultant

Classes concentrate on grammatical analysis, understanding, analysing and appreciating the literary qualities of the set texts and translation. However, the teaching of classical languages has gained from developments in modern language teaching, so it is not as different as you might expect. You may go on visits to museums or sites with links to the classics.

SUBJECT COMBINATIONS

If you are thinking of a degree in Latin or Greek and have the opportunity to take the language for A level, then you should. If you are thinking of studying both languages at university, you don't have to offer classical Greek A level, but a modern language alongside Latin would be helpful. Greek combines well with most A levels including history, modern languages or English. If you are considering a degree in archaeology then mathematics or a science, especially chemistry, would be useful as archaeology uses scientific techniques for the analysis of archaeological sites and remains. If you are considering medicine then plenty of anatomy and pathology terms are in Greek or Latin so it could be a useful subject along with your sciences.

It is possible to combine all A and AS levels with other equivalent qualifications such as BTEC Nationals or OCR Nationals and they could form part of Diplomas.

HIGHER EDUCATION OPTIONS

As the opportunity to study Latin or classical Greek is not always available in schools, some universities now teach them from scratch offering different routes to beginners and those with the A level .

For classics degrees (Latin and Greek), you usually have to offer one or both of the languages (if only one, Latin is the usual requirement). There are a few classics courses where AS levels in Greek or Latin are accepted and one or two where GCSEs in Greek or Latin are accepted.

Degree-level study

The following options are open to you at degree level:

- a single-subject degree in either Latin or Greek (although often you can also study the other language as a minor or through options)

- a degree in classics (Latin and Greek) – again, you can usually vary the proportions of the two languages, or concentrate more on one or the other as you progress through your degree.

In both these types of degree, you will spend much of your time reading Latin or Greek literature, developing your understanding and appreciation of the language. Naturally, the number and variety of writers that you study will expand greatly from your A level work. You may also have the opportunity to study the history of Latin or Greek. Some courses allow you to study the Latin used after the end of the Roman period (about AD 476) up to the Middle Ages (ending about AD 1500). In addition to language and literary work, you study Greek and Roman history, culture and society, mythology and religion, and art and architecture. Most degree courses are very flexible and allow you to choose the proportion of the time that you wish to devote to each of these topics.

Degree subject combinations

You can combine the study of Latin or Greek with many other subjects especially English, history, philosophy, archaeology and modern languages, although you will find combinations with computing and business. Combining the study of a classical language with the modern languages that have developed from it can be very interesting. You can combine classics with modern Greek and with other modern languages like German, French and Italian.

Other higher education qualifications

There are no foundation degrees directly related to Greek and Latin but related subjects available include history, heritage and archaeology. There are no HNDs or HNCs in Latin or Greek.

Relevance to other subjects?

The study of classical Greek and/or Latin can lead to many courses at university. It is a foundation for ancient history, classics, classical studies, languages, history, English, law, philosophy and theology.

Even if you don't think that you will want to take Greek or Latin beyond A level, don't rule it out at this stage. Your study of a language rather different from English, the alternative language-learning techniques demanded, and (for Greek) the mastery of a different writing system, provide good evidence of your intellectual abilities. Studying a more unusual language provides a good talking point at interviews!

Important advice

There is variation and flexibility in the exact texts and periods covered by different classics degree courses and a wide variety of courses in related areas, classical civilisation for example. You must think carefully about exactly which aspects of your studies of Latin or Greek you most enjoy and then find a degree course that fits your interests.

CAREER OPTIONS

Into work after A levels

Latin or Greek A levels are unlikely to lead directly to related work although if you work in law, you will find Latin useful. However,

> *'I was surprised to find that I use my Latin every day in my job.'*
> Bill, trainee solicitor

the different disciplines and techniques involved in studying a 'dead' language in a more formal way suggest a clear, logical mind and a good memory. The study of classical languages will also help you in any language study you might do now or in the future. You could consider careers that are open to anyone with good A levels, such as banking, insurance, accountancy, retail or national or local government.

Into work as a graduate

Working with Greek or Latin

There are only a few careers in which you can really use Latin or Greek and these, as you might expect, are concerned with passing on your knowledge to others.

- **Teaching Latin or Greek in schools** – this is the main possibility and the independent school sector offers most opportunities. If you are interested in teaching younger age groups (below A level), you would need to offer another subject such as history, religious studies, a modern language or English.

- **Teaching in a university or college** – this is usually coupled with research, and postgraduate study will be necessary.

- **Archaeology** – there may be some opportunities for graduates in Latin or Greek to work as archaeologists, discovering and studying the material evidence of early history. The work ranges from organising digs (excavations), through charting out farmland that may have once formed a Roman settlement, to the assembly and treatment of new pieces of evidence in museums. You would need to undertake further training, but work experience can be gained through taking part in digs during vacations or at weekends. Remember that you will be in competition with graduates who have specialist archaeology degrees.

- **Library and archive work** – there may be some opportunities in specialist classical libraries or archives. Further training would be required after your degree.

- **The heritage industry** – there may be opportunities to work in specialist museums or as tour guides or historic interpreters using your knowledge of classics.

Working outside Greek and Latin

Very few classics graduates end up working in a directly related area. However, most find that their skills are respected and valued by employers in other fields. Employers recognise that classics graduates can think clearly and logically and, because of this, careers in HM Revenue and Customs or as tax advisers are a popular destination for classics graduates. Classics graduates go into a wide variety of jobs such as research, education, IT, librarianship or museum work, and many go into management and administration, the Civil Service, banking, insurance, advertising, publishing and journalism.

A degree in Latin or Greek would be a good background if you are thinking of a career in law (the study of Roman law is included in many law courses), or you could enter accountancy training at the graduate stage.

SOURCES OF INFORMATION

Joint Association of Classical Teachers
www.jact.org

Friends of Classics
www.friends-classics.demon.co.uk

Websites

www.classicspage.com

www.onlinelatinschool.com

www.ancientgreekonline.com

'We cannot possibly understand our modern world unless we understand the ancient world that made us all.'
Denise, studying history, Latin and French A levels

Health and social care

Health and social care is a huge and varied area of work, covering a wide range of professions. There are many opportunities in health and caring: this course gives you a broad understanding of health and social care principles, how the sector operates and the opportunity to develop skills in this area of work.

It is a broad-based qualification that encourages you to study in a practical way. The course helps you to develop a range of vocational skills that will be useful to you either for higher level study or in work and training. This A level is available as a double or single award.

WHAT DO YOU STUDY?

The topics listed give an idea of what could be covered. The exact content of AS and A2 specifications differs according to exam boards, so you will need to check with your school or college about the exact modules available to you.

- **Communication** – it is essential to develop and maintain good relationships in this area of work.

- **Human health and development** – basic anatomy and physiology of the major organ systems of the body and how body systems depend on one another to function.

- **Development** – from birth to death, theories of development and the range of factors that can influence growth and development, including genetic, environmental and socioeconomic factors.

- **The caring system** – how this works and how to promote quality and effective care in a positive environment.

You will have the option to take other units depending on your school, college and the exam board. Options include:

> *'I like the fact that everything you do is applied to real life. Going on a placement in a care home has given me confidence.'*
> Janet, aged 17, studying health and social care, biology and psychology

- **child development** – needs and provision for early-years clients, working in early years care and education

- **caring for older people**

- **meeting individual needs**

- **nutrition and dietetics** – health as a lifestyle choice, the role of exercise in maintaining health and well-being, complementary therapies

- **understanding human behaviour** – psychological perspectives

- **anatomy and physiology** – common diseases and disorders, diagnosis and treatment, complementary therapies

- **caring for people with disabilities** – understanding mental disorder and mental health issues

- **social issues and welfare needs, social trends**

- **public health and environmental health**

- **health and safety in care settings**

- **working in health and social care.**

The A2 will include a research project on a subject of your choice. You will learn why research is carried out in health and social care, research and analysis methods and how to present results, as well as the ethical issues involved.

HOW DO YOU STUDY?

You undertake a mixture of assignments, project work, surveys, attend talks from visiting speakers, do role-play, group work and work experience. You will learn and use a variety of transferable skills throughout the course. These include collecting, analysing and interpreting data, communicating your findings in different ways, and identifying and developing the links between different parts of the subject. You will have the opportunity to go into various care and health settings locally to investigate topics for yourself, apply what you have learned in class and find information for your coursework units. There may be opportunities for work placements within caring or health establishments and you will use these experiences to support your studies.

SUBJECT COMBINATIONS

Health and social care can be usefully combined with biology or human biology or other science A levels to support applications to nursing or other paramedical careers. Combined with psychology or sociology, it could support social work or teaching applications. Note that if you are considering a career in medicine you will need to have two or three science A levels including chemistry.

It is possible to combine all A and AS levels with other equivalent qualifications such as BTEC Nationals or OCR Nationals and they could form part of Diplomas.

HIGHER EDUCATION OPTIONS

Degree-level study

You could consider a wide range of courses, including health sciences, health studies, nursing, midwifery, community, health and well-being, biology, health promotion, exercise and health, sports and exercise studies, teaching, social work, and paramedical degrees such as physiotherapy, occupational therapy, paramedic science, speech and language therapy, and radiography. Your options will depend on your choice of units. Some competitive courses such as physiotherapy might ask for additional AS or A level study in biology, chemistry or physics and may specify certain subjects at GCSE.

Degree subject combinations

There are lots of different options for combined study in areas such as health science or studies and biology. You can combine with subjects that are related, such as sport and exercise studies, but also with subjects such as marketing and business studies.

Other higher education qualifications

There is a wide selection of foundation degrees covering many different areas related to health and social care. Examples of these are health and social care, complementary healthcare, food, nutrition and health, exercise health and fitness, health and active lifestyles, health, fitness and personal training, health informatics, healthcare science, mental health, maternal and newborn health, dental nursing, paramedic science, beauty therapy and spa management, sports therapy, animal health and veterinary health.

HND and HNC courses are available in various specialisms; examples include health and social care, fitness, health and exercise, post-exercise and health sciences. There are also DipHEs in operating department practice and health promotion.

> 'I was interested in nursing, but it's made me think that this isn't for me. I want to go into management but in a caring job.'
> Sue, taking A levels in health and social care, business and sociology

Relevance to other subjects?

The wide range of skills you will acquire from the health and social care course could be transferred to other areas such as hospitality and catering, leisure, recreation, tourism or business.

Important advice

Make sure that you are taking the right selection of units for any careers you are considering. Don't forget that GCSE and A level subjects and results could be important for entry to further study, so if you need to retake subjects you should try to do this as soon as you can. It is important to research carefully into the range of higher education courses available to you. Any work experience you can get in the health and social care field is advisable, as it will help your applications.

CAREER OPTIONS

Into work after A levels

There will be opportunities in areas such as childcare (you will need further study to become a nursery nurse) but other jobs such as playgroup assistant or nanny may be available. There are also opportunities to work as care workers in residential homes or health care assistants in hospitals. You could also consider becoming a classroom or teaching assistant, although you normally need to be aged 18 to start training. Your knowledge of health and social care could be applied to administrative jobs in the health service. There are also opportunities in the police, ambulance service and also jobs like airline cabin crew where your study could be put to good use with further training.

Into work as a graduate

Working in health and social care

Health studies and science courses can vary in their content and may cover options such as health promotion, health information science or health service administration, which could lead into administration and management careers in the health service or the caring sector. Social care or social science courses can lead to management or administration (see the entry for sociology). You could enter careers for graduates of any discipline, which could cover a wide range of business and management areas. If you have done a more vocational course specialising in, for example, nursing, podiatry, radiography or social work, then the routes into work are well defined, although you could undergo further postgraduate study to qualify in some of these careers.

Working outside health and social care

A good working knowledge of how social and caring services work could lead you to consider jobs in administration. This could involve dealing with the public, which would make good use of your communication skills. Your knowledge of the human body could lead to careers in leisure and fitness or medical sales. Other jobs you could consider would be the police, ambulance service or Armed Forces.

SOURCES OF INFORMATION

General Social Care Council
www.gscc.org.uk

NHS Careers
www.nhscareers.nhs.uk

Websites

www.socialworkcareers.co.uk

www.communitycare.co.uk

www.socialworkandcare.co.uk

'It's made me aware of all the opportunities available to me. I hope to go into nursing when I finish.'
Alice, taking A level health and social care with biology and sociology

History

'Those who cannot remember the past are condemned to repeat it'

George Santayana (1863-1952)

It is said that we can learn from the past to avoid the same mistakes in the future. The study of history is concerned with when and why things happened and attempts to analyse the significance of past events. The best reason for taking a history course is that the past fascinates you and you enjoy studying it. History combines the excitement of exploration and discovery with the sense of reward that comes from successfully confronting and making sense of complex and challenging problems. The purpose of historical inquiry is not simply to present facts but to search for an interpretation of the past. Historians attempt to find patterns and establish meaning through the study of evidence. It provides skills and understanding that will always be valuable in any career.

WHAT DO YOU STUDY?

The topics listed give an idea of what could be covered. The exact content of AS and A2 specifications differs according to exam boards, so you will need to check with your school or college about the exact modules available to you.

It is a requirement of all history A level specifications that students study British history. There is a wide variety of history specifications for A level. Periods of history can be covered in depth over at least 100 years, or topics could be organised around themes. You might also carry out an in-depth historical inquiry of your own choice. Options on courses include world history, economic and social, modern and medieval history and there are wide choices available in each specification.

Examples of long in-depth historical periods are:

- India: from the Mughal Empire to the British Raj, c1700-1857

- The making of modern Germany, c1800-1900.

Examples of shorter or thematic papers could include:

- The reign of Peter the Great of Russia, 1682-1725

- Britain and appeasement, 1919-1940

- A new Roman Empire? Mussolini's Italy, 1922-1945

- The impact of Stalin's leadership in the USSR, 1928-1941

- The impact of Chairman Mao, China, 1946-1976

- The campaign for African-American civil rights in the USA, 1950-1968

- The USA and Vietnam, 1961-1975

- British society, 1959-1975

'There are a lot of essays to write in history but I found the research needed for a project to be very interesting. You don't often get to choose what you write about and I often found myself going much deeper than needed because I was so interested in the topic.'
Peter, aged 20, studying for a degree in war studies after A levels in geography, history, politics and general studies

- The Reformation in Europe, c1500-1564
- The triumph of Elizabeth: Britain, 1547-1603.

It is not essential to have studied history at GCSE in order to do the A level. Some degree courses in history require a modern language at GCSE.

HOW DO YOU STUDY?

History A level involves being able to read and absorb information quickly. There is never enough class time to cover every aspect of every topic, so the more reading you can do on your own the better. Class discussions form an important part of the course but they must be backed up by note-taking and reading. There will also be field study trips to places of historical interest.

SUBJECT COMBINATIONS

If you want to study history at degree level then the A level is the obvious choice, although it's not a strict requirement for many degree courses. You will need to develop skills in research analysis and interpretation to study A level history so you might want to choose other subjects that will provide supporting knowledge and skills.

Government and politics will add to your understanding of political ideology and the British political system, which will be useful if you are studying modern history. Sociology and economics also cover a number of topics relating to developments in the Western world, requiring the ability to research and interpret data critically. A level English will help the development of your essay-writing skills. You might also want to consider modern foreign languages or classics.

It is possible to combine all A and AS levels with other equivalent qualifications such as BTEC Nationals or OCR Nationals and they could form part of Diplomas.

HIGHER EDUCATION OPTIONS

Degree-level study

There are many history and history-related degree courses. The largest number of courses are in British and European history, although they do not all cover all periods. As at A level, course topics relate either to periods, geographical areas or themes. Some interesting options on courses include the social history of medicine, gender history, the crusades, intellectual and religious history, financial history, the history of technology and industrial relations. You do not have to opt for a degree covering the periods that you studied at A level so you have the opportunity to try something new.

If you are sure that you want to specialise from the start, there are specialised degrees like ancient history, economic and social history, heritage studies, American history, medieval studies, Jewish history, peace/war studies and the history of Scotland, Wales or Ireland. Some modern history courses offer a year studying in Europe and some offer related work experience.

Degree subject combinations

History can be combined with many other subjects. The most widely available are English, geography, languages, philosophy, politics and sociology. However, practically any combination is possible and modular courses are also available.

Other higher education qualifications

There are foundation degrees in history and heritage management studies; garden history and heritage horticulture; historic building conservation; libraries, museums and archives; history, heritage and archaeology.

There are no HNDs or HNCs in history although there are some courses for which an

A level in history would be good preparation. HNDs or HNCs in information or office management, for example, would put to good use your experience of collecting and analysing information.

Relevance to other subjects?

Even if you don't continue with your history studies, you will find that A level history is a well-respected qualification for many courses. In subjects like law, modern languages, English, politics, sociology, economics and business you will find opportunities to use your writing and analytical skills.

Important advice

History is a popular degree. It would be an advantage to try and visit historical places that relate to your studies or interests. These include not only the great historic houses but sites such as Quarry Bank Cotton Mill in Cheshire, the Potteries Museum in Stoke-on-Trent and Ironbridge Gorge in Shropshire. Visit the various folk and local history museums around the country (especially larger ones like St Fagan's National History Museum near Cardiff, where rural Welsh houses and workshops have been reconstructed). Do some research into them beforehand, so that you know what to look for once you get there. You should be prepared to do a lot of reading in your spare time. The monthly magazine, *History Today*, will give you a taste of different historical periods and topics before you study them in detail, as will the wide range of historical programmes on TV.

CAREER OPTIONS

Into work after A levels

The wide range of skills and knowledge that you will develop as a history A level student will be helpful in finding employment. You will be able to think and argue logically, write well and be able to organise and analyse

large quantities of information. These are the kinds of skills needed to work in areas such as administration, management, sales and marketing. With further training you might find work in libraries or archives.

Into work as a graduate

Working in history

There are only a few careers in which you can use your historical knowledge directly:

- **teaching** – teaching history is the most direct way to use and develop your subject knowledge. To teach in state schools you need to take a PGCE to give you qualified teacher status (QTS). Secondary schools are your most likely destination, but with the National Curriculum there may be jobs in primary education

- **museum work** – work in museums (usually after postgraduate training)

- **archive work** – archivists are employed either by the Government (in record offices) by the media or industry. Again, further training in information management would help your prospects.

Working outside history

You will find history graduates working in many areas of management and administration because their eye for detail, research skills and ability to form logical arguments can make them ideal organisers of both people and resources.

They also work for local and national government, in finance, marketing, sales and the media.

History is often seen as a good preparation for a career in law (shown by the fact that some universities recommend A level history rather than A level law as an entry qualification to law courses).

SOURCES OF INFORMATION

The Historical Association
www.history.org.uk

Websites

www.bl.uk/learning/histcitizen/index.html

www.spartacus.schoolnet.co.uk

www.historytoday.com

Archaeology

Archaeology is the study of past human societies from the investigation of material remains. In archaeology A level, you study the techniques of modern archaeological research and its place in society and 'themes' that are wide ranging in both time and geographical distribution. You look at archaeological sources and methods. The periods you might study include prehistoric Britain (Neolithic to Iron Age), Ancient Egypt, the Roman World or the Maya. The course encourages you to develop your capacity for critical thinking and to see the relationships between different aspects of archaeology. In the final unit, you will undertake your own archaeological investigation, a piece of coursework based on personal research and fieldwork. This investigation normally focuses on your local environment, using local resources and using the archaeological methodology learned elsewhere in the course. The course includes field trips to archaeological sites. Archaeology combines well with many other subjects like science, art, technology, geography, history, sociology, anthropology and religious studies.

'When I graduated, I found employers were very aware of the competencies that we historians develop during our studies. My job is to analyse information and data relating to finance, and what impressed my employer was that I could easily adapt the skills I used at university.'
Jerry, financial analyst with a BA in history

History of art

In history of art A level you study the work of artists, sculptors and architects, concentrating on the Western world. Works are studied in the light of the political, economic, social, religious and cultural context in which they were created. For example, did the artists work as servants of a religious or political leader, or did they see their art as personal expression? You learn about the artistic tradition in which the artists worked, and study the techniques that are used in painting, sculpture and architecture.

WHAT DO YOU STUDY?

AQA is the only exam board currently offering history of art (art of the Western world).

For AS you will cover the following topics:

Visual analysis and interpretation

You will learn to look at works of art such as painting, sculpture and architecture. You will learn how to interpret paintings taking into account such things as composition; colour, light and tone; materials and techniques. You will examine how sculpture can vary according to materials, techniques and processes, size and how architecture is influenced by site and location, materials and scale, and location.

Themes in history of art

You acquire a knowledge and understanding of historical art themes in relation to examples of works of Western art and architecture, artists and architects drawn from classical Greece to the end of the 20th century (500 BC-2000 AD).

All works of art are studied in relation to the following themes and you look at each work in the light of these.

- **Materials, techniques and processes** – how works of art are produced.

- **Form and style** – how the formal features of art and architecture contribute to its style and meaning and how different styles have evolved.

- **Form and function** – the purpose and appearance of, for example, a building, and how to evaluate it taking into account its role as a functional building as well as an artistic work.

- **Historical and social contexts** – how to interpret works of art in the light of history and social history.

- **Patronage** – what influence artistic patronage has on works of art.

- **Social and cultural status** – how these influence art.

- **Gender, nationality and identity** – how styles evolve due to these factors.

At A2 you will continue your investigations and interpretations concentrating on one period in each of the two units. The periods are shown below and your teacher will choose the appropriate one.

In each topic you are required to have a detailed knowledge of formal features, materials, techniques and styles, and of the individual artists, sculptors and architects of the period. You will be examined on your understanding of the historical, social, economic and cultural contexts of the period as well the philosophy and art historical concepts of the time.

'If you want to get into art conservation, make sure you get some sciences, especially chemistry, at either GCSE or A level.' Jennifer, taking a postgraduate qualification in fine art restoration after a degree in history of art

Unit 3

Art and architecture: in 15th-century Europe

European painting, sculpture and architecture in the 15th century, for example the works of Botticelli, Da Vinci, Brunelleschi, Bosch and Raphael.

Art and architecture in 17th-century Europe

European painting, sculpture and architecture in the 17th century, for example the works of Rembrandt, Vermeer, Wren, Van Dyck and Inigo Jones.

Art and architecture in 19th-century Europe

European painting, sculpture and architecture in the 19th century, for example the works of Blake, Turner, Constable, Rodin, Rousseau, Barry, Pugin, Gilbert Scott.

Art and architecture in Europe and the USA between 1946 and 2000

European and American art and architecture 1946-2000, for example the works of Hirst, Emin, Hockney, Warhol, Moore, Hepworth, Foster, Goldfinger and Gropius.

Unit 4

Art and architecture in 13th- and 14th-century Europe

European painting, sculpture and architecture in the 13th and 14th centuries, for example the works of Bellini, Van Eyck, Pisano and Giotto.

Art and architecture in 16th-century Europe

European painting, sculpture and architecture in the 16th century, for example the works of Michelangelo, Palladio, Holbein and Bruegel.

Art and architecture in 18th-century Europe

This topic deals with European painting, sculpture and architecture in the 18th century, for example the works of Hogarth, Adam, Vanbrugh, Gainsborough, Roubiliac and Reynolds.

Art and architecture in Europe and the USA between 1900 and 1945

For example, the works of Lutyens, Epstein, Matisse, Picasso, Magritte, Klee and Miro.

There is no GCSE history of art and you are not expected to know a great deal about art before you start the A level. You don't have to be good at painting or drawing but it may help you if have experience of art, photography, history, languages, politics or sociology at GCSE. The most important thing is a real interest and enthusiasm for art history.

HOW DO YOU STUDY?

History of art is based around the detailed study of works of art. You can expect a lot of group work, discussing images of the works, whether they are paintings, sculptures or buildings. There will be study visits to galleries in the UK and possibly in Europe, such as Florence, Paris, Amsterdam and Barcelona. You will need to develop the ability to write intelligent and clear essays analysing the works. The subject is assessed by written papers throughout.

SUBJECT COMBINATIONS

If you are thinking of studying history of art at degree level, it is a good idea to combine the A level with subjects that complement your work. Art and design, English, history, classical civilisation or religious studies would provide invaluable background knowledge. Languages (especially French, German or Italian) also combine well. Even if you don't consider yourself 'artistic', you may find history of art a useful accompaniment to other subjects. For example, combining history of art with a science-based subject may not seem an obvious choice but can be a help with careers such as archaeology and art restoration or conservation, which require scientific skills. The history of art A level provides a useful background for an art Foundation course.

It is possible to combine all A and AS levels with other equivalent qualifications such as BTEC Nationals or OCR Nationals and they could form part of Diplomas.

HIGHER EDUCATION OPTIONS

It is not essential to have studied A level history of art in order to study it at a higher level.

Degree-level study

A history of art degree will extend your studies much further than the Western world. You may spend some of your time focusing on a single artist or artistic movement, but you will have the opportunity to study topics such as world cinema, photography and the art of other civilisations. Some courses include practical studio work in art or design. Many courses offer a study period abroad, ranging from a week, to a term or a year. Most of these visits are to Europe, although North America and Australia are possibilities. A related course is a degree in the arts market, if you are interested in developing in the appraisal of arts and artefacts.

Degree subject combinations

History of art is available with related subjects such as fine art and subjects like English, history and languages.

Other higher education qualifications

There are no history of art foundation degrees although some art and design courses have a module in art history. There are also courses in building, architectural stonework, furniture and book conservation.

There are no HND or HNC subjects in history of art but plenty of practical art courses such as fine art, graphics and building restoration.

There are also design history courses available at postgraduate level. If you are thinking about the practical study of art, you should consider taking an art Foundation course, which will help you get into a practical design course.

Relevance to other subjects?

The history of art A level will be useful for entry to humanities and social science degrees.

Alternatives to a history of art course include design history, visual studies or visual culture, which look at all the visual aspects of society not just 'art', and so include the study of advertising, fashion design, television and film. Other alternatives are degrees in architecture, archaeology, art conservation, furniture restoration, museum and gallery studies, and arts administration.

Important advice

The best preparation for the study of art history at a higher level is to visit as many galleries, museums and churches as you can. Many art collections are now available on the web so you don't have to travel far. Most art galleries are free and you may find some near you.

CAREER OPTIONS

Into work after A levels

If you intend to go into work straight after A level history of art you may find work as a junior assistant in a gallery, auction house, design company or antiques business. You could consider part-time study to further your knowledge in these areas. There may be Apprenticeships in these areas of work.

Into work as a graduate

Working in history of art

Careers in history of art often require further postgraduate study.

Possible careers include:

- museum, gallery or the antiques business
- arts administration or management
- auctioneer or valuer
- picture researcher
- specialist art or architecture librarian/archivist
- theatres, arts centres, arts sponsorship for large companies and the arts support schemes run by local authorities and central government
- heritage industries – many tourist attractions, historic houses or industrial archaeology sites have an 'art dimension'
- specialist travel and tourism (e.g. lecturing on art tours)
- art and design publishing, broadcasting and journalism
- conservation and restoration.

Working outside history of art

You will find the skills and knowledge gained on a history of art degree useful for the many careers open to graduates in any subject, such as buying, marketing and selling, finance and administration. Teaching is another option.

SOURCES OF INFORMATION

Association of Art Historians
www.aah.org.uk

The National Gallery
www.nationalgallery.org.uk

ICON (the Institute of Conservation)
www.icon.org.uk

Websites

http://cgfa.acropolisinc.com

www.chart.ac.uk/vlib

'It makes you appreciate what a rich cultural history we have .This will really help me when I go to art college to train to be a designer.'
Sandra, aged 18, taking history of art A level with art and history

ICT and ICT (Applied)

Here you get the opportunity to see how computer technology is affecting the world we live in. The practical use of software for problem solving and information by individuals, organisations and within society is the focus of the course. You will get an understanding of the ICT industry, the career opportunities available and the application of ICT principles. You will learn how to present and handle information, understand the function and forms of software and hardware, and how to plan and develop solutions to ICT problems. You will also learn to look at ICT from the user's perspective, including technical support and software development.

The course helps you to develop a range of skills that will be useful to you either for higher level study or in work and training.

Note that it's not about learning how to use spreadsheets and word processors but focusing more on using those applications to provide solutions for clients.

WHAT DO YOU STUDY?

Specifications vary and you may have the opportunity to choose different options depending on your school or college. The areas you could cover are as follows.

ICT and society, the information age – information is coming at us every day and impacts on all aspects of our lives. You will study the technologies available such as the internet, multimedia, broadband, wireless and digital communication. You will learn how these technologies impact on daily life and how the gulf is being bridged between those that have and don't have access to this technology.

The digital economy – e-commerce and how commercial websites are set up and operate. How the e-marketplace works, issues affecting e-consumers such as security and privacy.

The knowledge worker – IT professionals are knowledge workers, working with huge amounts of information and working out priorities, analysing and assessing information, and having to make decisions up against strict deadlines. You will learn how to extract the right information from huge amounts of data and make informed decisions about it, also about potential information overload.

How organisations use ICT – how organisations are structured, how they use and exchange information and how to evaluate ICT systems within organisations.

Using ICT to communicate, communications and networks – how organisations write, present and manage information, evaluating business documents and analysing communications systems within companies, such as internet and intranet networks.

Data handling, using database software – how data and databases are used within organisations, finding, selecting and manipulating data, presenting information effectively using a database, understanding the use of databases in organisations. You may create your own relational database.

> *'You never stop learning; your degree is only the first step in a long journey.'*
> Ash, aged 21, graduate software engineer with a BSc in computer science

Managing ICT projects – learning about project management, working to a brief, breaking a project up into individual tasks, planning ahead to use all resources effectively, learning how teamwork helps this process.

Programming – how different programming languages are used for different purposes, such as Visual Basic, Pascal, Delphi, C++, Prolog, Lisp, SmallTalk, Java, VB.NET, HTML and web application languages, and database query languages like SQL. You may undertake an in-depth programming project.

System design and installation/ configuration – how to design systems to meet user needs and understand and implement safety and security procedures. You will set up a computer system to a set specification individually or with other students, undertaking modifications to the hardware and software of existing systems, and creating and maintaining records of everything that you do for the project.

The following options could also be available:

- software development – design
- interactive media products
- artwork and imaging, computer artwork
- web development and management
- technical support
- systems analysis
- program design, production and testing
- customising applications
- development and maintaining ICT systems for users
- supporting ICT users
- ICT solutions for people with individual needs
- advanced spreadsheet design
- numerical modelling using spreadsheets
- problem solving using ICT
- publishing.

N.B. A level computing is described on page 66.

HOW DO YOU STUDY?

You will build up a portfolio of coursework, undertake assessments, and complete practical exercises and tests. You will go on work placements and study visits to see ICT in action. The portfolio of assignment work, which builds throughout the course, is a major feature of assessment. This portfolio will include items that you have created, for example, documentation, and will use different types of media such as e-books. You will work on your own to solve problems as well as undertake research assignments to given timescales. It will be an advantage to have your own access to email and the internet.

SUBJECT COMBINATIONS

ICT goes well with subjects like business studies, media or languages. As ICT is such an important study area, you could combine it with health and social care, travel and tourism, engineering, or more traditional subjects like history, geography and sciences. Some pure computing degrees do require an additional specified A or AS level in maths or a science and if you are considering adding maths or product design, this could lead to engineering courses at degree level.

It is possible to combine all A and AS levels with other equivalent qualifications such as BTEC Nationals or OCR Nationals and they could form part of Diplomas.

HIGHER EDUCATION OPTIONS

Degree-level study

ICT allows progression to many related degree courses such as computer network technology, computer games development, business information technology, information and communication technology, business systems, internet business development, e-commerce and internet systems, and multimedia technology and design. The content of courses varies as some will be more technical, concentrating on artificial intelligence, robotics or software engineering, while others will be geared towards business computing systems. It is important to look at the course content closely to see what is offered. The course title may not tell you the exact content of the course.

Degree subject combinations

There are many combinations available with ICT courses. You could combine with a business studies subject to broaden your expertise, or perhaps maths or statistics. ICT goes well with a wide range of subjects including humanities, social sciences and languages. There are new degrees in IT management for business combining both business management and ICT skills.

Other higher education qualifications

Foundation degrees are available in computing, applied computing and in related areas such as computer networking, system support, information systems design, interactive computing, internet technologies, business computing, computer aided design, software applications development, multimedia and computer games design.

The HND courses available include: business computing systems, computer science, computer forensics, computing systems security, computing technology, software engineering, mobile computing and network management, and security and computer networking.

Relevance to other subjects?

ICT gives you a thorough knowledge of business and IT systems as well as problem-solving and analytical skills. You could consider subjects like business studies or financial management, banking, insurance, travel and tourism, and leisure and recreation.

Important advice

It is a good idea to find out about the facilities and equipment that will be available to you when you are researching higher level courses. Some companies offer sponsorship for ICT degrees, so you should find out about these as soon as you can – many have early closing dates. It is also a good idea to investigate specific course requirements to find out whether additional A or AS subjects are advisable or certain GCSE subjects are required for entry to these courses. If you don't choose to do an ICT degree, there are opportunities to take postgraduate qualifications in ICT.

CAREER OPTIONS

Into work after A levels

You could enter employment as a trainee in jobs such as networking, technical support and systems design, helpdesk professional, PC support, database or network administrator. Your skills could open up opportunities in business administration or any area where knowledge of ICT is essential. There may be Apprenticeships available.

Into work as a graduate

Working in ICT

Depending on the content of your degree, these are the types of jobs that would be open to you:

- **account manager** – acts as the interface between ICT and the users or customer, advising on the best solutions for different types of application
- **software engineer** – specifies, develops, documents and maintains computer

software programs in order to meet client or employer need

- **database administrator** – responsible for the usage, accuracy, efficiency, security, maintenance and development of computerised databases

- **applications developer** – writes and modifies programs to enable a computer to carry out specific tasks, such as stock control or payroll, typically for technical, commercial and business users

- **systems operator (technical support)** – takes the specification for the requirements of a computer system and designs the system including hardware, software, communications, installation, testing and maintenance

- **systems developer** – sets up the computer operating systems and standard software services essential to the operation of any computer

- **information technology consultant** – gives independent and objective advice on how best to use information technology to solve business problems. The work includes analysing problems, making recommendations and implementing new systems

- **computer virus expert** – works in a virus lab, identifying, unravelling and fixing computer viruses. A thorough knowledge of programming and applications is required for this

- **network engineer** – responsible for the management of a computer network. This will include software installation and configuration, upgrades, diagnostics and troubleshooting.

Working outside ICT

You will have a good knowledge of ICT systems and applications, excellent communication skills, be able to think logically and have team-working skills. You could use these skills in many aspects of business including administration, sales and marketing. Teaching is another option and ICT is currently a shortage subject.

SOURCES OF INFORMATION

BCS, The Chartered Institute for IT
www.bcs.org

e-skills UK
www.e-skills.com

Website

www.computing.co.uk

> *'I can't think of any jobs where you don't need a good knowledge of ICT. It is around us in our daily lives as well as in the business world.'*
> Sam, aged 23, management trainee with a BSc in IT with business studies

Law

In A level law you will study the English legal system. You learn how the rules with which we live are established, developed and administered. You explore many different areas of law and then assess the effects of these laws in everyday life. Both real and hypothetical cases are examined to highlight how the law works in practice. A level law provides you with a good general insight into the institutions and work of the English legal system and the people who work within it. It also gives you lots of transferable skills.

WHAT DO YOU STUDY?

The topics listed give an idea of what could be covered. The exact content of AS and A2 specifications differs according to exam boards, so you will need to check with your school or college about the exact modules available to you.

Depending on the exam board, you study some or all of the following.

The legal system:

- **functions of law** – protection of rights/freedoms, balancing conflict of interests

- **how the law is made** – custom, precedent, EU law, legislation and its interpretation

- **legal disputes resolution** – the criminal and civil courts, tribunals, arbitration

- **the judiciary** – the role of judges and magistrates

- **the courts** – the criminal and civil courts and the role of the European Court of Justice, the jury system

- **the penal system** – sentencing and the treatment of offenders, and police powers

- **the legal profession** – the work of barristers, solicitors and legal executives, other sources of advice and funding.

Criminal law:

- **the ingredients of an offence** – commission of the physical act, the mental element

- **homicide** – murder, manslaughter, corporate manslaughter

- **offences against the person** – assault, assault occasioning actual bodily harm, wounding and grievous bodily harm

- **offences against property** – theft, robbery, burglary, criminal damage, fraud offences

- **defences** – insanity, intoxication, self-defence, provocation, duress

- **other topics** – principles of criminal liability, law and morality, law and justice, being an accessory to a crime.

Civil law:

- **civil law offences** – the law of 'tort' (a wrong or harm caused to someone), negligence and liability, trespass, nuisance, defence.

Contract law:

- **how a legally binding contract can be made and unmade**

- **contracts** – formation of contract, contractual terms, invalid contracts, discharge of contract

- **consumer protection**.

> *'Go to your local magistrates' court and sit in the public gallery. It will give you an instant introduction to law. That's what hooked me.'*
> Vincent, studying a BA in law

HOW DO YOU STUDY?

You need to be able to write well, think logically and have a good memory. You must be prepared to study and understand a lot of written material. The law is ever changing and so you discuss and analyse new or proposed legislation. You will also get involved in debating. You will write essays that explore the relevant concepts and analyse them to reach a conclusion. In addition, you have to apply legal principles and cases to hypothetical problems and assess how appropriate they are to their solution. There will be visits to local and regional courts and you might get to visit places like the House of Commons, the Royal Courts of Justice and the Old Bailey.

SUBJECT COMBINATIONS

The ability to express yourself clearly both orally and in writing is essential for the study and practice of law. You may wish to combine law with English or history to help develop these skills, and these are useful for entry to law degrees as many universities prefer essay-based subjects. Subjects such as business studies or economics can help you to understand the context in which legal work is carried out. Psychology, sociology, and government and politics can also provide a good foundation for further study in law-related subjects. A modern foreign language could open up the opportunity to study in another country and even gain a legal qualification there.

It is possible to combine all A and AS levels with other equivalent qualifications such as BTEC Nationals or OCR Nationals and they could form part of Diplomas.

HIGHER EDUCATION OPTIONS

An A level in law is not essential for study of the subject at university. Some university law departments sometimes prefer students to start their degree course as a beginner in law so you must check this when researching courses. However, students who have studied law at A level can find that it gives them a head start at university.

Note that some universities use the National Admissions Test for Law (LNAT) to help them to select candidates – you can find out more about this at www.lnat.ac.uk.

Degree-level study

Law degrees consist of a core of essential topics, which are those you need to take and pass if you want to obtain the maximum exemption from professional examinations. They are:

- obligations (contract)
- obligations (tort)
- criminal law
- public law
- property law
- equity and the law of trusts
- European Union law.

In addition you might take options in family law, commercial law, tax law and environmental law. Some degrees include the legal practice (for solicitors) or Bar exempting courses (for barristers). As well as law degrees leading to a professional qualification, there are a number of other law-related courses such as criminology and criminal justice. The latter focuses on the people and institutions of the criminal justice system and how they respond to criminal behaviour. These subjects provide a good background for careers in the police and prison services and within the criminal courts.

Degree subject combinations

The core topics take up approximately half of your time, so it is sometimes possible to obtain full professional exemptions if you study law in combination with another subject. This is something to check carefully as you plan your UCAS applications. Perhaps the most popular subjects to combine with law are those that provide some complementary experience and therefore broaden your career prospects. Examples are politics, economics, sociology, psychology, languages and business studies. Many law degrees now offer a European or wider international perspective, in which you study the law of the European Union, or the law and language of one or more other countries. This is important as increasingly legal practice crosses national boundaries.

Other higher education qualifications

There are many legal and related foundation degrees available, including law; criminology; criminology, policing and forensics; crime and community safety; finance and law; business with law; legal practice; legal studies; paralegal practice; police studies; offender management; and youth justice.

At a few institutions you can study for an HND or HNC in subjects such as law, business law, legal studies, business and law, and legal practice. Such courses are more vocational than degree courses, and can form a good preparation for a legal career outside the main legal professions – as a court or police officer, for example. Within the legal profession you could go into paralegal jobs, such as a legal executive or secretary, which could eventually lead to part-time study to qualify in law.

Non-graduate route to law

There is a route to qualifying as a solicitor via the non-graduate Institute of Legal Executives (ILEX) route. This is the route for people who work in legal employment and study part time. It can be followed after A levels, foundation degrees or HNDs.

Relevance to other subjects?

The law A level develops your ability to think logically, make balanced judgements based upon clear evidence, and understand the social effects and consequences of such judgements. It is a good basis for almost any social science course at a higher level, including sociology, psychology, politics, economics or business studies. Your practice in essay writing and mastering factual information would make you a good candidate for other subjects such as history, geography, English or classics.

IMPORTANT ADVICE

Take this A level because you are fascinated by the subject not because you are thinking ahead to the career possibilities. Be aware that there is a range of approaches to law at universities, with a spectrum stretching from 'black letter' law (the basic principles of law which are generally accepted and undisputed) degrees to welfare rights law, so you must research courses before applying.

Although law is an academic subject, it requires students to consider the practical effect of the theory by applying it to real-life situations. Go and sit in the public gallery at a local court to appreciate the impact that law has on everyday life. If you can, get some work experience with a law firm or lawyer.

CAREER OPTIONS

Into work after A levels

You won't come away from the law A level as a fully qualified lawyer. However, the course does provide valuable background knowledge if you want to work for a law firm in a support role and train part time. For example, you can go on to qualify as a legal executive, who does support work in a solicitors' firm. Then, if you wish, you can take up further training to become a solicitor. A level law is not a requirement for that route into the profession.

Into work as a graduate

Working in law

To specialise within the field of law it is necessary to gain additional qualifications after your degree:

- **barristers** – they represent their clients in the courts. They must first take the one-year, full-time Bar Professional Training Course (BPTC), followed by a pupillage (Apprenticeship) within a set of chambers for at least one more year

- **solicitors** – these draw up contracts, assess cases, provide advice and recommend courses of action to clients. First they must take the one-year Legal Practice Course (if they have a law degree) followed by a training contract with a law firm. Non-law graduates have to study for a Common Professional Examination (CPE) or a Graduate Diploma in Law (GDL) then follow the law graduate route

- **conveyancers** – these are specialised property lawyers, drawing up and transferring leases or deeds for houses etc. You would need to do further study to become licensed

- **the police** – the police force is a possibility and as a police officer you would apply your legal knowledge on a day-to-day basis. There are also administrative and specialist support jobs within the police.

Working outside law

A law degree is well respected for many business or management careers. For example, all limited companies must have a company secretary, who has to take on a number of legal responsibilities. You might choose to enter another profession such as accountancy or human resources where knowledge of law could prove useful.

SOURCES OF INFORMATION

The Bar Council
www.barcouncil.org.uk

Institute of Legal Executives (ILEX)
www.ilex.org.uk

The Law Society
www.lawsociety.org.uk

Websites

www.lawcareers.net

www.lnat.ac.uk

www.skillsforjustice.com

'It is hard but once you get to grips with it, it becomes fascinating. You have to stick with it and really concentrate on the whys and wherefores. I hope it will help me in a business career.'
Stephen, taking A levels in law, business and psychology

Leisure studies

The leisure industry is fast growing and every changing, covering everything from theme parks, cinemas and museums to leisure centres, outward bound activities, fitness centres and spas. The course gives you an in-depth understanding of all aspects of leisure, both from the point of view of industry professionals and from the customer's perspective. You will study the structure of the industry, leisure facilities, lifestyles and lifestyle management, and current issues in leisure. The course combines research, investigation and practical application to a wide range of leisure situations and prepares you for a career in the industry either through higher education or straight into employment. It also equips you with interpersonal and practical transferable skills that will be invaluable in any career.

This A level is available as a double or single award.

WHAT DO YOU STUDY?

This A level is offered as a double award by AQA (12 units) and a single award (six units) by OCR and Edexcel. Check with schools and college to see what options are available to you.

The leisure industry today – how the leisure industry works, what career paths are available, and how the industry might develop in the future.

A people business – investigating why customer service is so important and how interpersonal skills are used in dealing successfully with customers. You will learn about the leisure customer, how to handle complaints and how to measure, monitor and evaluate customer service procedures and practices.

Leisure industry practice – safe working practices in the leisure industry; marketing and budgeting; quality measures and key business systems used in leisure organisations.

Working in leisure – exploring the employment and training opportunities within the industry. You will cover human resources issues such as recruitment and selection and motivation of the workforce.

Current issues – investigating factors currently affecting the industry and analysing how they will affect the industry in the future.

Here are some examples of the other options that may be available to you:

- fitness training for sport
- leisure and the media
- leisure in the community
- lifestyles and lifestyle management
- outdoor leisure
- event management
- leisure in the outdoors.

You might also have the chance to gain industry-related qualifications such as first aid, sports leaders, YMCA gym instructing or coaching awards, which will help you gain employment.

> *'Remember that it's a people business, so you must really like them!'*
> Daniel, aged 19, apprentice leisure trainee at a health club

HOW DO YOU STUDY?

There is a mixture of coursework and assessed projects, plus some external exams. You will go on study visits to leisure and recreation sites. You may take part in activities such as coaching a group of young people, or outdoor adventure activities to give you an insight into how they are organised. In addition, there will be work experience, work shadowing, and links with local employers, case studies and research, as well as practical projects.

SUBJECT COMBINATIONS

Physical education, psychology, business studies, travel and tourism, modern languages or geography are good combinations.

It is possible to combine all A and AS levels with other equivalent qualifications such as BTEC Nationals or OCR Nationals and they could form part of Diplomas.

HIGHER EDUCATION OPTIONS

Degree-level study

There are leisure management degrees and you also find them combined with related subjects like events management, hospitality, sports and tourism. There are specialised leisure degrees, for example entertainment management, adventure sports management, extreme sports management and spa management. Many courses offer a compulsory or optional sandwich placement and some have links with universities abroad, offering overseas placements.

Some professional organisations, such as the Institute of Sport and Recreation Management (ISRM), validate courses allowing graduates membership and professional status.

Degree subject combinations

It is possible to study a number of combinations of subjects, especially if you consider a combined or modular course. There are some directly related combinations like sports development but there are many other subjects such as geography, English, languages, media, history, business studies or computing.

Other higher education qualifications

There are many foundation degrees available including: leisure management, hospitality management, tourism and leisure management, sport and leisure management, outdoor leisure management, personal trainer, spa management, outdoor education, and adventure tourism management.

There are HND and HNC courses available providing a mix of practical experience and theory. Examples of courses are leisure management, leisure management (outdoor activities), sport and leisure management (health and fitness), and hospitality management (leisure and tourism).

Relevance to other subjects?

There are many related areas to consider including hospitality and tourism or business and management. Psychology is another option and there are degrees combining sport and leisure with psychology and education, as well as degrees in sport psychology.

Important advice

Try to get some work experience in the industry as this will give you a good insight into the work. Think about getting some industry-related qualifications in, for example, lifeguarding, sports coaching and leadership awards. It is also important to look carefully into higher education courses in leisure, sports studies and recreation as they vary a great deal. Some sports science courses, for example, may ask for a science A or AS level.

CAREER OPTIONS

Into work after A levels

An A level in leisure studies is a good foundation for a range of jobs in sport and leisure centres, local government, and leisure and recreation businesses. There are opportunities to go straight into the industry in jobs such as health and fitness instructor, personal trainer, pool lifeguard, leisure or sports centre assistant, sports retail, outdoor education tutor, coach, play leader, or jobs in administration within the industry. There would also be opportunities in the Armed Forces. For some of these jobs you will need further training, for example, an NVQ in exercise and fitness to become a fitness instructor. Some jobs will offer training towards these qualifications and career development training from professional bodies such as the Institute for Sport, Parks and Leisure (ISPAL) or ISRM.

You may also find Apprenticeships available where you can combine work and training and you might even be able to work your way up to degree level study via this route.

Into work as a graduate

Working in leisure

The industry has expanded rapidly in recent years and this is likely to increase, especially with the growth in health spas, fitness centres and active lifestyles. Consumer expenditure on sports and leisure has doubled in the last decade and this has led to an increase in opportunities and jobs in health and fitness clubs, leisure centres and sports clubs.

Apart from trainee management jobs there are positions in the marketing, public relations, sales and sponsorship sides of the industry, which could involve working in a head office rather than a local centre. There will be opportunities both in the UK and abroad. Skills in this area will be transferable to jobs in the travel and tourism sector. You may find employment with hotel groups, or in jobs like an event organiser. You could also specialise in leisure retail or health and beauty management in places like spas. You will also find openings in the gambling industry, another form of leisure.

Working outside leisure

You will have gained excellent customer service and communication skills as well as sales and marketing skills. These could be transferred to careers in business, administration and management.

SOURCES OF INFORMATION

Fitness Industry Association (FIA)
www.fia.org.uk

The Institute for Sport, Parks and Leisure (ISPAL)
www.ispal.org.uk

Institute of Sport and Recreation Management (ISRM)
www.isrm.co.uk

SkillsActive
www.skillsactive.com

Websites

www.visitbritain.org

www.leisuremanagement.co.uk

'I like the way you learn skills that you know will be useful in jobs. My work experience at the local pool has been really interesting. I'm getting things to put on my CV all the time.'
Caroline, taking A levels in leisure and business studies

Mathematics (including statistics and mechanics)

Mathematics is a challenging subject and a vital tool that supports the study of other subjects. The A level shows you how mathematics is used to describe and predict a diverse range of things, for example, the way the economy works, the motion of the planets, the speed of a chemical reaction, the behaviour of large groups of people and the way decisions are made in business. Some A level topics follow on from GCSE. You study them in greater depth and then tackle harder and more complicated problems. You will also study new areas, with their own specialised techniques for solving whole new types of problems. Mathematics is a continuous discipline, which means that techniques introduced in one topic must be understood before the next.

WHAT DO YOU STUDY?

The topics listed give an idea of what could be covered. The exact content of AS and A2 specifications differs according to exam board, so you will need to check with your school or college about the exact modules available to you.

N.B. New A levels in mathematics and further mathematics are currently being designed for first teaching in September 2012.

Mathematics can be divided into two areas: pure and applied. Most courses consist of about half pure mathematics and half 'applied' topics like mechanics, statistics or discrete mathematics. Exam boards allow choice between the areas by providing a range of optional modules. However, although the specification may allow choice, you might have to study what your school or college offers.

These are the main subjects covered:

- **pure mathematics** – algebra, functions and graphs, geometry, trigonometry and vectors, logarithms and powers, linear and quadratic equations, sequences and series, calculus and numerical methods. Pure mathematics is the foundation for much of the work you do in other areas as well as being the starting point for the study of mathematics at a higher level

- **statistics and probability** – collecting and presenting data, combining probabilities, conditional probability, probability distributions, mean value and spread, frequency tables, cumulative frequency, hypothesis testing, correlation and regression. Statistics is used in all areas of science and the social sciences, including psychology, economics, business studies and management. This topic is good preparation for work or further study in any of these areas, especially as many degree courses include a compulsory module in statistics

- **mechanics** – description of the way that objects move in terms of distance, speed, acceleration and time and how these are related, the action of forces on stationary and moving objects, momentum and energy, vectors and circular and oscillatory motion. Mechanics is important in physics and engineering and in subjects like

The maths department offers lots of extra help, which I wasn't aware of before I got here; there are weekly 'maths surgeries' where postgrads are available to help you, a scheme where first years can buddy up with a mentor and tutors who are very supportive.'
Henry, first year BSc maths

architecture, physical geography and environmental science. It is the starting point for the study of more advanced topics at a higher level including relativity and elementary particles

- **discrete/decision mathematics** – network diagrams, linear programming, route inspection problems, critical path analysis and algorithms. Discrete/decision mathematics is used in economics, management studies and computer science.

In addition there are other A/AS levels in mathematics:

- **further mathematics** – this course is for more able mathematics students who enjoy the subject and have a real flair for mathematics. In further mathematics courses, the ground covered is both broader and more difficult than the ordinary curriculum. In some cases, it consists of taking more of the optional modules in the ordinary curriculum but studying them in greater depth. You will need GCSE mathematics at grade A*, A or B in order to study further mathematics

- **statistics** (*available as a separate A or AS level*) – provides a second subject for mathematics students but also an excellent option for anyone wanting to continue with a mathematical subject to at least AS level. A useful choice for degrees where statistics would be useful like psychology, sociology or business studies

- **use of mathematics** (*available as a full A level from 2011*) – involves the application of advanced mathematics in real contexts. It includes the use of computers and graphical calculators. Students are encouraged to apply mathematics in their other studies and interests. It is for students who don't want to undertake a detailed study of mathematics but would find a working knowledge useful in their further training or study.

HOW DO YOU STUDY?

Learning mathematics means learning how to use it to solve problems and the only way you can do this is through practice. Classwork involves the teacher explaining new material and then working through examples. You follow this up by tackling new problems, which become more difficult. Some of this work will be done in class, but you should also expect to put in at least five or six hours per week outside lesson time. You do most of your work using pen and paper with the help of calculators (although some modules may be non-calculator) and you will use computers to model systems and try out ideas on a larger scale. Some exam boards require you to complete a project. Many people find that the change from GCSE to A level mathematics is a big one. As this subject builds continuously on previous work, it can become difficult if you get behind. You must have a very thorough grasp of the fundamentals, so that you can concentrate on the new material.

Calculators

All the awarding bodies assume that you will use a scientific calculator in some examinations although there will be some non-calculator papers as well. Check with your teachers for advice on which calculators are acceptable.

SUBJECT COMBINATIONS

Mathematics is used as a tool in many other subjects, from engineering and physics to social sciences and business. Depending on what you want to do, you can combine it with any other subject. If you are thinking of studying mathematics or a related subject at a higher level, you should think about combining it with a science. Physics is a useful preparation for degree courses that include applied mathematics. As well as overlapping with mathematics in some topic

> 'Numeracy is becoming more important in so many careers now. A level maths will make you very employable.'
> Carol, HR manager

areas, physics also uses mathematics more than any other subject, so it can provide valuable practice and support.

Other sciences, and subjects like economics, also involve mathematics. You might consider further mathematics, as this covers more ground and gives extra depth to your understanding. Further mathematics is for very able mathematicians who want to undertake additional study. A level mathematics and physics are required or preferred for physics and most engineering degrees. If you are interested in these subjects, it is important that mechanics forms part of your A level course. If you intend to study A level biology, psychology, geography, sociology, computer studies, economics or business studies, you will find that the statistics in A level mathematics or statistics will be useful.

It is possible to combine all A and AS levels with other equivalent qualifications such as BTEC Nationals or OCR Nationals and they could form part of Diplomas.

HIGHER EDUCATION OPTIONS

A good pass at A level or equivalent is essential if you want to study mathematics successfully at a higher level. If you do not have mathematics at a high enough level you could consider a foundation year (see below).

There are different types of mathematics degrees. There is a four-year degree called MMath. Even though the first 'M' stands for 'master', this is an undergraduate degree. The first two years are the same as the BSc, but the final two years are more demanding. If you enter university on one degree you can transfer to the other and as the MMath is tougher than the BSc, students who do not maintain a good average grade in their first two years usually transfer to the BSc in their third year. Many of those who complete the MMath go on to higher degrees.

You will also find MSci degrees, which are comparable with masters level study.

Degree-level study

Mathematics at degree level is a natural continuation of A level work in some ways. However, the rate at which you cover new material is much faster, and degree-level study is more abstract than at A level and more difficult to relate to common experience.

The size of the subject means that most mathematics courses are flexible, particularly in the second and third years. There are also many specialist courses that allow you to concentrate on one area from the start. These include courses in the main areas of the subject, like pure mathematics, applied mathematics and discrete mathematics. Other courses concentrate on particular application areas like engineering mathematics or business mathematics, mathematical physics and mathematics education (which leads to a teaching qualification in addition to a degree). Some courses offer a year abroad spent studying at another university.

N.B. Some universities offer a foundation year for those not up to undergraduate level standard in mathematics. If you complete this successfully you can transfer to a mathematics or mathematics-related degree.

Degree subject combinations

Most combined and modular schemes include mathematics. You may want to combine mathematics with a completely different subject to provide variety, but there are also plenty of opportunities to take combined courses in which mathematics and the other subject support and complement each other. Such subjects include physics (there are also specialist mathematical physics courses) or statistics.

Other higher education qualifications

There is a foundation degree in computing and mathematics and related subjects like accounting, business, engineering and IT.

There are no HNDs in mathematics, but again consider related areas such as business, accountancy, engineering and IT.

Relevance to other subjects?

Mathematics A level is accepted as a good entry qualification for almost any other subject at degree level. Mathematics is needed for most physics and engineering courses and is strongly recommended or compulsory for many chemistry courses. Although not always a requirement for courses in biological sciences, it can be very useful, especially if courses contain statistics. Statistics is useful for social science courses such as psychology, geography, sociology, business studies and economics, and is required for some of the more mathematically orientated economics courses. Mathematics is useful for computer science and is compulsory for some of the more theoretical courses.

Mathematics can provide useful support for courses in economics and business studies. A level mathematics can be used as an alternative to A level physics for some courses. For example, the A level requirements for medicine, dentistry and veterinary science are usually for mathematics or physics in addition to chemistry (usually compulsory) and biology (usually recommended).

Important advice

In order to succeed in mathematics you must work consistently over a long period. You get into a regular routine of work that will allow you to build up your skills and knowledge. If you are considering a gap year before a mathematics degree it is important to check with universities to see how they

view it. Some universities feel that you lose continuity in your studies. If you decide to take a gap year, it would be wise to keep up your mathematics during your time out and revise it just before starting your course.

CAREER OPTIONS

Into work after A levels

An A level in mathematics is in great demand by employers. Even when a job does not require specific mathematical knowledge, employers find that the discipline learned through studying mathematics helps you think clearly and logically. You will find people with A level mathematics working in areas that make obvious use of mathematical skills, such as accountancy, banks and financial services, but you are equally likely to find them working as a retail manager in a shop or department store, or as a website or computer games designer.

Into work as a graduate

Working in mathematics

There are many areas where you can use the expertise developed during your degree. These include the following:

- **finance and accountancy** – this is the single largest career area for graduates in mathematics and statistics. Accountancy will require further training and there are opportunities in private practice, local and central government and business. Banks and other financial services companies like to recruit mathematics and statistics graduates to their management training schemes

- **IT** – some graduates go into mathematical computing, but the majority go into more general areas such as programming, systems analysis or consultancy

- **actuarial work** – graduates start as trainees and take professional exams

- **management** – mathematical techniques are used as management tools for solving a variety of complex problems in production, distribution, marketing and financial investment

- **technology** – industries such as aerospace, renewable energy and telecommunications employ mathematics graduates for analysing data and working on the design of products or industrial control systems

- **education** – there is a demand for qualified mathematics teachers so you may qualify for financial help with your training

- **research** – nearly 23% of mathematics graduates go on to further study or research in mathematics. However, the number finally making a career in research is very much smaller. Some large companies and government organisations also employ research mathematicians, but again the numbers are small compared to the number of graduates.

Working outside mathematics

As most jobs involve some use of numerical or financial data, mathematics graduates are well placed in the job market, provided that they can bring other skills like communication, team working and management potential. Many employers are more interested in a mathematician's ability to analyse and solve problems than any specific mathematical training. Employers include local government, the Civil Service and all areas of industry and business.

SOURCES OF INFORMATION

PSI (Statisticians in the Pharmaceutical Industry)
www.psiweb.org

Institute of Mathematics and its Applications
www.ima.org.uk

Royal Statistical Society
www.rss.org.uk

Websites

www.mathscareers.org.uk

www.orsoc.org.uk/about/careers.htm

Media (communication and production)

If you are fascinated by how TV programmes, adverts or feature films are put together then this course is for you. You will gain an understanding of production processes in the media industries and the different techniques used in video, film, audio and printed media. You will be able to learn skills and put them into practice in video production, sound production, publishing or multimedia production depending on your school or college. You will create your own media products as part of the course.

This is a broad-based qualification that encourages you to study in a practical way. The vocational skills that you learn on the course will be useful to you either for higher level study or in work and training.

WHAT DO YOU STUDY?

This is only available as a single award offered by Edexcel.

Industries, texts and audiences – you will look at the media industry, its products or texts, e.g. newspapers, magazines, TV and radio, voiceovers in documentaries or television advertisements, and the audiences that receive and use these products or texts. You will examine how media organisations work, how they construct their products around targeted audiences, and how those audiences understand and use the products that are offered to them.

Skills for media production – this is your opportunity to practise and improve your own creative, technical and evaluative skills in your chosen areas of media production. You will look at the skills required for researching media products and evaluating them. This will involve audience research, looking at different methods of researching, recording and evaluating your results.

You will look at your existing technical and production skills and identify the skills that you need to learn or improve. You will acquire knowledge and understanding of relevant technology and develop skills in the techniques required to create a media product in the medium in which you are working.

Media production brief – you will put into practice the skills that you have developed in other units by creating a media product to an externally set brief. You will learn about pre-production, production and post-production and will develop your technical skills.

Research and development for media production – you will devise an original idea for a production. You will research the content, audience and viability of the idea and apply that research to its development by experimenting with the technical and creative elements of the proposed production. You will present the idea, together with your research and development work, through an oral 'pitch' followed up by a written 'treatment'.

Media production project – you will produce a media product demonstrating all the skills and knowledge that you have gained. Your product must appeal to the right audience and be original. You must take into account your clients, deadlines, budgets and your team of people. When it is completed, you will need to evaluate the effectiveness of your product.

> *'I made a radio documentary about the music business as part of my course. This helped me get into my current job.'*
> Chris, aged 24, production assistant in radio after a degree in media studies

Professional practice in the media industries – you will reflect on what you have achieved in previous units and report on the products and the process of production, following a given structure. You will take into account past and current professional practice in the chosen medium and genre, and the relevant professional codes and constraints that might have affected your work and working practice. The report can be in any format – written, spoken, a programme or on audio or DVD.

N.B. See also A level in media studies on page 164.

HOW DO YOU STUDY?

There is a mixture of practical and creative work combined with research and coursework. The course is assessed internally and externally through assignments, projects and case studies. You will watch films and television programmes as part of the course, but with a critical eye. You will go on study visits to media companies or have the opportunity to participate as a member of the audience of a live television studio recording.

SUBJECT COMBINATIONS

It is possible to combine media (communication and production) with many different subjects, such as English language or literature, history, psychology, art or business studies. If you are considering a technical or engineering career in the media, maths and physics would be useful. Film or media studies may overlap with some of the content and you would need to check this if looking at

> *'What was so cool about this course was that you get visiting teachers who actually work in the industry. It gives you the opportunity to find out the reality of the media world.'*
> Seb, aged 18, taking A levels in media, history and business

subject combinations for higher education. There may be opportunities to take some related NVQs in media depending on the facilities available at your school or college.

It is possible to combine all A and AS levels with other equivalent qualifications such as BTEC Nationals or OCR Nationals and they could form part of Diplomas.

HIGHER EDUCATION OPTIONS

Degree-level study

You will find a wide range of media degrees available; in fact, well over 1,900 media-related courses are currently on offer at degree level. You must look at the content carefully. Some are more like general arts degrees, concentrating on the media as an academic subject; others involve more technical skills such as radio, TV or video production, and further still, others could involve subjects like graphic design, photography or illustration.

Degree subject combinations

Media studies combines well with subjects like communication and cultural studies and there are combinations available with specialisms such as creative writing, television, film and video production, and web design. You will find that it can be combined with most courses including arts, business, languages and social sciences.

Other higher education qualifications

There are foundation degrees available in many specialist areas such as broadcast media, animation, multimedia, design for games, editorial and news media design, digital media, computer games and interactive media, media advertising, media composition, film and television production, digital imaging and design for media, new media design, radio production, media production, moving image, journalism, wildlife education, and media and television production.

HND and HNC subjects in media tend to offer more specialist and practical training, such as interactive media, media production, media technology, digital film-making, practical journalism, design for interactive media and visual communication.

Relevance to other subjects?

Your course contains elements that are relevant to lots of other courses. Look at specialist courses in advertising, public relations and journalism. Arts and humanities degrees as well as more business-orientated courses are other possibilities. Depending on your choice of units, you will have developed writing or technical skills in film and broadcasting, so you might wish to consider more applied vocational courses in these areas.

Important advice

In an industry where making contacts is extremely important, any work experience or work-shadowing that you could do in media would be very useful to you. It is also a good idea to investigate the type of course that you might be interested in; try to find out what happened to the graduates of that course. Did they get the types of jobs that you are interested in? Don't be afraid to ask what the unemployment rate is among recent graduates and how long it takes to find a suitable job.

CAREER OPTIONS

Into work after A levels

It may be possible to get some trainee or Apprenticeships in the media depending on the area that you're interested in. You may find trainee positions in journalism or photography but you would need a good portfolio. You may find junior jobs in the film and music industry and it is worth looking at Apprenticeships available through Skillset. You could consider administration jobs as a way into the media, although it might be advisable to get some qualifications in administration or business studies. The majority of students will look at higher education courses where they can gain more experience and make useful contacts for media-related careers.

Into work as a graduate

Working in the media

This is a fast-moving industry and a popular career choice. Graduates do find jobs in the media but these are people who have prepared themselves, are well motivated and have managed to pick up useful work experience and contacts. Many people get involved in university radio stations or student newspapers to help build up their portfolios. Media graduates can get into jobs such as assistant editors in publishing, production assistants with TV and radio companies, or runners for film companies. More go into administration, sales and marketing jobs within the media. You might also want to consider some postgraduate training to improve your chances.

Working outside the media

You will have good communication skills both verbally and visually, and with the written word. You will also have studied marketing and market research in some depth. These skills could be transferred to careers such as sales and marketing and in many areas of business and finance, where communication is important. A media degree is acceptable for many other non-media jobs and past graduates have entered IT, teaching, business and finance.

SOURCES OF INFORMATION

British Film Institute
www.bfi.org.uk/education

Film Education
www.filmeducation.org

Skillset
www.skillset.org/careers

Websites

www.bbc.co.uk/jobs

www.itvjobs.com

www.ukfilmcouncil.org.uk

'Make sure you do your research thoroughly before you finally decide. Go to as many open days as you can and look at the facilities. Don't be afraid of just emailing or ringing up universities for information and advice.'
Josie, aged 24, working in marketing after a broadcast journalism degree

Media studies

Media and communications are one of the UK's biggest industries. Media reflects and influences all aspects of our society. In media studies you will gain an understanding of all types of media including film, music, newspapers, radio, magazines and games. You will examine media technologies such as blogs and websites. You will develop an understanding of media products and how they are produced, distributed and 'consumed'. You will learn theory and critical analysis as well as some of the practical and technical skills involved in producing media products.

WHAT DO YOU STUDY?

The topics listed give an idea of what could be covered. The exact content of AS and A2 specifications differs according to exam boards, so you will need to check with your school or college about the exact modules available to you.

Media products and their audiences – films, TV, radio, newspapers, magazines, games software and web-based media; their target audiences, how they are produced, distributed and 'consumed' by their audiences. The forms and conventions of different media genres, such as broadcast fiction, film fiction, documentary, lifestyle, music, news and sport.

Media issues – media regulation, the relationship between the media and society, censorship and violence, advertising, global media, media and collective identity, and media in the online age.

Key media concepts – you may carry out a textual analysis of a piece of media such as a radio play or TV drama. You will analyse how the piece is put together and different techniques used in the production. For a film this could be camera angles, lighting, and sound and editing techniques.

'Media studies links with a wide variety of subjects.'
Alex, aged 17

Practical techniques – learning the technical skills to create media products and creating your own. You might create a video, DVD, music jingle or a website.

A GCSE in media studies is not required for this course but you would be expected to be familiar with a wide range of media products.

N.B. See also A level in media (communication and production) on page 160.

HOW DO YOU STUDY?

Case studies are used throughout the course to provide examples of different media forms and styles as an effective way into discussions and debates. Practical classes involve learning how to research and create a piece of media. You might make a trailer for a TV soap, documentary or thriller, an advertisement, a short interview or news round-up for a radio broadcast, a design for a new women's magazine or create a website. When you are presenting results of any research or project you will use appropriate technologies such as a PowerPoint presentation, a blog website, a podcast or a DVD or memory stick with 'extras'.

You are expected to keep up to date with developments in the media and be active and critical when viewing or using any type of media. Approximately 50% of the marks are now allocated to coursework across the specifications.

> 'It's good to learn about something that everybody encounters every day.'
> Craig, aged 16

SUBJECT COMBINATIONS

Media studies complements many subjects because it covers such a wide range of subjects. If you are thinking of studying media at a higher level, then English, communication and culture, sociology and psychology could prove useful. For practical courses in media production, it may be an advantage to have an art and design A level, or even maths and sciences for the more technical courses.

It is possible to combine all A and AS levels with other equivalent qualifications such as BTEC Nationals or OCR Nationals and they could form part of Diplomas.

HIGHER EDUCATION OPTIONS

An A level in media studies is not required in order to study the subject at a higher level.

Degree-level study

Courses in media studies vary greatly. You will find some are more general humanities type courses and others are more practical. Many institutions offer practical courses in subjects such as multimedia, digital animation and media production. Some of these might ask for either an art Foundation course and/or a portfolio for entry.

You will also find more specialist courses such as journalism or broadcast journalism. If you don't want to specialise at first degree level there are opportunities for postgraduate study in media specialisms such as journalism.

Degree subject combinations

The subjects most widely available in combination with media studies are English, history and politics. If you want to get a job in the media, which can be difficult, it would be a good idea to combine media studies with a subject that might help you to get a start in your career, such as business studies, politics, modern languages, the digital industries or sciences. You can take media studies as part of a modular course, allowing you to study a wide range of other subjects.

Other higher education qualifications

There are foundation degrees available in many specialist areas such as broadcast media, animation, multimedia, design for games, editorial and news media design, digital media, computer games and interactive media, media advertising, media composition, film and television production, digital imaging and design for media, new media design, radio production, media production, moving image, journalism, wildlife education, and media and television production.

Media studies can be taken at HND or HNC level and courses include interactive media, media production, media technology, digital film-making, practical journalism, design for interactive media and visual communication.

Relevance to other subjects?

Media studies A level helps you to develop useful skills relevant to a number of other subjects. Your ability to analyse and criticise visual, written and audio information in relation to cultural and social factors would help with subjects such as English, history of art, drama and theatre studies, design courses, archaeology, anthropology, philosophy and modern languages. Your understanding of the political and social influences at work in the media would also help you in the study of most social science courses, such as sociology, psychology, politics or history.

> 'It makes you learn more about the world you live in.'
> Shiana, aged 17

Important advice

There are many media courses on offer. If you are even remotely considering a career in the media, you should make sure that the course you choose offers the balance that you want between practical and theoretical work. It is a good idea to check out the range of practical facilities offered, such as recording equipment and editing facilities. Make sure you research the destinations of graduates from your chosen courses. If you are interested in studying a non-media related subject at a higher level, you should make sure that the universities or colleges you are considering will accept media studies. Don't forget that if you are planning a career in the media you should be building up experience now, even if it is on the school website or hospital radio.

CAREER OPTIONS

Into work after A levels

Media studies is useful in many areas of work, particularly if they involve communication and up-to-date media knowledge. The media industries are difficult to get into, so your A level won't guarantee you entry. Unless you are prepared to start at the bottom as, for example, an office assistant or runner and work your way up, you will need further qualifications and experience.

In media you will need to be good at networking and making the right contacts to progress in your career. You may find that there are some Apprenticeships available.

Into work as a graduate

Working in the media

It is hard for media studies graduates to get started in the media. Any contacts made during your degree may eventually become very useful so it is important to keep up your contacts, keep networking and get as much work experience as you can. Companies like

> 'It's good because it involves the practical and theoretical.'
> Emily, aged 17

the BBC offer work experience placements, which are worth looking at, and you may be able to arrange your own work placement or internship. If you are hoping to enter TV or film production, you should be prepared to get further training, or to start in a junior position. You may find it useful to arrange and finance extra training yourself to get you the right skills and knowledge.

Don't forget that the media industry is a very broad one and covers not only the obvious jobs in journalism, interactive media, film and TV. There are also opportunities in animation, computer games, advertising, facilities (specialist technical services to film and TV), photo imaging and publishing.

Here are some examples of popular jobs in the media:

- **talented 'creatives' in advertising** – these are always in demand, as they provide an essential source of imagination in the creation and selling of products

- **journalism** – in radio, TV, newspapers, magazines or digital media

- **production/broadcasting assistants** – in film and television they help to run the producers' and directors' offices, involved in programmes from planning to post-production

- **technicians** – technical jobs arranging lighting or sound in studios or on location for outside broadcasts

- **researchers** – these work mainly on factual research for programmes, including films and documentaries.

Working outside the media

There are many career areas where you could make use of your knowledge and skills. Your understanding of how images are created and the effect that they have on consumers would be useful in public relations. Marketing may also be a good choice, as it involves identifying the kind of product that the public would like to buy, and managing the packaging, advertising and selling of that product. You will have developed good communication and teamwork skills, which could be applied to many areas of business.

SOURCES OF INFORMATION

British Film Institute
www.bfi.org.uk/education

Film Education
www.filmeducation.org

Skillset
www.skillset.org/careers

Websites

www.bbc.co.uk/jobs

www.itvjobs.com

www.ukfilmcouncil.org.uk

'A level media studies has been an insightful experience into the media we come across in everyday life. It is my favourite of all my A levels and I have gained personally from studying it.'
Sarah, aged 17

'I've found it so far very enjoyable and enlightening and would recommend it to anyone.'
Stephanie, aged 17

Modern foreign languages

You may think that English is the international language of business but in practice it accounts for about 30% of the world gross domestic product (GDP) according to the World Bank. Neglecting languages in business means ignoring significant potential markets. Apart from the business aspect, language study not only gives you language and communication skills, but also a way of understanding a society and its culture.

A range of modern foreign languages is available at A level, including French, German, Spanish, Russian, Italian, Greek, Japanese, Chinese, Polish, Turkish, Arabic and Urdu.

You are expected to develop a much deeper understanding of how the language works than at GCSE. You are encouraged to learn languages within the context of the culture, society and way of life of the countries where they are spoken, including current issues affecting the country. You might also focus on how the language is used in business; the top business languages required by UK employers are currently (in order) French, German, Mandarin Chinese, Spanish, Polish, Russian, Arabic, Portuguese, Japanese and Korean (CILT 2010).

French is the most popular choice. France is one of our nearest neighbours and for a country so close, French culture, philosophy, literature and view on life are quite different from our own. Studying French brings you into close contact with the country's traditions and gives you direct access to its rich literary and artistic traditions.

German has many similarities to English, and some English learners find it easier to pronounce than French. One major difference between German and either English or French is that German grammar makes more use of 'inflection' – changes of word ending to indicate a change in meaning (as in English singular and plural, for example). This means that getting started can seem more difficult than with a language like French, but once you are over this hurdle, you can progress at a similar rate. Once you have the basics, German can provide you with an understanding of a culture with a complex political history and a rich literary, musical and dramatic tradition. It is also spoken by some eastern Europeans.

Spanish is a language that you may find quite easy, especially if you have already studied French (although it gets more difficult later). It is the world's fourth most widely spoken language (after Chinese, Hindi and English) and has the advantage of opening up the language and literature of most of Latin America as well as Spain. Spanish is an important language in the USA as well.

Italian, like Spanish, will be easier for you to learn if you have already started French. It is perhaps less likely than French, Spanish or German to be useful to you in your career (it has fewer speakers than the 'big three') but is still an important business and cultural language.

Russian is more difficult than the other frequently taught languages, not least because it has a different alphabet. However, most learners soon master this and find it to be a rewarding language to learn. Not only does Russia have one of the world's great literary and artistic traditions, but the opportunities to use Russian at work are increasing all the time as the country opens up to the rest of the world.

China, with a population of 1.3 billion, is playing an increasingly powerful role in global trade, diplomacy and culture. Although a difficult language to master, Mandarin Chinese is becoming a popular A level. The grammar is simple, but to speak the language you need to be able to master the system of tones that governs meaning. Beginners are likely to find this easier than learning the characters, of which there are thousands.

Polish has become popular since Poland joined the EU. Many Poles work in the UK, and UK citizens are setting up businesses and buying property in Poland.

You might want to consider one of the non-European languages now available at A level. As well as providing the opportunity to study cultures outside Europe, they open up many employment opportunities. This is particularly the case for languages connected with areas of economic importance like India and the Far East.

WHAT DO YOU STUDY?

The topics listed give an idea of what could be covered. The exact content of AS and A2 specifications differs according to exam boards, so you will need to check with your school or college about the exact modules available to you.

Command of a second language is usually broken down into four skills – writing, reading, speaking and listening (understanding the spoken language).

Writing – the ability to communicate in the written language using the appropriate style and form for the communication required. This may involve tasks such as writing a reply to a formal or informal letter, job applications or writing a promotional leaflet. You may be expected to express your ideas in the form of essays and short-answer questions on a wide range of topics including social issues, the arts, education or literature, written in your chosen language.

Speaking – the ability to express yourself clearly and correctly through spoken language. You will be encouraged to develop a wide vocabulary and practise speaking in the language as often as possible in order to

develop a comfortable and grammatically accurate style. All specifications require an oral exam, and you will be given plenty of practice at taking part in general conversation as well as speaking on specific topics.

Reading – you will be encouraged to read texts regularly in your chosen language. Some of these may be literary texts in the form of plays, poetry or prose. You will read newspapers and magazines in the chosen language to develop your vocabulary and comprehension. You will be tested, mainly in the chosen language, with comprehension questions of various types. Some have short answers or are multiple-choice questions, but others require more extensive writing. One purpose of this is to demonstrate your understanding of what you read; in the case of literary work, your appreciation is assessed as well as your understanding.

Listening – gaining skills in listening and understanding the language, including its informal use by native speakers. This is usually done using material taken from the media such as radio, satellite TV, cinema, DVDs or the web. While working on all these skills you learn about the society, culture, education, institutions and economy of the country or

> *'In an increasingly competitive job market, proficiency in a foreign language can give you added value when applying for jobs.'* Danny, graduate recruitment consultant

countries where the language is spoken. The exams will effectively test your knowledge of these issues as well as your command of the language. Study of literature is a smaller item in the specifications than it used to be, having largely been replaced by the study of present-day society and issues. However, literature – including that of the past – is itself a part of society and most students will study some texts.

Unless you are a native speaker of the language in question, a good pass (GCSE at grade A or B) in the language is usually required in order to take the A level. Some schools offer languages for beginners at A level.

HOW DO YOU STUDY?

There are many ways that you can spend your time in class when learning a language: this is partly because different ways of learning reinforce each other, and variety helps to cater for your learning style. You will work individually and in groups with written texts from newspapers and magazines, and multimedia recordings. You will watch recorded programmes and films and then discuss them, working on the vocabulary that you learn and the grammatical points that they illustrate. Outside of class, there is a good deal of time spent committing things to memory – especially vocabulary. There may be the opportunity to go on a trip to the relevant country or you may be able to go on an exchange programme and live in the country for a while.

SUBJECT COMBINATIONS

If you are thinking of specialising in modern foreign languages at degree level, you may prefer to make an early start by studying

two languages for A level (although you can nearly always start a second language as a beginner at degree level). If you take two languages, you should find that the skills and knowledge relating to the workings of one language will help you with the other. This is also the case if you combine a modern foreign language with an A level in classical/ancient Greek or Latin. You could combine a language with many other subjects including business, ICT and sciences.

It is possible to combine all A and AS levels with other equivalent qualifications such as BTEC Nationals or OCR Nationals and they could form part of Diplomas.

HIGHER EDUCATION OPTIONS

There are opportunities to study language degrees without having an A level in the language and you will learn the subject from scratch (also known as *ab initio*). However, for French degrees virtually all institutions require A level French. The same applies to a lesser extent to German and Spanish. For other languages universities will expect students to be beginners. However, a language A level, even in a different language, will help as it proves you have language learning skills and experience.

Degree-level study

Language study at degree level varies considerably from one place to another. At some, you would find a big difference from your A level studies as you would spend a large proportion of your time studying literature. At others, the focus remains on practical language use and the study of contemporary society.

A popular option is to build on your existing skills and knowledge by continuing with your A level language and starting a new one alongside it. At some institutions you can choose from a wide range of languages that may not have been available to you at A level, such as Scandinavian languages, Portuguese, Arabic, Chinese, Japanese or African languages.

Another option is a regional studies course, which allows you to study one or two modern foreign languages alongside the economic, political, social, legal and cultural climates of that country or region. European studies is the most widely offered. It is assumed that you already have a strong grasp of your major chosen language, unless it wasn't available to you at A level.

On nearly all language degrees you will spend some time abroad. This is usually the third of your four years. The way that you spend this year depends in part on your own preference, but also on the arrangements that have been developed over the years. For example, students going to France are most likely to work as an English language assistant in a secondary school or college, while those going to Russia usually spend their time on special courses of study at a university. However, opportunities to work as an employee in a business or similar organisation are also possible.

Degree subject combinations

Modern foreign languages can be usefully combined with a wide range of other subjects. With increasing economic, political and cultural contacts throughout the world, a carefully chosen combination can increase your employment options. Economics, business studies, marketing, politics, a science subject or law could be particularly appropriate. Combined subject degrees are available almost everywhere. Some institutions have created specialised 'European' or 'international' degrees in subjects such as engineering, sciences and law (where you may study French or German law and language, or European Union law, as well as English law). In these, your language study is more likely to be integrated with your study of the other subject than it is in a standard two-subject degree course. You will find specialised combined degrees to cater for emerging markets: Chinese, for example, can be combined with business studies, ICT and marketing.

Other higher education qualifications

There is a foundation degree in modern foreign languages with public service interpreting.

There are some HNDs and HNCs in tourism management offering options in modern foreign languages.

Chartered Institute of Linguists qualifications

The Chartered Institute of Linguists runs qualifications in translating and interpreting. These can be studied full or part time.

Relevance to other subjects?

Even if you decide not to study modern foreign languages by themselves at a higher level, you will find your study valuable. A knowledge of a modern foreign language at A level would help in the study of English, especially English language, history, politics and philosophy. If you are interested not just in one or two languages but language in general, you might consider a degree in linguistics, in which you study the development of human language: its structures, history and use. Since linguistics study must be backed up with examples from particular languages, knowledge of a modern foreign language will be very useful to you; you can also combine language study with linguistics.

Important advice

No matter how much classroom work you do, there is no substitute for experiencing a language first hand. Try to visit a country where your chosen language is spoken and spend time listening to it and speaking it, as well as absorbing the country's culture. It's easy to listen to the radio on the internet and this can only help you with your studies.

Nearly all universities have language centres, so even if you decide not to study your languages as part of a degree, you are likely to have the opportunity to continue your studies part time at a university language centre.

CAREER OPTIONS

Into work after A levels

You will find the level of language that you achieve with A level study is an advantage when you apply for practically any sort of job, especially with companies trading internationally. There are some opportunities to go straight from A levels into a job where your language skills will be used every day, such as working for an airline as cabin crew or ground staff, or within the travel industry, perhaps as a rep for tour companies at home or abroad. You must try to maintain and improve your language skills as they can get rusty. Also languages are constantly evolving so you need to learn new words as they arise.

Into work as a graduate

Working in modern foreign languages

Language-based careers are a popular choice for language graduates. You normally have to undertake further specialist training if you wish to become a professional linguist.

There are three traditional language-based career roles – interpreters, translators or teachers. These can be combined in a number of careers:

- **interpreters** – these translate the spoken language, normally into their own mother tongue. Interpreters provide an essential link between businesses or governments during negotiations or they may work translating for foreign nationals abroad. The work may be face to face or over the telephone. This kind of work requires further training and fluency in two foreign languages preferably including a degree in an unusual language. There is a shortage of interpreters with English as their first language and two other languages, especially in the UN and European Parliament

- **translators** – these work with the written language and the normal practice is to translate into the native language from the second language, not vice versa. They are often self-employed and work mainly for businesses. Some translators group together to form agencies offering translation in a wide range of languages

- **teachers** – language teachers are always in demand so the more subjects or languages you are able to teach, the more valuable you are likely to be

- **linguists** – within the Diplomatic Service, linguists can be both translators and interpreters. They may find themselves working in the UK or within an embassy abroad, where they play an important part in daily communication between countries and the trading, cultural and political decisions that are made

- **travel and tourism** – there are many opportunities here, whether you are working in the UK or abroad, ranging from tour guide to management positions. You could be using your languages on a daily basis and your knowledge of the country and culture to help you communicate effectively.

Apart from these jobs, in a recently survey it emerged that 74% of employers want language skills. Here are some examples of jobs where languages will be useful:

- **computer games translator** – translating computer games into other languages

- **website translators** – more and more websites are multi-lingual or need to have a version for different language speakers

- **football analyst** – watching and analysing the latest European football matches and producing reports on the failures and successes of the team. These are passed on to traders to aid investors in betting more successfully

- **international relocation manager** – working for large international companies to help staff relocate to new countries. You organise housing, schools for their children and removals

- **luxury yacht sales manager** – selling yearly memberships to 'high net worth individuals' who want to be charted on a route around the world on their private yacht and waited on by their own staff

- **tour organiser** – organising tours for musical groups like orchestras or theatre companies; organising and booking venues, hotels and transport

- **journalist** – using your language skills to research and write articles for magazines

- **press conference assistant** – interpreting for foreign language speakers at press conferences. Think of all the football players and managers who may need this service

- **recruitment consultant** – recruiting globally in a wide range of employment sectors.

You will find languages skills in demand in most areas of work. Examples of areas using languages skills include: IT, creative and media, national and local government, hospitably and tourism, manufacturing, construction, property management, engineering, finance and business.

Working outside modern foreign languages

Graduate linguists are good candidates for most jobs open to graduates in any subject

as they are flexible thinkers, imaginative and creative. They also have an understanding and appreciation of other cultures. Many find that they do not use their languages at the start of their career – for example, they may be engaged in general management training. If they maintain their language skills there could be opportunities to use them later on.

SOURCES OF INFORMATION

Chartered Institute of Linguists
www.iol.org.uk

CILT, the National Centre for Languages
www.cilt.org.uk

Websites

www.languageswork.org.uk

www.ilovelanguages.com

www.thirdyearabroad.com

www.vistawide.com/languages

'Travel is made easier when you have studied languages. My languages degree allows me to teach young children, making them more aware of language and culture.' Simon, French teacher with a degree in French and German

Music

If you are a keen musician, this course gives you the chance to develop your musical abilities and knowledge in a wide variety of ways. You will be able to demonstrate your skills in musical performance and study musical theory, composition and the history of music. Some specifications allow you to study world music, folk music, jazz, and music for film and TV as well as the classical music of Western European cultures. Students learn to work together well in addition to developing performing, composing and critical or analytical skills. The course is valued by employers and universities because it reflects versatility, creative ability and good communications.

WHAT DO YOU STUDY?

Music A level specifications are broadly alike, but have different emphases within them. Most allow you to choose where you want to place the emphasis of your own studies. You study a number of the following, depending on the course options you choose. Some offer different pathways for composers and performers.

Listening – developing your ability to listen to and analyse music through a variety of exercises such as dictation, analysis of performance errors and stylistic description of samples of music.

Performing – preparing a recital lasting between 5 and 16 minutes (depending on the exam board), there may also be ensemble playing and technology-based performances.

Analysis and appreciation of the elements of music – learning about musical structures and techniques such as sonata form, rhythm, harmony and counterpoint (the combination of two or more simultaneous melodies, as in a fugue).

History of music – studying one or two topics relating to the music of a particular period or type. Examples of topics set include music for film and television, popular music and jazz, and the Western classical tradition (compulsory in some specifications). Other topics include choral music in the Baroque period, jazz genres, music theatre (a study of

the musical from 1940 to 1980) and British popular music (from 1960 to the present day). The scope of a topic is often quite wide, since it includes the influences of music from other periods or countries on the music in your study.

Composing – learning the techniques of musical composition, partly through the imitation of styles, in which you have a degree of choice. Examples of styles might include choral harmonisations in the style of J. S. Bach, keyboard accompaniment in the early Romantic style, minimalism or more recent developments such as the popular song, folk, club dance, hip-hop, music theatre and world music. As well as composing, you will carry out exercises in arrangement – the preparation of a given piece of music for a particular instrument or group of instruments. Your work will be submitted for the exam in the form of a folio and/or a recorded version, and you may be required to write a commentary on your work. Some exam boards require composition as part of a formal examination.

'It was great to have the opportunity to explore and learn about music from all continents, historical periods and styles. The fact that you are being taught by staff who are leaders in their areas of study is highly fascinating and encouraging, because they pass their enthusiasm on to you.'
Anna, BMus graduate

A good grade (B or above) in GCSE music is often required before you can study the A level. You will be expected to play a musical instrument to a certain standard, which can vary between Associated Board of the Royal Schools of Music grade 4 and 6, depending on your school or college.

HOW DO YOU STUDY?

In some ways, music is like a language. You have to learn how it is put together (techniques such as harmony and types of musical form) and how it conveys feelings, mental images and moods. As with learning a language, improvement comes largely from exposure and lots of practice. Much of your time will be spent listening to music, discussing and analysing what you have heard and developing your ability to listen actively. Your ability to analyse different pieces of music depends on your experience of a wide variety of different types of music, so as well as your set work you should go to as many live music events as possible. If your course involves performance, you will have to spend quite a lot of time practising your instrument or instruments. You will have the chance to perform and record your own compositions as well as those of others.

SUBJECT COMBINATIONS

Music can be combined with any other A level. If you are thinking of studying music in higher education, especially if you are thinking of a singing career, languages are very useful. If you are considering a course in music technology or electronic music, mathematics, physics or computing will be useful.

It is possible to combine all A and AS levels with other equivalent qualifications such as BTEC Nationals or OCR Nationals and they could form part of Diplomas.

HIGHER EDUCATION OPTIONS

A good pass in A level music is usually required in order to be able to study it at a higher level. For many courses you have to pass a performance test and/or offer a pass at a high level (usually grade 8) in the Associated Board of the Royal Schools of Music graded examinations.

Degree-level study

Depending on your interests you can take a music degree course at university, where you will be studying alongside students in other disciplines, or at a music college (conservatoire), which is geared more towards performance.

Music courses usually lead to either a BA (Bachelor of Arts) or BMus (Bachelor of Music) degree. The BMus is much the same as a BA but when an institution offers both a BA and a BMus, the BA is typically broader in scope while the BMus concentrates more on composition, history or performance. You should check the course details carefully. You would probably spend the first two years of a music degree course developing the skills and knowledge that you gained at A level, your understanding of music theory and history, and your performance skills. In the final year, you have the chance to concentrate on the aspects of music that you find most interesting.

Your specialised options might include the study of a particular period of musical history: works written for choirs, the piano, stringed instruments or another family of instruments; non-classical music, such as jazz or rock; or the use of computers in music composition. Some institutions also offer the chance to spend part of your time studying abroad in a conservatoire or university.

Conservatoires: as mentioned earlier, these are for more performance-based degrees and have a separate application and selection process. There are seven conservatoires:

Birmingham Conservatoire
Leeds College of Music
Royal College of Music
Royal Northern College of Music
Royal Scottish Academy of Music and Drama
Royal Welsh College of Music and Drama
Trinity College of Music.

You can search for courses based on instrument and/or music genre on the Conservatoires UK Admissions Service (CUKAS) website, www.cukas.ac.uk.

A few universities offer degrees in electronic music, music technology or e-music. In these, your study of traditional music techniques is complemented by learning about methods of producing music using new technologies. Other courses specialising in particular types of music include, jazz and popular and commercial music and world music.

Degree subject combinations

University-based courses give you the opportunity to study music as part of a combined degree scheme or modular course, with a wide range of other subjects. You might consider a performing arts or creative arts course, in which you can usually study a combination of drama, music and visual art. Alternatively, you can combine music with any other subject including business, maths, English, history or modern languages. You could also study music as part of a Bachelor of Education (BEd).

Other higher education qualifications

There are foundation degrees in music, commercial music, music and sound technology, music technology, music management, music production plus performing arts, media composition and musical theatre.

HNDs and HNCs are available in music performance, music business, music production, music technology, sound engineering, events management, and urban and electronic music.

Relevance to other subjects?

An A level in music doesn't have to lead to a music course at a conservatoire or university. Many people find that their musical knowledge and understanding of the 'language' of music is extremely useful in subjects such as drama, modern foreign languages, philosophy, linguistics and communication studies. There are also specialised music technology courses and music industry business courses.

Important advice

The selection procedure for a higher level course in music can be very tough. In addition to a general interview you are likely to be asked to perform a piece of music and to take a listening test and a sight-reading test, or something similar. Make sure you are prepared for this.

CAREER OPTIONS

Into work after A levels

An A level in music may not lead directly to a music career but it can give you an advantage in careers where musical knowledge would be useful. Provided you don't mind starting as a junior, running errands and making the tea, you might find work in the recording industry, for a music magazine or website, or at a radio station. A level music can be used as a general qualification for entry to careers in many businesses or organisations.

Into work as a graduate

Working in music

Many careers relating to music involve additional training and experience before they can really take off properly. These include the following:

- **performing** – as a soloist, part of a small ensemble or larger orchestra, or as a piano accompanist for other performers. This sort of work requires a very high standard, continual practice and often unsocial working hours. There is also a good deal of competition and you will have to take whatever work you can get. If you have the relevant experience and ability, you may be able to supplement your performing income with private or school teaching

- **media** – there is an increasing demand for music of all types for broadcasting on radio, TV and the internet, and therefore a number of career opportunities in the areas of presenting, writing (for computer games, for example) and in music technology generally

- **teaching** – including private tuition to individual students, as well as class teaching in schools. For teaching in state schools, you will need a recognised teaching qualification. You may also gain work as a peripatetic teacher, moving round to different schools to give lessons

- **musical technician** – as a technician rather than a performer, you might be responsible for sound quality or technical equipment either in the recording studio or as part of a team at a performance

- **music business management** – organising performances, contracts, rehearsals and publicity on behalf of musicians. You might work for a large symphony orchestra, jazz band or pop band

- **composing** – not many people earn a living as composers and usually build up their careers gradually. They might work on commissions awarded by advertisers or television and radio producers, often spending weeks working painstakingly on pieces lasting only 15 seconds

- **music therapy** – working with adults and children with injuries or disabilities, making use of both the physical skills and emotional dimension of music to develop or restore people's abilities. You would need a further qualification for this.

Working outside music

Because of the option to teach, quite a high proportion of music graduates do work professionally in music after they graduate. Some use their practical skills and knowledge in other careers. Some of these will have a connection with music, including arts administration, libraries and publishing. Others take further training and enter completely different careers.

SOURCES OF INFORMATION

British Association for Music Therapy
www.bsmt.org

Incorporated Society of Musicians
www.ism.org

Royal Academy of Music
www.ram.ac.uk

'I like the variety, it's not just classical music and you learn to appreciate all types of music. It's broadened my taste in music and I've listened to things I wouldn't have touched before.'
Nigel, A levels in music, history and English

Music technology

Technology in music is now part of our everyday life. It is used in all areas of music from classical through to hip hop, grime and grindie. Music technology teaches you how to use this technology to arrange and compose music. The A level gives you the opportunity to develop your musical abilities, study composition and arrangement, and acquire skills in sequencing and multi-track recording.

Music technology A level is part of the A level music curriculum. In order to get onto the course, you must be able to play an instrument to a reasonable standard. Schools and colleges have varying requirements but, in general, it ranges from Associated Board of the Royal Schools of Music grades 4 to 6 with a reasonable knowledge of music theory, usually at grade 3 or higher. GCSE music may be a requirement unless students have previous experience. No experience in music technology is required.

WHAT DO YOU STUDY?

The topics listed give an idea of what could be covered. The exact content of AS and A2 specifications differs according to exam boards, so you will need to check with your school or college about the exact modules available to you.

Sequencing, recording and producing – learning the skills required to produce accomplished musical performances in a range of styles using sequencing software, and using the processes of multi-track recording to produce finished mixes in a range of musical styles. You will also learn how to record live instruments.

Arranging and improvisation – this involves taking a motif or melody and developing it into a full arrangement to be presented as a score or finished recording on CD.

Composing using technology – developing the ability to use computer software and multi-track recording techniques to create compositions to a brief.

Listening, analysing and producing – developing the ability to analyse the musical, technical and stylistic features of music and considering the impact of technology on music.

History of music and specialist areas of study – studying the history and development of Western classical music in relation to technology. Other topics you might study depending on the options chosen include popular music covering areas such as rock and roll, rap and hip hop, reggae, heavy rock, soul, indie rock, punk and jazz. You might also study music for the moving image, which includes music for films and television, and words and music (the relationship between words and music). In the current specification, albums by The Who and Madonna, and film music from *Batman* and *Goldfinger*, are studied.

HOW DO YOU STUDY?

Much of your time is spent in practical study, creating recordings and sequencing using a range of technology (depending on the pathway chosen). You will have the opportunity to record original compositions

'I was able to use the recording studio facilities to record local bands in my spare time. This will help my CV and I will have a portfolio of professional demos ready for when I graduate.'
Michael, on a BSc in music technology

and develop arrangements from lead lines and short motifs. You will learn how to recognise musical features and stylistic elements through listening to a wide range of music, from Western classical to popular music and jazz. As well as the coursework set by your teacher, you should spend as much time as possible listening to a broad selection of music, learning to recognise the musical structure and the technology used.

SUBJECT COMBINATIONS

If you wish to study music technology at a higher level, you might select other A levels from mathematics, physics, ICT, electronics or music depending on the content and requirements of the course. Some courses will require music A level in addition to music technology, or require you to reach a certain standard of performance (which could include an audition).

It is possible to combine all A and AS levels with other equivalent qualifications such as BTEC Nationals or OCR Nationals and they could form part of Diplomas.

HIGHER EDUCATION OPTIONS

Degree-level study

Music technology is a popular area of study and attracts students from both musical and technical backgrounds who want to learn about both cutting-edge technical and creative developments in the field.

There is a variety of degrees available with varying titles including music technology, creative music technology, and e-music. Degrees can be based in music colleges or music or engineering departments at universities, depending on the content. Some are technical and concentrate on the practical skills of sound engineering, whereas others are a mixture of music and music technology; many require some competence in performing music at certain levels. They may

be BMus, BSc, BEng or BA degrees depending on the content. There are related courses in sound technology and sound engineering and production, music technology software development, smart systems and music technology, music systems engineering and a degree in music informatics, which combines new music with new technology, including music composition and analysis, studio recording, computer music, interactive multimedia and artificial intelligence.

There is a list of courses accredited by the Association of Professional Recording Services (APRS) available on their education website, JAMES (Joint Audio Media Education Services; see sources of information). The courses are accredited as they meet industry needs, so could help you get employment after you graduate.

Degree subject combinations

Music technology combines well with music, performing arts and media courses. There are specialist combinations available with electronic engineering, pop music, radio broadcasting and film production. You could consider combinations with management or ICT and you will also find music technology combined with science subjects.

Other higher education qualifications

Foundation degrees are available in music technology, creative sound design, commercial music technology, creative sound technology, creative music production, entertainment technology, music and sonic arts (music technology), live sound, music and sound technology, and music production.

There are HNDs and HNCs in music technology, applied multimedia, music production, media technology (music and sound engineering), multimedia integration, and urban and electronic music.

Relevance to other subjects?

Depending on your interests you could consider popular, commercial music or media studies. There are also sound engineering and electronics courses. If you are interested in the music business, there are courses in music industry management and music journalism.

Important advice

Music technology degrees vary in their content and specialism, so you must research the different courses to find out which is the best for you. Course requirements also vary as well as the standard of musical performance required, so be sure to contact universities and colleges directly to find out what would be suitable for you. It is also important to ask them what sorts of jobs their graduates go into.

CAREER OPTIONS

Into work after A levels

You might start as a junior in a recording studio, or as a runner or messenger in the music or TV industries. You might find work in a radio station, the film industry, assisting with live sound at concerts and the theatre, or possibly administration work with music and other media publications. There would also be opportunities in music, computer or electronics shops. (See also the information under this heading in the music entry.)

Into work as a graduate

Working in music technology

Depending on the content of your degree, here are some of the careers you could consider:

- audio production
- audio sales
- audio systems maintenance
- equipment design
- events management
- independent musical composition and performance
- media production
- music and sound support for live performances
- music education: teaching, lecturing, research, technical support
- music for new media (interactive games, the web)
- music production
- music, sound design and post-production for film, television and radio
- research and development
- software design
- sound design
- sound engineering
- studio engineering
- studio management
- television and radio engineering and production.

Some of these areas cross over into the more creative aspects of music. The work could be freelance and/or on short-term contracts, so you are likely to be self-employed.

Working outside music technology

You would have knowledge of IT and engineering so you could consider working in the IT or engineering industry, which might require further training. If you have a strong interest in the music industry, there could be opportunities in music management and administration, arts administration, journalism and marketing.

SOURCES OF INFORMATION

Association of Professional Recording
Services (APRS)
www2.aprs.co.uk

BPI
www.bpi.co.uk

Websites

www.jamesonline.org.uk (for list of accredited
higher and further education courses)

www.computermusic.co.uk

www.soundonsound.com (online magazine)

*'You must be able to read music for the A
level, it will give you a head start.'*
Bill, aged 17, studying music technology,
mathematics and music

Performing arts

The course is all about the performing arts industry and the different careers and progression routes through it. You will be able to specialise in one or two areas. You don't necessarily have to be able to dance, sing, act and play an instrument to a high standard for this course, although if you can do more than one it will be helpful. It would be helpful to have already achieved a GCSE in dance, drama, music or expressive arts for this course.

This applied A level is a broad qualification that encourages you to study in a practical way. It is designed to help you develop a range of vocational skills that will be useful to you either for higher level study or in work and training.

N.B. There is also a course entitled performance studies (OCR).

WHAT DO YOU STUDY?

This course is available as a single award.

N.B. A level in drama and theatre studies is described on page 88.

Specifications vary, but in all you will investigate the industry and jobs within it, develop your own performing arts skills, and get involved in all aspects of organising and producing productions.

Investigating the performing arts industry – looking at how the business part of the industry works, how decisions are made and how it is financed and marketed.

Knowledge and understanding of the past and the important developments that have taken place in the performing arts – this will be useful to you in developing your skills, creating your own performance pieces and discovering what has influenced your own work.

Exploring skills for performance – assessing and building up your own skills in one or more of the specialisms offered: dance, drama, music, music technology or the technical and production aspects of performance. This will depend on your own interests and what is available in your school or college.

Exploring repertoire – researching stylistic conventions, interpretation of repertoire.

Creating work for performance – creating your own performance or showcase; this could be something totally original or adapted from another source. You work with others in a project management team through the whole creative process, culminating in the event itself, which improves your skills in all the different areas.

Performance practice – learning what is involved in performing work as a performer, including safe working practices.

Professional practice: production demonstration – learning about carrying out a production role in response to a brief or commission, developing your production skills and demonstrating them in practical work, producing a final product or providing a practical application in performance. You might work as a member of a production team (for example, front of house, stage management, or lighting and sound technician) or design something for the

'I only feel alive when I am in the theatre. I am prepared to take any job as long as I can work there.'
Sam, drama student, after a first degree in history

production such as a costume, mask, prop, puppet or set.

Employment opportunities in the performing arts and how to get work – looking at the different jobs and opportunities available, how people and companies promote themselves, and also topics such as terms and conditions of employment. You need to learn about effective self-promotion, attitudes, survival skills and self-employment.

HOW DO YOU STUDY?

You will study through a programme of assignments, which will include practical performing, and there will be tests, set assignments, projects and case studies, some of which will be assessed externally. You may keep a working log detailing all aspects of the development process of an assignment or project including research, exploration, practical application and ongoing evaluation. In group work you may have to prepare supporting documents explaining how the performance was prepared and how you were involved in the creative process.

You will go on visits to performing arts venues and see productions. There may be speakers from the industry.

SUBJECT COMBINATIONS

A levels in media studies and English language would combine well, and also subjects such as history and psychology.

It is possible to combine all A and AS levels with other equivalent qualifications such as BTEC Nationals or OCR Nationals and they could form part of Diplomas.

> *'What I found really nerve-racking was that theatrical agents came to the drama school shows. They take notes all the way through!'*
> Paul, actor with a degree in performing arts

HIGHER EDUCATION OPTIONS

Degree-level study

Courses are divided into practical performance or technical courses, and more academic studies. There are courses in performing arts where you can study one or two types of performing arts; and specialised drama, dance and music colleges where you would concentrate on one. Technical courses include stage management and costume design. The more academic courses tend to be at universities, but not exclusively; you will find some excellent courses at universities that are academic as well as offering performance skills.

Apart from courses entitled performing arts, other course titles to look out for include: contemporary and performance practices, performance design and practice, acting for stage and screen, media performance, musical theatre, and acting and stage combat.

Degree subject combinations

Performing arts can be combined with many different subjects. Popular combinations are with media studies, English, management and education.

Other higher education qualifications

You will find a wide variety of foundation degrees, which provide employment-related courses in many specialisms within the sector. Examples include:

- contemporary circus and physical performance
- creative industries (performing arts)
- festival, site specific and street arts
- music performance
- music production

- performance and events production
- performing arts (drama)
- performing arts (acting)
- performing arts (dance)
- performing arts in the community
- performing arts (contemporary theatre)
- performing arts (music theatre)
- popular music
- stage management
- technical theatre.

There are some HNDs and HNCs in performing arts and examples are:

- performing arts
- performing arts (acting)
- performing arts (dance)
- performing arts (music)
- performing arts (performance)
- performing arts (musical theatre)
- popular music.

Relevance to other subjects?

Look at degrees in arts administration, leisure and recreation, hospitality management, and events and exhibition management.

Important advice

You need to get as much experience of performing arts as you can, either in or outside of education. If you do not intend to become a performer, there are opportunities to learn about technical support. Join a local drama group and get experience of stage management, costume and make-up. Get involved with school and college productions.

CAREER OPTIONS

Into work after A levels

Most students who want to perform or learn technical skills will go on to higher education.

'The show must go on, even if you aren't feeling up to it. You need self discipline and real determination to succeed.'
Luke, student on a performing arts degree

You will need to get more experience and training and make useful contacts. Jobs available after A levels could include administration and support in performing arts organisations, box-office work and other front-of-house work in theatres. There may be some practical junior jobs available in costume, scene construction or props. Apprenticeships might also be available at this level.

Into work as a graduate

Working in performing arts

If you start work as a performer you will need to attend auditions and build up your experience. You may need to find yourself an agent to help you get work. If you have studied technical skills, this is a similar route: you will start at a junior level and build up experience and contacts. With a performing arts background you could go into teaching, which would require further training. There are opportunities in arts administration and community arts work (promoting performing arts in the community). You could also consider retailing (music shops, costume hire companies) and general administration or management in performing arts.

Working outside performing arts

As you will have learned valuable transferable skills on the course, such as communication, you would be able to go into many areas of work including business and retail. Sales and teaching would give you a good opportunity to use your communication skills. (See also the music, and drama and theatre studies entries.)

SOURCES OF INFORMATION

Association of British Theatre Technicians
www.abtt.org.uk

Council for Dance Education and Training
www.cdet.org.uk

Incorporated Society of Musicians
www.ism.org

National Council for Drama Training
www.ncdt.co.uk

Philosophy

If you have ever seen *The Matrix* film trilogy and wondered about some of the issues in the films you will already have had an introduction to some of the key questions studied in philosophy. Why are we here? What is the truth? Do we just fit in with the way things are or question them? If you have watched the *Lost* series this may well have thrown up similar questions.

The word 'philosophy' comes from the ancient Greek word meaning 'love of wisdom'. The Greeks founded philosophy and the issues they considered are still pursued by philosophers today. As an A level philosophy student you will be asking questions like: Is there anything that we can really know with certainty? What is justice? How is the human mind related to the body? Are there any absolute moral values?

The point of philosophy is not so much to answer such questions (although you may find more satisfying answers than you had before) but to learn how to analyse and approach them. Developing such skills will be worthwhile for your further studies and in your daily life. The skills that you will develop through your study of philosophy, such as arguing logically and lateral thinking, are extremely relevant to our information-based economy and are transferable to many other academic subjects.

WHAT DO YOU STUDY?

The topics listed give an idea of what could be covered.

AQA is the only board offering this specification.

On the course you will gain an understanding of some important philosophical ideas, their historical presentation and their contribution to modern thought.

You will strengthen your capacity for analysis, reasoning and judgement; spot flaws in logic; learn how to argue logically and confidently; understand views different from your own; and be able to oppose others' arguments.

The AS specification will give you a broad introduction to the study of philosophy and its key themes.

You will cover the following themes:

- reason and experience
- why should I be governed?
- why should I be moral?

- the idea of god
- knowledge of the external world
- tolerance
- the value of art
- god and the world
- the debate over free will and determinism.

At A2 you will develop your understanding of key philosophical concepts, themes, texts and techniques and specialise further, choosing two themes to study in depth and focusing on philosophical problems through the study of a key text.

- **Philosophy of mind** – What is the mind? What is its place in nature? What is the relationship between mentality and physicality? How are mental states identified, experienced and known?

'It teaches you to think and question everything. It fits in very well with my other subjects.'
Violet, aged 18, taking A levels in philosophy, maths and physics

- **Political philosophy** – This theme covers philosophical questions concerning how human well-being can be helped or hindered by the organisation of society and political structures.

- **Epistemology and metaphysics** – Epistemology: do we know anything for certain? Is there any difference between knowledge and belief? Metaphysics: the branch of philosophy responsible for the study of existence. It answers the question 'What is?' It encompasses everything that exists, as well as the nature of existence itself. It says whether the world is real, or merely an illusion. It is a fundamental view of the world around us.

- **Moral philosophy** – Are there moral truths and if so what is their nature?

- **Philosophy of religion** – How should we understand religious belief? Are the claims made by religious believers a distinctive kind of theory or hypothesis? If so, are the arguments used and conclusions reached reliable? How do these aspects of religion weave into the fabric of religious belief and inform our understanding and evaluation of it? To what extent do different religions compete with or even undermine each other?

- **Philosophical problems** – You will study classical philosophy texts and look at the problems raised by these philosophers. You will need to be familiar with the text and will be required to develop and explore the problem areas identified within it. You will be expected to use this knowledge as a springboard for wider discussion and engagement of issues, and apply your acquired knowledge to philosophical problems raised in the text. The texts are works by Hume, Plato, Mill, Descartes and Nietzsche.

There is no GCSE in philosophy although OCR offers religious studies GCSE with an emphasis on philosophy and ethics. However, for the study of this subject at A level you will need an enquiring and open mind, as well as the ability to write in good, clear English.

HOW DO YOU STUDY?

Class discussion based on your reading is an important aspect of studying philosophy, as it has been for hundreds of years. Be prepared for the reading to be difficult at first, until you get used to the way that philosophical arguments are presented. There may also be the preparation and delivery of student presentations and group topics. As you might expect, your written work will be in the form of essays and you will be expected to undertake a lot of independent study. The subject is stimulating but also demanding. You must be able to work hard to grasp some difficult concepts and then be able to cope with class discussions that will test your understanding and your viewpoint.

SUBJECT COMBINATIONS

You are unlikely to be asked for particular A level subjects if you apply for a university course in philosophy, although mathematics may be a preference for courses involving formal logic. Otherwise, your ability to form logical arguments would be helped, and in turn reinforced, by studying subjects such as English, history, politics, psychology and critical thinking.

It is possible to combine all A and AS levels with other equivalent qualifications such as BTEC Nationals or OCR Nationals and they could form part of Diplomas.

HIGHER EDUCATION OPTIONS

It is not necessary to have an A level in philosophy in order to study it at a higher level.

Degree-level study

Philosophy degree courses vary a great deal in content. Some place a great deal of emphasis on the traditional study of the great philosophers of the past, such as Aristotle, Plato and Descartes. Others focus on modern issues relating to politics, psychology, education and religion. All of them encourage you to form and defend your own ideas. Most courses begin with a year spent introducing you to the main strands in philosophical argument and other courses are even broader to begin with, starting with a general foundation course covering other humanities subjects as well as philosophy. As you progress through the course you will find yourself with an increasing number of options, with some third years having no compulsory topics. Options could include history and the philosophy of science, feminist philosophy (theories about the position of women in society), aesthetics (how we judge beauty and art), or the works of particular philosophers such as Hegel, Nietzsche or Wittgenstein. You can specialise in European or mental philosophy.

Degree subject combinations

On many courses you have the option of continuing to study philosophy alongside another subject, and there is a wide range of subjects in the arts, humanities and sciences. Some of these are modular degree schemes in which you have a more or less free choice from a wide range of subjects. There are also several degrees combining three subjects out of philosophy, politics, economics, psychology and history. These degree programmes are designed so that the subjects throw light on each other, although you can usually select options in order to weight your own course in the direction of just one of the subjects.

> 'If you think you might want to go into teaching, it's a good idea to combine philosophy with a more commonly taught subject.'
> Alan, philosophy teacher at an FE college, with a degree in philosophy and history

Other popular combinations are politics, economics, religious studies, history and modern languages.

Other higher education qualifications

As foundation degrees are vocational, there are none in philosophy. You might want to consider those available in law, politics or community studies.

There are no HNDs or HNCs in philosophy. An HND in legal studies or business law is one possibility, as it gives you plenty of opportunity to use your experience of logical argument and can provide the foundation for a career in law.

Relevance to other subjects?

Philosophy helps you to think about and understand important and complex ideas and issues, and encourages you to look at them critically and sensibly. You will be able to use ideas from present-day thought as well as evidence taken from the works of thinkers throughout history. This experience would provide a good basis for many subjects, including politics, law, theology/religious studies, economics, history, sociology, linguistics, drama and classics. Also look at subjects like human rights or international relations.

Important advice

You cannot be a lazy thinker in philosophy and your commitment to the subject will be clear from the amount of reading that you do. Interviews for higher level philosophy courses often involve discussion of what you have read, not just the books on the set texts for your A level subjects. The more you read in philosophy, the better you will become at forming intelligent arguments of your own.

CAREER OPTIONS

Into work after A levels

Philosophy is not a vocational subject so won't lead straight into a particular career. It does help you to become a clear and critical thinker who can put together a reasoned, intelligent argument. These skills are valuable to employers in many areas, including administration or any job requiring organisational skills. You would be an effective member of any team where the powers of persuasive argument are important such as in marketing or sales.

Into work as a graduate

Working in philosophy

Careers linked directly to philosophy are limited. The nearest you can get to working as a philosopher is by teaching or lecturing in schools, colleges or universities. If you want to teach in a state school you will need to offer an additional National Curriculum subject such as history, or government and politics, as well as studying for a postgraduate teaching qualification (PGCE). Only if you become a philosophy lecturer or writer will you get the chance actually to 'do some philosophy' of your own. This could involve further study at postgraduate level.

Working outside philosophy

Most philosophy graduates go on to work in areas that enable them to use their ability to ask intelligent questions, analyse a problem and come up with a reasoned decision. Many philosophy graduates find employment in management or administration, where the ability to make informed decisions (often on other people's behalf) is extremely important. Others use their powers of argument in sales, advertising and marketing, targeting potential buyers for a product and finding the most effective way of selling it. Financial jobs are also a possibility as are jobs in law or politics. Some graduates go on to work in journalism, the media, publishing or social work.

SOURCES OF INFORMATION

Royal Institute of Philosophy
www.royalinstitutephilosophy.org

Websites

www.alevelphilosophy.co.uk

www.philosophynow.org

> 'A philosophy degree has trained the individual's brain and given them the ability to provide the skills we require and clients demand. These skills include the ability to be analytical, provide clear and innovative thinking, and question assumptions.'
> Evelyn, director of a management consultancy

Photography

In photography A level you study different aspects of photography allowing you to display your creative abilities and understanding of different areas of the subject. This will give you opportunities to specialise in areas other than lens-based imagery, such as digital imaging and the moving image. The specifications are both theoretical and practical. On the theoretical side, you study cultural, historical and contemporary practice and its use as a means of visual expression and communication. On the practical side, you learn how to choose and treat subjects for photographs as well as how to take, develop and print images of your own.

WHAT DO YOU STUDY?

The topics listed give an idea of what could be covered. The exact content of AS and A2 specifications differs according to exam boards, so you will need to check with your school or college about the exact modules available to you.

Most of the course is based around coursework. You will cover a broad range of topics, which could include:

- portraiture
- documentary photography/ photojournalism
- landscape photography – urban, rural and coastal
- working from objects – for example, still life and the natural world
- experimental imagery – how photographic images can be changed and manipulated to create striking effects
- photographic installation, video, television and film.

In addition, you could also cover some of these topics as you work through the course.

Exploring visual characteristics – how to represent people and human situations, inanimate objects and the living world through the medium of photography.

Digital photography.

Interpretation of the subject – the different ways of representing the subject of a photograph and the effects they create.

Light sources – how to manipulate light for effective photography.

Cameras and related equipment – understanding and assessing the photographic equipment available.

Sensitive materials and processing – the detailed techniques and knowledge required for developing photographs.

Colour photography – how it is created and how its technology differs from that used for black-and-white photography.

Photography in the mass media – the role played by photography in communicating information to the public, and the creation of images as a means of entertainment.

The moving image – similarities and differences between photography and film, video and television, as a means of communication.

How to interpret and work to a brief.

It is not essential to have GCSE photography to take the A level.

HOW DO YOU STUDY?

Practical work is extremely important part in this subject. The work involves selecting and

> *'Make sure you learn dark-room skills as this forms the basis of everything you do.'* Suzanne, studying A level photography with communication studies and English literature

preparing subjects, whether in a studio or natural setting, in landscapes or cityscapes, then checking and adjusting lighting before taking the final photograph. You then develop, edit and print the photographs. The pictures that you create during this time will contribute to your exam portfolio, which should show a variety of techniques and subjects. Theory work involves classroom discussion of photographs and other visual media, together with note-taking and essay writing. You will visit photography galleries, exhibitions and trade shows.

Research and development of ideas form an important part of the coursework. You will need to be self-motivated and work outside of lecture time. You might be asked to provide your own equipment, such as an SLR camera, filters, tripod and memory stick, although sometimes these can be borrowed from your school or college.

The assessment will include producing a portfolio of work, controlled assignments (where you will be given preparation time and then controlled time to finalise your work) and you may have to prepare a personal investigation with a related written personal study.

SUBJECT COMBINATIONS

If you want to study photography beyond A level, you will be expected to have a good portfolio. It would be useful to choose other A levels that will help you with this. An obvious choice is art and design, although you must ensure that the subjects do not overlap too much, as the two A levels might not be accepted for entry to higher education.

Media studies includes the investigation of visual images as a means of communication, so could be a good choice. If you want to broaden your studies and increase your job opportunities, consider languages or business studies as these are useful in most careers. Finally, if you think that you might aim for a career in technical photography (medical or forensic photography, for example), physics, chemistry or mathematics would make good choices.

It is possible to combine all A and AS levels with other equivalent qualifications such as BTEC Nationals or OCR Nationals and they could form part of Diplomas.

HIGHER EDUCATION OPTIONS

A good portfolio of photographic work is a major entry requirement for higher level photography courses. Most people produce this as part of a one-year Foundation course in art and design, which is available at many colleges and schools of art, as this is the usual entry route. However, some exceptional students can get in with just A levels or equivalent.

Degree-level study

Photography can be studied as a single subject. Apart from degrees entitled photography, you will also find course titles such as contemporary lens media, lens-based photo media, photographic art, photographic practice and visual communication (photography).

Courses vary in the amount of practice and theory involved, but most provide the option of specialising in particular areas of photography during the second or third year. This could include medical, landscape, nature, portrait, industrial, still life and cinema photography. There are also courses specialising in documentary, marine and natural history photography, fine art, photography for fashion and advertising, press and editorial photography and photojournalism.

Degree subject combinations

There are options to combine photography with related subjects such as video, fashion and brand promotion, public relations or digital imaging as well as with many other subjects. Studying for a combined degree may increase the options open to you after your degree. Look at subjects such as business studies or languages, which would benefit your future career whatever you decide to do.

Other higher education qualifications

Not to be confused with the preparatory art Foundation courses, foundation degrees are available in photography, action photography, photography and digital imaging, commercial photography, contemporary photography practice, creative and editorial photography, digital photography, fashion styling and photography, lens-based photo media, photography and digital imaging, photography and digital design, wildlife education and media and video.

There are HNDs and HNCs available in photography and digital photography.

Again, as with degrees, for some courses you may first need to take a one-year Foundation course in art and design.

Relevance to other subjects?

Other subjects where photography A level would be an advantage are media studies, film studies or cultural studies, history of art, or any art and design specialism, such as graphic design, fine art (painting and drawing) or sculpture.

Important advice

It is never too soon to start gathering work together for your portfolio. Get into the habit of carrying a camera around with you to take advantage of photo opportunities. The work that you do outside of your lessons is just as important as what you do in class.

CAREER OPTIONS

Into work after A levels

You could go on to train as an assistant to a professional photographer, gaining experience as you go along. Starting salaries are often low, but you get the opportunity to learn on the job and, if you're lucky, to make use of the facilities or equipment. There could be opportunities in camera and photographic equipment shops and you might also want to consider a job on the reproduction and development side of photography. This could be a high-street laboratory or professional development laboratories, responsible for anything from holiday snaps to wedding pictures or commercial photos. Provided that you have a good enough portfolio and your own equipment, you might consider approaching local newspapers for work, photographing newsworthy events. This would be on a freelance basis, but again it is good for building up your experience and portfolio. There could also be opportunities to work for the police or the Armed Forces.

Don't forget to see if Apprenticeships are available.

Into work as a graduate

Working in photography

Professional photographers work in studios or on location. Some are employed by newspapers, industrial or architectural companies or by businesses compiling professional portfolios for models or actors. Many photographers are self-employed (at least 50%), and are responsible for finding

> 'You have to have your own website to promote yourself.'
> Will, freelance photographer

their own work, running their business and the creative photographic work itself. Photographers specialise in many different areas and the direction that you eventually take could be by careful planning or by chance. Specialist areas include product or food photography (for cookery books and magazines, or any product that must be made to look as attractive as possible), fashion styling, police work (creating photographic records of criminals, scenes of crime and evidence) or travel photography. Digital imaging is an important area, using photographic materials as the basis for the kind of computer-enhanced images that we see around us in advertising, on DVDs and in films. Finding work in photography can be difficult as it is very competitive, so a creative, imaginative and committed approach to the job search is the key to success. You will need to have a good quality portfolio in order to approach employers, develop a creative CV and even set up your own website.

Working outside photography

As competition in professional photography is intense and careers insecure many photography graduates use their skills in a slightly different context. For example, an understanding of the power of the visual image is important for anyone working within advertising. They can work as photographic archivists, responsible for the organisation and storage of photographic history or documentary evidence, which must be easily accessed when needed by publishers, newspapers or even the police. There are also jobs within areas of film and television, including direction, production, editing, computer graphics, set design/dressing and lighting. Here the work is far more concerned with the moving image rather than the static one, but a sense of form, colour, light and framing are all just as essential.

SOURCES OF INFORMATION

Association of Photographers
www.the-aop.org

British Institute of Professional Photography
www.bipp.com

British Journal of Photography
www.bjp-online.com

Royal Photographic Society
www.rps.org

'Take your camera with your everywhere; you never know when an opportunity might come along.'
Michael, taking A level photography with government and politics and business

Physical education

Studying physical education gives you the opportunity to develop a theoretical understanding of the physiological, psychological and sociological factors that underpin sporting performance as well as gaining practical experience. It is a well-respected academic subject, offering you the opportunity to explore sport on a national and international level. It has never been so much in the spotlight with the current focus on healthy lifestyles and of course the 2012 Olympics. The specifications focus on participation and performance in physical activity as part of a balanced, active and healthy lifestyle.

WHAT DO YOU STUDY?

The topics listed give an idea of what could be covered. The exact content of AS and A2 specifications differs according to exam boards, so you will need to check with your school or college about the exact modules available to you.

- **How the human body works** – the anatomy and physiology of the human body and how the body responds to physical activity and assessing fitness; physiological, biomechanical and psychological factors in sport.

- **Performance** – analysis and critical evaluation of the factors that improve or optimise performance; factors affecting the nature and development of elite performance.

- **Sociocultural and historical effects of participation in physical activity** – the current state of sport both in the UK and globally. Participation in sports and recreation, including healthy lifestyles and contemporary health concerns.

- **Acquiring, developing and evaluating practical skills in physical education** – in some specifications the practical demonstration of skills is from a choice of activities including combat, invasion and target games, gymnastics, dance, athletics, outdoor and adventurous activities, and swimming.

It is not necessary to have taken GCSE physical education in order to study this A level. However, if you have taken this GCSE course and/or biology, you may find it useful in the transition to A level work.

HOW DO YOU STUDY?

It involves a mixture of practical and theory work, with the opportunity to work on your own sporting performance. You will learn theory, observe sporting performances and may analyse your own performance on video or by keeping your own personal diary.

The assessment is a combination of practical assessment, coursework and exams.

SUBJECT COMBINATIONS

If you are considering a degree in physical education (or sports science) then at least one science from biology, human biology or chemistry is recommended. Physical education also goes well with subjects such as history, sociology and psychology. If you are considering sports or leisure management, business studies or leisure studies A levels would be good choices.

It is possible to combine all A and AS levels with other equivalent qualifications such as BTEC Nationals or OCR Nationals and they could form part of Diplomas.

HIGHER EDUCATION OPTIONS

Degree-level study

There are four core areas involved in studying physical education (or sports science) at degree level:

- sports psychology
- exercise physiology – nutrition, diet etc
- exercise and health
- biomechanics – the analysis of physiology during sporting activities.

You will find specialised sports science or sports studies courses available, such as sports and exercise science, physical education and coaching, sports coaching, sport/exercise psychology, sports rehabilitation, sports massage, sport technology, sports medicine and even equine and human sports science. There are also courses in sports development and active lifestyles promotion (working to develop opportunities for participation in sport and healthy living for all sections of the community) as well as sport management, which can get very specialised, e.g. sports management (golf). Degree titles vary and can include physical education and health and fitness in their titles. There are also physical education degrees incorporating teacher training.

Degree subject combinations

You can combine sports science or sports studies with related subjects, like human biology, or with management courses, such as tourism, leisure or outdoor recreation. You could also consider combinations with business, ICT or languages.

Other higher education qualifications

Foundation degrees include areas such as sports science, sport health and fitness, sports development and coaching, fitness instruction and sports massage, sports journalism, outdoor leadership and sports therapy.

Specialist courses are available in football coaching, football development, rugby coaching and performance, golf management and golf coaching.

You could consider related courses in leisure and tourism management, spa management, or surf science and technology.

There are a number of HND and HNC courses available providing a mixture of practical work and theory. Courses available include sport and exercise science, sports studies, sport and recreation management, sports and leisure management, and sports performance and coaching.

Relevance to other subjects?

Look at courses in leisure and recreation management, and hotel and hospitality management. You could also consider courses in psychology or sociology, youth work or teaching.

Important advice

In order to keep up with the practical component of the course you should follow a training regime (or continue with any existing programme that you may have).

This should include general cardiovascular work together with some resistance training. A general pattern of healthy living, such as a healthy diet excluding cigarettes and alcohol, is regarded as essential.

As there are so many related higher level courses in the sports, fitness and leisure sector it is advisable to start researching courses as early as possible to find the ones most suitable for you. Remember to ask about the destinations of the graduates from any courses you are considering.

CAREER OPTIONS

Into work after A levels

A knowledge of physical education could help you work within the sports and leisure industry in support jobs such as leisure centre assistant. You might also consider sports coaching, lifeguard or personal fitness instruction work (depending on any extra qualifications you may have gained). Retail sports shops or jobs in IT and administration connected to the sports industry could also be options. You may find there are Apprenticeships available.

Into work as a graduate

Working in physical education

About one in five sports science graduates go into professional jobs in sports straight after graduating.

Health and fitness industry – this is a major career option for graduates in sports studies so you might consider a career in the management of fitness, leisure centres, health clubs or spas. You might start as a personal trainer, which can offer a good route into the industry. You may also find jobs in local or national government such as active lifestyles officers who promote healthy living and lifestyles in the community.

Coaching – this ranges from high-level activities (such as the Olympics) to providing for the needs of young people in the community. It also connects with the popular world of personal development training, especially in large corporate companies. Local councils are increasingly recognising the need for young people to be able to access sporting facilities, and the need for professional coaching in this area is now widely acknowledged. With the 2012 Olympic Games approaching this is becoming an expanding area.

> *'It's such a satisfying job. I organised some 'Walking for health walks' locally. It got people out of their cars and provided a chance to experience the health benefits of a short stroll.'*
> Neil, active lifestyles officer, with a degree in sport studies

Sports development officer – promotes sports locally within the community, often targeted at a particular group, for example young people. You would work for local or national government.

Teaching – you would need to study for a Postgraduate Certificate in Education (PGCE) after your degree unless you choose a BEd or BA with Qualified Teacher Status (QTS).

Outdoor activities manager or leader – managing an outdoor activities centre, offering instruction to a wide range of people; or becoming a leader where you offer people instruction and encouragement.

Sports marketing and media – this ranges from being an events manager and being involved with the general business of putting on events, to gaining sponsorship or becoming an agent for sportspeople. This often involves establishing links with the corporate and business world and is a rapidly developing area.

Postgraduate study – just over 16% of sports science graduates go on to further study, which could be in sport performance, sport and exercise medicine, sport development, sport management, sports therapy, sports injury, or sport events management. Sports science graduates wanting to qualify as a physiotherapist will need to take a pre-registration postgraduate course.

Working outside physical education

Your degree could equip you for careers in management, banking and insurance, the social services, the police, the fire service and the Armed Forces.

SOURCES OF INFORMATION

British Association of Sport and Exercise Sciences
www.bases.org.uk

Sports Wales
www.sports-council-wales.org.uk

Sport England
www.sportengland.org

Sportscotland
www.sportscotland.org.uk

UK Sport
www.uksport.gov.uk

'I just loved the psychology aspect of the course as it helped me improve my own performance and those of the younger pupils I coach.'
Russell, taking A levels in physical education, biology and sociology

Physics

Physics relates to everything in our world and beyond in the universe. What is out in space? Are there really aliens? It is also more down to earth and includes items that we take for granted in the modern world like mobile phones, the internet, PCs and the power that runs them. It is an exciting and creative science, which is constantly evolving as new discoveries are made.

Studying physics is all about observing natural phenomena, trying to understand them and predicting what might happen in new and unknown situations. You learn about a wide range of theories explaining and predicting the way in which the physical world behaves. It's a broad subject involving experience and observations, theory and maths, ICT, materials and information theory. As a physics student, you must be able not only to follow and construct logical arguments but also to use your imagination and intuition to see how what you have learned can be applied to new situations. Physics is continually developing with new theories and practical techniques so offers a unique base from which to meet the demands of new technologies in our ever-changing world.

WHAT DO YOU STUDY?

The topics listed give an idea of what could be covered. The exact content of AS and A2 specifications differs according to exam boards, so you will need to check with your school or college about the exact modules available to you.

All physics specifications include the following:

- **the properties of matter** – solids, liquids and gases; mechanical, thermal and electrical properties explained in molecular terms

- **the properties of materials** – including density and Young's modulus

- **mechanics** – including motion along a straight line, projectile motion, Newton's laws of motion, energy and power

- **oscillations and waves** – mechanical and electromagnetic waves, sound and optics

- **quantum phenomena** – photoelectricity, energy levels and photon emission, wave–particle duality

- atomic, nuclear and thermal physics

- **fields** – force fields, gravitational fields, electric fields, capacitors, magnetic fields, electromagnetic induction, particle accelerators, fundamental particles

- **electricity** – electrical quantities, resistance and resistivity, circuits and components, alternating current, direct current circuits

- **further mechanics** – including momentum, circular motion and simple harmonic motion.

You will also study a range of other topics, which will include more advanced theoretical work and some specific applications of physics. You may also learn practical techniques such as planning, implementation, analysis, evaluation and communication.

'I like maths and love the way that you work so logically in physics. It's also all about the world we live in and if you are curious about how the world and the universe work, you will never get bored.' Gawain, taking A levels in physics, maths and chemistry

Examples are:

- **medical physics** – imaging, ultrasound and other techniques for the diagnosis and treatment of illness

- **astrophysics and cosmology** – the study of stars, galaxies and other heavenly bodies

- **telecommunications** – commercial and industrial applications of radio waves and digital techniques

- **energy** – the production and conservation of energy

- **applied physics** – rotational dynamics, thermodynamics, engines.

There are physics specifications driven by real-life applications, focusing on the practical activities and applications of physics. Examples are physics in context and advancing physics (which was developed with the Institute of Physics).

These courses cover topics such as the study of digital imaging in medicine, human perception, digital communications, designer materials, wave and quantum behaviour, photons, space and time, gravitational fields, the expanding universe, liquid nitrogen, plasmas, electromagnetic machines, electric and magnetic fields, fundamental particles, ionising radiation and radioactive tracers.

A good grade (C or above) in physics or double science at GCSE is usually required to study A level physics. You will also need to be able to use mathematical formulae confidently.

N.B. There is also an A level in electronics (see the engineering entry).

HOW DO YOU STUDY?

You learn through a combination of theory and practical work.

Theory is taught through lectures explaining conceptual physical models. You develop your understanding of much of the theory by applying it to increasingly complex problems, and you will be expected to read textbooks and scientific journals to increase your understanding.

Practical work is used to learn experimental techniques, to place the theory in context and to help develop a deeper understanding of physical phenomena. You will learn the selection and use of different types of equipment, processing of data, making observations and measurements, and the analysis and evaluation of results.

SUBJECT COMBINATIONS

Physics combines well with other science subjects, but maths will be particularly helpful and relevant as there is so much maths involved in the study of physics. You should take A or AS level mathematics if you are thinking of a degree in a physics subject or engineering. Further maths is useful for some engineering courses, such as aeronautical engineering. Physics A level combines well with chemistry, leading to medical courses and many technology and science-based courses like chemical engineering, energy engineering, environmental forensics, materials engineering, nanoscience and technology, renewable energy and sustainable technologies, and textile science and technology.

Physics could also be combined with A level engineering or design and technology for engineering design or product design courses.

There are foundation years available for some courses, which are designed to fill gaps in maths and physics and prepare you for entry onto the first year of a degree, so you might still get in.

It is possible to combine all A and AS levels with other equivalent qualifications such as BTEC Nationals or OCR Nationals and they could form part of Diplomas.

HIGHER EDUCATION OPTIONS

Degree-level study

Traditional physics courses give you a solid grounding in modern and classical physics along with the associated mathematics and experimental techniques. Important areas covered include mechanics, relativity, quantum mechanics, electromagnetism, optics, atomic and nuclear physics, and solid-state physics. Teaching is through lectures and lab work, backed up by tutorials and/or problem-solving classes. The three-year courses are broad in scope, while the four-year courses lead to the qualification of MPhys or MSci and aim for the greater subject depth you need if you want to practise as a physicist in research or in industry.

There could be specialised options, such as astrophysics, chemical physics, industrial physics, geophysics and particle physics with cosmology. In some cases these extra specialised courses may be specified in the degree name, for example physics with computing, or physics with astrophysics. Maths features in all physics courses, both as a language through which physics is expressed and as a method for the development of the subject and for problem solving. Some courses offer particularly mathematical or theoretical streams, while others tend to specialise in the more applied and technological aspects of the subject. Some applied physics degrees are sandwich courses, which involve placements in industry. There are some sandwich courses available in pure physics, where the placement could be with a wide variety of employers or research establishments, for example British Aerospace, the National Physical Laboratory or Proudman Oceanographic Laboratory. Or your placement could be abroad, for example at the high-energy research centre (CERN) in Geneva, the Swiss Federal Institute for Snow and Avalanche Research in Davos, or the Max Planck Institute for Solid State Physics in Stuttgart.

Degree subject combinations

You can combine physics with virtually any subject, although some subjects are closely related, like electronics, astronomy or mathematics. If you think you might not want a purely technical career, combining physics with management, business studies or a modern language would be a good preparation for careers in management, business or industry.

Other higher education qualifications

There are foundation degrees available in physics, which could lead into linked degree courses or employment. There are no HNDs or HNCs in pure physics, although they are available in electronic engineering.

Relevance to other subjects?

Physics A level is useful for many related degrees, such as engineering, materials science or geophysics. There are also courses in engineering physics, which are designed to combine education and training in the branches of physics that have been identified as important for the development of a professional engineer. Many medicine, dentistry and veterinary science courses specify A level physics or mathematics as a requirement. The mathematical basis of physics makes it a good preparation for many other subjects. For example, there is increasing emphasis upon scientific research methods and statistical analysis in courses such as psychology, sociology, economics and business studies, so they could be other options.

Important advice

Have a look at the content of courses to see which ones inspire you. There could be sponsorship for physics or engineering degrees. This is competitive, and sometimes the closing dates are before the UCAS closing dates.

CAREER OPTIONS

Into work after A levels

There may be some related jobs such as a laboratory technician, and there may be technical Apprenticeships available. Having studied physics you will have good problem-solving, research and report-writing skills, so you could consider opportunities in many other career areas including business and finance.

Into work as a graduate

Working in physics

Physics graduates can use their particular skills and knowledge in working for a wide range of employers including:

- **engineering and electronic companies** – researching and developing new products

- **utilities providers** – particularly telecommunications, power and transport

- **energy** – this could be in traditional fields, such as gas, oil and electricity, improving fuel efficiency and output, or research into new or renewable sources like wind farms

- **medical physics** – magnetic resonance imaging (MRI) scanners, lasers used in surgery, ultrasound, therapeutic radiography for treating cancer

- **materials industries** – including steel, plastics and ceramics producers and companies using these materials

- **radiation protection** – monitoring emissions and ensuring the safe disposal of radioactive waste. This could be within the nuclear power industry, the NHS, or the Radiation Protection Division of the Health Protection Agency

- **defence** – employed by agencies and contractors of the Ministry of Defence, might design and implement new weapons systems and technology, and intelligence systems (e.g. through communication satellites)

- **space science** – researching other planets, building satellites and space probes, collecting information about the universe and its origins

- **schools and colleges** – physics teachers are in demand, and there is extra financial help available for teacher training in science subjects

- **research** – in research scientist jobs for government departments and commercial companies.

Many physics graduates move on to further study after their first degree (roughly a third), taking courses such as PhDs and MScs in subjects ranging from theoretical physics to computing science, environmental science and sound engineering.

Working outside physics

Physics is a subject providing strong academic and technical training. The IT industry employs many physics graduates as software engineers, programmers, systems analysts and IT consultants. As a physics graduate you could enter a wide variety of careers including accountancy, technical sales and marketing, banking, finance, local and national government.

SOURCES OF INFORMATION

Institute of Physics
www.iop.org

Science Museum
www.sciencemuseum.org.uk

Website

www.physlink.com

> 'A physics degree will get you anywhere. Employers love problem solving and analytical skills and people who are good with numbers and computers.'
> Martin, taking BSc physics

Psychology

Psychology is the study of human experience and behaviour. It tries to help you understand both your own and others' behaviour. If you have ever wondered why you feel stressed out, forget important information or laugh at jokes you don't understand, then psychology can provide you with answers. As a student of A level psychology, you are introduced to the main branches of the subject and the issues that they address. Ultimately, these are all concerned with understanding what people think and do, and why. The new specifications for psychology have fulfilled the criteria for it being considered a science.

WHAT DO YOU STUDY?

The topics listed give an idea of what could be covered. The exact content of AS and A2 specifications differs according to exam boards, so you will need to check with your school or college about the exact modules available to you.

- **Method** – how psychologists collect, analyse and interpret data about thought and behaviour.

- **Perspectives** – different approaches to the study of the mind and behaviour.

- **Social psychology** – how the individual and social forces interact.

- **Cognitive psychology** – how we obtain, process and remember information; language and its relation to thought, including memory and eyewitness testimony.

- **Individual differences** – personality, intelligence, normal and abnormal behaviour, mental illness and its treatments (including anxiety disorders and autism).

- **Culture and identity** – whether human abilities are related in any systematic way to human groupings by culture, race or gender.

- **Biological psychology** – how our biological and physiological make-up relate to thought and behaviour; issues include motivation, emotion, awareness,

sleep and stress, factors affecting stress, coping with stress and managing stress.

- **Developmental psychology** – how we change during the course of our lives, including social and cognitive development, language acquisition, childhood, adolescence and old age.

- **Comparative psychology** – the similarities and differences between human and animal thought and behaviour; the extent to which what we learn about animals can be applied to humans; ways in which evolutionary ideas can be used to explain human and animal behaviour.

- **Health psychology** – how our physical and psychological well-being may be interrelated; addictions and eating disorders.

- **Educational psychology** – how we learn and how this might be influenced by how we are taught.

A GCSE in psychology is not needed to study A level psychology but you will need GCSEs at grade C or above in English, mathematics

'The most rewarding aspect about my experience of reading psychology was that the course was unlike anything I had expected, particularly in its scientific rigour. It was really challenging and very hard work.'
Mark, BSc psychology graduate

and possibly a science. Maths is especially useful, because of the statistics involved in psychology.

HOW DO YOU STUDY?

A lot of work in psychology involves discussion of different theories of why people think and behave in the way that they do. You are encouraged to form your own ideas and opinions and to back these up with evidence from your own experience as well as research carried out by others. You should be prepared to do a lot of reading and research in your own time. The best psychology students are those who try to apply their knowledge in the real world. You also spend some time learning how to carry out research and methodology in psychology, including how to design an experiment or other research project and how to draw conclusions from your results.

SUBJECT COMBINATIONS

Most institutions do not specify particular A levels for psychology degree courses, although for some biology is quoted as being desirable. Some courses involve quite a lot of experimental design and analysis, however, and mathematics and sciences are often mentioned as being preferred. Other courses don't involve much quantitative work, and for these any A levels of a suitable grade are acceptable. GCSE maths and English, and sometimes a science, are often essential requirements for entry to degree-level study in psychology.

It is possible to combine all A and AS levels with other equivalent qualifications such as BTEC Nationals or OCR Nationals and they could form part of Diplomas.

HIGHER EDUCATION OPTIONS

An A level in psychology is not essential for study of the subject at a higher level, but it is definitely preferred now that the A level is more widely available in schools and colleges. Most degree courses now assume some prior study of psychology.

Degree-level study

A psychology degree can be orientated towards science (when it will usually be a BSc degree) or arts (usually a BA), the main difference being the amount of emphasis on experiment and quantitative analysis. A BA course will include some quantitative work but will focus more on theories and topics within psychology that rely less on statistical data or quantitative investigation. Such topics include the ethics of psychology (the potential power that a psychologist has in terms of knowledge about people's behaviour and emotions, and how this power can be abused), or theories of how we may develop particular personalities.

Instead of a straight psychology degree, you might consider a course that is more focused, such as health, forensic, social or sport psychology. There are some broader courses available such as behavioural science (usually combining psychology and sociology, sometimes with animal behaviour, biology or anthropology) or cognitive science (combining psychology with computer science – especially artificial intelligence, the modelling of thought processes using computers).

If you are considering becoming a psychologist, you must make sure that your course is recognised by the British Psychological Society (BPS) (see sources of information for contact details).

Degree subject combinations

Psychology is available in many combined degree schemes, so it can be studied in combination with practically any other subject. You could consider subjects that are connected or complementary such as sociology, criminology, social anthropology, child development or exercise psychology. There are also more mainstream subjects available such as computing, mathematics, business studies, English, geography and management.

Other higher education qualifications

There are foundation degrees available in animal behaviour and psychology, applied psychology, psychology and crime, equestrian psychology, psychology and counselling, and psychology with sociology.

There is an HND in applied psychology and sports, exercise and health sciences, which will contain some elements of sports psychology.

Relevance to other subjects?

You will find your A level in psychology useful in other subjects at degree level. It provides grounding in research methods, analytical skills, essay technique and logical problem solving, all of which will be useful for subjects such as sociology, economics and geography. If you are more interested in people, then counselling could be another option.

Important advice

If you are considering a career in psychology, you should check that your chosen degree programme has been validated by the BPS as giving the Graduate Basis for Chartered Membership (GBC), especially if you want to work in the National Health Service. If the course that you take doesn't provide this, you may have to sit more exams after leaving university to meet the entry requirements for professional psychology training.

'It relates so well to real life and you start to understand why people behave as they do.'
Jonathan, A levels in psychology, biology, physical education and sociology

CAREER OPTIONS

Into work after A levels

If you intend to go into work straight after A levels, you are likely to find that many employers value the knowledge and skills you have gained from the psychology A level. Your communication and research skills will be valuable in business, sales and marketing, the media and the health sector.

Into work as a graduate

Working in psychology

There are many options if you want to become a professional psychologist but you will need to undertake postgraduate study for nearly all of them. You are likely to have to get some practical work experience before you start your specialist postgraduate training.

- **Clinical psychologists** work directly with patients in a hospital or as part of a community healthcare team. They may also undertake research.

- **Counselling psychologists** help individuals, couples, families and groups who are having problems with normal life. They help people to understand their problems and make their own decisions. They may work in GPs' surgeries, counselling organisations, academic and business settings, or privately.

- **Educational psychologists** work with children and young people who may have learning difficulties or behavioural problems.

- **Forensic (criminological and legal) psychologists** work with other professionals in the courts and prisons. Their work ranges from assessing the mental competence of offenders to participating in the day-to-day running of prisons.

- **Health psychologists** assess people's attitudes, behaviour and thinking about health and illness. They work with other health professionals to help in communication with patients, and investigate how people's beliefs may affect their treatment.

- **Neurophysiologists** try to understand the relationship between the brain and psychological processes. They work towards the rehabilitation of patients who have suffered brain injuries, or perhaps have had their brain function affected by conditions such as strokes. They may be employed in the NHS or in the private sector.

- **Occupational or industrial psychologists** advise firms on the recruitment and training of staff in organisations and on improving the working environment.

- **Sport psychologists** work in competitive sport and recreation, increasing awareness of the relationship between the mind and physical performance.

Working outside psychology

Even if you don't want to become a psychologist, you might use some of your psychology skills in your chosen career. Your understanding of individual and group behaviour will be especially valued in social work, human resources, sales, marketing, careers guidance, and general administration and management.

SOURCES OF INFORMATION

British Psychological Society (BPS)
www.bps.org.uk

Careers in Psychology
www.careersinpsychology.co.uk

Religious studies

Religious studies provides you with a better understanding of world religions, philosophy and ethics. You certainly don't need to be religious to study it and students of any or no faith at all will find it an extremely challenging subject. You may study different religions in depth or concentrate on issues such as war, terrorism, morality and aspects of politics. You will gain an understanding of other people's views and how to look at things from another person's viewpoint. You will gain useful debating, discussion and research skills.

WHAT DO YOU STUDY?

The topics listed give an idea of what could be covered. The exact content of AS and A2 specifications differs according to exam boards, so you will need to check with your school or college about the exact modules available to you.

Specifications have a wide variety of options, some let you focus on one or two religions, some cover the philosophy of religion and ethics while others are more theology based and centre on the Bible. The following gives you some idea of possible options.

- **Philosophy of religion:** this covers the philosophical arguments about the existence of God and the problems with these arguments. It includes studying about the nature of God and the need to prove God's existence, arguments for the existence of God based on apparent order and purpose in the world, the problem of evil, scientific explanations, life after death, religious experiences, miracles and atheism.

- **Religious ethics:** this covers the relationship between morality and religion and the various ethical dilemmas people may face. It includes studying ethical theories, ethical language, objectivity, subjectivism and relativism, utilitarianism, situation ethics, justice, law and punishment, war and peace, medical ethics and sexual ethics.

Throughout these topics examples are drawn on from world religions, the media and contemporary society. You will consider scholarly contributions to these topics, such as those from Aquinas, Paley, Swinburne, Hume, Kant, Plato and Aristotle.

- **The history of Christianity:** the early Christian church – starting with the church as portrayed in the New Testament through its development and expansion to the fifth century AD. The medieval and modern Christian Church – monasticism, the Reformation, non-conformity, Christian theology in developing countries.

- **Religion, art and the media**

- **Studies of the Old and New Testaments or scriptures from other religions**

- **Religion and contemporary society**

- **Specialism in a world religion:** including Buddhism, Christianity, Hinduism, Islam, Judaism and Sikhism.

It is not essential to have studied GCSE religious studies in order to take the A level – the examination boards clearly state that the course is intended to be accessible to

'I enjoyed my degree, it taught me how to think logically, research effectively and also how to understand people. It certainly helped me get first job.'
Simon, trainee investment banker, with a degree in theology

students of any background. A good grade in GCSE English or history would indicate that you could cope well with the researching and writing involved.

HOW DO YOU STUDY?

In lessons the key concepts will be explained and there is a large element of group discussions and topical debates. There is extensive use of IT and there will be visiting speakers. You would be expected to do a lot of private study, reading set texts and researching other books around the subject. You will apply your knowledge to developing the skills of analysis, evaluation, empathy and essay writing.

SUBJECT COMBINATIONS

Religious studies can be combined with almost any other subject. If you are considering religious studies at a higher level, you might consider studying an ancient language, classical civilisation or philosophy. More common combinations are history, sociology, drama, English literature, media studies, psychology and business studies.

It is possible to combine all A and AS levels with other equivalent qualifications such as BTEC Nationals or OCR Nationals and they could form part of Diplomas.

HIGHER EDUCATION OPTIONS

It is not essential to have an A level in religious studies in order to study it at a higher level, but normally at least one essay-based subject is required.

Degree-level study

Religious studies generally examines religion as a worldwide phenomenon. It includes the study of the major world religions. You study the history of the religions, the moral issues that they address, and their place in the world today.

Theology or divinity degrees concentrate on Christianity. You might be advised to learn Biblical Hebrew and/or New Testament Greek, and the emphasis is on the study of Christianity from its inception to the present day. This includes an examination of its cultural, ethical, philosophical and historical developments.

Biblical studies deals specifically with the Bible, its content and the changing approaches to it over the centuries.

Specialised courses are available in Islamic studies, Jewish studies, Jewish history and there is a new course entitled religion in the contemporary world, which combines humanities and social sciences to explore the complex relationships between religion and society.

Degree subject combinations

There are many joint degree courses available and you can combine theology or religious studies with most subjects. The most popular options are history, English, philosophy, sociology or languages. You could also combine with related subjects like church history.

Specialist degrees such as Islamic studies offer combinations with Arabic, theology and Latin, and Jewish studies can be combined with Hebrew or holocaust studies.

Other higher education qualifications

There are some foundation degrees available but they are geared towards those wishing to work in the church: theology and ministry, and pastoral mission.

There are no HNDs or HNCs available but many universities and colleges, including theological colleges, run Diploma and certificate courses of various kinds, some of them part time or as evening classes. Some offer courses for the University of Cambridge

Certificate in Religious Studies and many run their own courses, most of which are intended for those planning a career in the Christian ministry.

Relevance to other subjects?

There are many other degree courses you could consider with a religious studies A level, such as American studies, combined studies, English, history, law, philosophy, politics, psychology, social science and teaching. It is acceptable as an entry qualification for any humanities or social science course. Anthropology, which involves looking at human culture in all its forms, including the role of religion and ritual in developed as well as 'primitive' societies, would be particularly enhanced by a knowledge of religion and religious behaviour.

Important advice

Make sure you research degree programmes carefully as some degrees just focus on one or two religions, whereas others cover many different faiths or broader issues. Some courses offer the opportunity to study abroad at another university or to study a particular religion during the summer vacation, for example in India. You should make sure the course matches your interests. If you are not sure whether you want to do your whole degree in religious studies, you might want to look at courses where you can combine subjects or have the option to add to or change your subjects after the first year.

CAREER OPTIONS

Into work after A levels

Religious studies A level is regarded by many employers as a reliable academic qualification. It suggests that you can communicate your ideas clearly and effectively and have strong written and verbal skills. It is a useful additional A level for many careers and

> '*I acquired certain techniques and methods for approaching and better understanding religious people, their ideas and traditions.*' Diana, BA theology graduate

would be acceptable for many jobs including business and administration, retail, the Armed Forces and social care.

Into work as a graduate

Working in religious studies

There are a number of career options relating to religious studies, most requiring some further training:

- **teaching religious studies in schools** – there are some openings for religious studies teachers in primary and secondary schools; to teach in state schools you either must have studied for a BEd degree or have followed a BA degree leading to QTS (Qualified Teacher Status), or have taken a one-year Postgraduate Certificate in Education (PGCE) after your first degree. Opportunities may be available to teach in colleges and universities

- **ordained ministry or other full-time careers in the church** – this requires additional training over a number of years. You must have total commitment and dedication

- **museum work** – you might be able to use your knowledge of different religious traditions and their historical development by becoming a specialist in the field of religious artefacts. A postgraduate qualification would help in this type of work

- **research and teaching in universities** – staff in universities usually carry out research as well as teaching, and there may be opportunities as research assistants. You could be involved in researching anything from ancient Hindu traditions to the modern evangelical movement in the USA.

'I enjoy religious studies because there is always a lot of discussion in class. The subject covers many aspects of life; such as miracles and war and peace and allows everyone to express their own point of view, without being judged. In this way, you always get different opinions on subjects that will relate to you in later life and which we can apply to everyday situations. We also complete an individual investigation in which we can independently research a topic that interests and appeals to us. This, combined with the other topics we study, helps me feel very confident and happy to study it.'
Amy, aged 16, taking A levels in critical thinking, psychology, religious studies and geography

Working outside religious studies

Only a few graduates in religious studies go on to a career with a religious organisation. Most use their skills in other areas, ranging from caring professions and charity work to business. Remember that a large proportion of graduate jobs are open to graduates in any subject, so if you are interested in a religious studies degree, don't worry about it being a disadvantage to you in the future. The critical thinking skills developed in a religious studies degree will help you at many levels in the world of work.

SOURCES OF INFORMATION

Board of Deputies of British Jews
www.boardofdeputies.org.uk

Hindu Council UK
www.hinducounciluk.org

Islamic Foundation
www.islamic-foundation.org.uk

National Society for Promoting Religious Education
www.natsoc.org.uk

The Buddhist Society
www.thebuddhistsociety.org

Website

www.reonline.org.uk

'Religious studies A level is a great course, which challenges you and develops your skills in essay writing, discussions and debates. The best part is that it is such an open subject, which allows you to bring in other subjects and aspects of life. I particularly enjoy the focus on personal relationships and topics such as law and punishment and abortion. I would recommend it to anyone because even though there is a lot of content, you don't realise it because it is all so relevant to everyday issues and situations.'
Amye, aged 18, taking A levels in religious studies, law and English language and literature

Science (Applied)

For this course you study how science is used in industry, commerce, research and for the benefit (or otherwise) of the environment. It concentrates on how to approach scientific problems and aims to develop the practical skills that you need to solve these problems. It gives you the opportunity to study science without specialising at this level. Your studies will be balanced between biology, chemistry and physics and you may have the opportunity to choose units that lead to a particular pathway.

You will develop a range of skills that will be useful to you either for higher level study or in work and training. This A level is available as a double and a single award.

GCSE science and maths are recommended to help you get the most from this course.

WHAT DO YOU STUDY?

The topics listed give an idea of what could be covered. The exact content of AS and A2 specifications differs according to exam boards, so you will need to check with your school or college about the exact modules available to you.

Investigating science at work – looking at the different ways in which scientists and their skills are employed, which could be in places such as pharmaceutical companies, hospitals, research laboratories, water and electricity suppliers or chemical companies. You will look at your local area to find out about jobs in science and how the industry contributes to the economy as well as our everyday lives. The importance of health and safety at work is covered.

Monitoring the activity of the human body/managing human activity – finding out how the body works and how physiological measurements are used to monitor the activity of the human body. You will look at imaging methods and ethical issues related to monitoring, diagnosis and treatment.

Finding out about substances/analysis at work – scientists are employed to analyse and identify all kinds of substances. These may be samples taken from the environment

(air, water, rocks, soil), living organisms, and from production processes in the laboratory or industrial manufacture. In any science-based activity or industry there will always be a need for analysis and quality assessment to track efficiency and provide positive feedback for continued improvement and productivity.

You will learn about the various types of analysis, including qualitative and quantative analysis, and other tests used to monitor energy and efficiency.

You will learn how to plan and carry out scientific investigations.

Here are some examples of the units offered by the different awarding bodies. You will need to find out what is offered by your school or college.

AS

Cells and molecules; chemicals for a purpose; food science and technology; forensic

> 'The organisation we studied was a zoo, which was really good fun. We looked at the conservation they do and the captive breeding programmes. We met people doing real jobs. You don't realise what goes on behind the scenes.'
> Tom, aged 17, taking A levels in applied science and biology

science; the physics of sport; energy transfer systems; choosing and using materials; and synthesising organic compounds.

A2

Applications of biotechnology; colour chemistry; controlling chemical processes; ecology, conservation and recycling; ecology and managing the environment; electrons in action; materials for a purpose; medical physics; physics of performance effects; sampling, testing and processing; sports science; the actions and development of medicines; the mind and the brain; the role of the pathology service; working waves (looks at a range of applications of electromagnetic waves, such as communications fibre optics, mobile phone networks and satellites).

HOW DO YOU STUDY?

You study in a practical way and concentrate on the knowledge, skills and techniques found in real-life situations. You study with a combination of practical portfolio building and tests, combined with lectures and workshops, experiments and investigations, fieldwork and visits, case studies, research assignments and detailed reports on science topics and issues. There will be industrial visits, and speakers from industry will come in to give you up-to-date information on the current labour market and issues that affect them. For the A2, you have the opportunity to carry out a practical investigation of your choice, which will give you practical experience and the chance to learn new skills.

SUBJECT COMBINATIONS

Think carefully about how applied science will fit in with your other subjects. There may be some overlap with other sciences such as biology, human biology and chemistry A level courses, and your teachers may recommend studying applied science instead of these subjects, rather than alongside them.

In addition, applied science can be used to support subjects such as physical education, psychology, sociology or other applied A levels such as health and social care or business. If you are aiming for a particular career path or degree course, you will need to check with the relevant university or college to find out whether your combination of subjects is acceptable.

It is possible to combine all A and AS levels with other equivalent qualifications such as BTEC Nationals or OCR Nationals and they could form part of Diplomas.

HIGHER EDUCATION OPTIONS

Degree-level study

The double and single awards in applied science are acceptable for entry to higher education and you could consider a whole range of science-based degrees depending on the units that you have chosen. Some courses may require 18 units in science, or ask for AS or A2 levels in certain subjects.

Courses you could consider include biological science, biomedical science, environmental science, forensic science, health sciences, and food or sports science. Engineering subjects are another possibility. It is worth investigating interdisciplinary or integrated science courses where you can study the central issues of science and how they relate to current issues. You could also consider degrees in nursing and teaching or other health-related careers such as radiography, occupational therapy or paramedic science.

Degree subject combinations

A scientific degree could be combined with a whole range of other subjects, such as business studies, languages, arts and humanities. If you are considering this, you must check that the content of the course will allow you to progress, especially if you are considering a pure science career.

Other higher education qualifications

You could consider a wide range of applied foundation degrees covering a wide area of scientific disciplines, such as animal science and welfare, applied science and technology, biological sciences, biomedical sciences, chemical sciences, equine science, food science manufacturing and technology, forensic science, healthcare science, marine science, marine sports science, nautical science, oral health sciences, paramedic science, pharmacy practice, sports science and injury management, and veterinary nursing science.

HND and HNC courses are available in a wide range of applied areas such as agricultural science, applied chemistry, beauty therapy sciences, biomedical sciences, chemical biology, countryside conservation, forensic science, life sciences, sciences (conservation biology), sciences (environmental hazards), and sport and exercise science.

Relevance to other subjects?

As you can see there are many science-related courses you could consider, many offering applied science. You will have gained analytical skills and the ability to think and present information in a logical way, so many other subjects could be open to you such as business, management and accountancy.

Important advice

There is such a wide range of science-based courses available – you need to do a lot of research to find out which ones are suitable for you. Don't forget to check out the facilities available at universities. If you are not sure where a course might lead in the future then ask what happened to previous graduates.

CAREER OPTIONS

Into work after A levels

You could go straight into employment as a laboratory worker in an analytical or quality control laboratory, hospital testing laboratory, educational science department, or a similar area of practical science. Other options could include dental technology or animal nursing. There may be Apprenticeships available, some of which could lead to degree level study.

Into work as a graduate

Working in science

Science graduates are in demand and highly valued. You will find scientists right across industry, in the health service, government establishments, and research and educational institutions. Obvious jobs are in research and development, but science knowledge can be useful in marketing and sales in science-based companies. The government employs scientists in administrative and consultancy capacities and there could be opportunities in related areas such as legal work (licensing drugs, for example) and information science. There is also a severe shortage of science graduates entering teaching and there are financial incentives to encourage them to train.

Working outside science

The course will provide you with good problem-solving skills as well as a good scientific and maths grounding, so you could consider trainee schemes in many areas including accountancy, banking, ICT and retail.

'I like the way that everything is connected to real life problems. It makes it easier to understand.'
Jonah, aged 17, taking A levels in applied science and maths

SOURCES OF INFORMATION

Biochemical Society
www.biochemistry.org

Bioindustry Association
www.bioindustry.org

Forensic Science Society
www.forensic-science-society.org.uk

Institute of Biomedical Science
www.ibms.org

Institute of Physics
www.iop.org

NHS Careers
www.nhscareers.nhs.uk

Royal Society of Chemistry
www.rsc.org

Future Morph (the Science Council)
www.futuremorph.org

Campaign for Science & Engineering in the UK
www.sciencecampaign.org.uk

Wellcome Trust
www.wellcome.ac.uk

Science in society

Everybody is affected by the big issues in science. Think about global warming and sustainability, food additives, genetic engineering and swine flu, TB and AIDS.

The course aims to develop the knowledge and skills for you to understand how science works, analyse current issues involving science and technology, and be able to communicate this understanding to others. It enables you to become 'scientifically literate'.

Science in society is relevant whatever subjects you are studying. If you are not specialising in science it gives you the opportunity to keep up to date with a fast-moving subject.

The course will enable you to:

- take an informed interest in media reports about issues and events involving science
- develop and be able to express an informed, personal point of view on these issues
- make use of your understanding of science in everyday contexts and in making decisions about your own lifestyle and choices in your life.

You will need to have studied science to GCSE level to take this course. The single science specification covers some of the elements in the science in society A level, so will be helpful to you.

WHAT DO YOU STUDY?

Science in society is available from AQA. There is also a science AS, only available through OCR. The specification for this AS is similar to that of the science in society AS.

In the AS there are two units. The first, called exploring issues, covers:

- the germ theory of disease
- impact of infectious diseases now
- transport issues
- medicines
- ethical issues in medicine
- reproductive choices
- radiation: risks and uses
- lifestyle and health
- evolution and the universe.

You will explore reading and writing about science through coursework, covering critical accounts of scientific reading and the study of a topical scientific issue.

Unit 2, called reading and writing, gives you the opportunity to research and report on a topical issue, and to review some popular scientific literature and then write about it.

In A2 you study:

- neurons and their interactions
- the functioning brain
- gene expression
- chemical cycles
- the radiation model
- energy: sources and uses
- biodiversity.

The final unit is a case study of a current issue. It is an exam where you are given some of the subject matter beforehand.

HOW DO YOU STUDY?

You will write essays, consolidate work done in class, and study the subject in newspapers and magazines, the web and on TV and radio. Assessment is through written examinations and coursework.

SUBJECT COMBINATIONS

Science in society can be combined with any subject whether science, arts or humanities.

It is possible to combine all A and AS levels with other equivalent qualifications such as BTEC Nationals or OCR Nationals and they could form part of Diplomas.

HIGHER EDUCATION OPTIONS

Degree-level study

If you have specialised in other subjects for a specific degree area, science in society will complement these A levels in your degree area of choice. It is especially useful for medical degrees, environmental sciences, human and biological sciences. It gives breadth to arts and humanities degrees and an added dimension to courses such as journalism or law.

Degrees related to science in society include philosophy, science communication and policy, and science and the media.

The following degree courses relate to science in society, but may require additional A level subjects: anthropology, disaster management, environmental studies, human sciences and sustainable energy.

Other higher education qualifications

There are no directly related foundation degrees, HNDs or HNCs in science and society, but you could look at a whole range of science, community and social studies courses as well media and journalism.

Relevance to other subjects?

Science in society contains elements of science and humanities so a wide range of related courses is available, depending on the other subjects studied.

Important advice

Look at science and technology related stories in the media and think about how the science is expressed and explained and how the story is written. Start analysing this and being critical of popular science items and articles.

CAREER OPTIONS

Into work after A levels

The mixture of problem-based learning and consideration of current issues makes the course a good additional qualification for many careers.

Into work as a graduate

Although your degree may not be directly related to science in society, the fact that you have studied this can help with many different careers in, for example, engineering journalism, technical writing, government, teaching, planning, law and even politics.

SOURCES OF INFORMATION

Science in Society (Nuffield Foundation)
www.scienceinsocietyadvanced.org

Institute of Science in Society
www.i-sis.org.uk

Sociology

Sociology is concerned with why society works in the way that it does, and the extent to which our behaviour and even our opportunities can be shaped by our social class, age, gender, disability and race. It questions the society in which we live in order to understand the relationship between individuals and institutions such as the education system, religion and the mass media. Each of us is a member of a variety of social groups. In A level sociology you are required to take a step back from your personal interpretation of the world and look at how you too may have been influenced or shaped by these groups.

WHAT DO YOU STUDY?

The topics listed give an idea of what could be covered. The exact content of AS and A2 specifications differs according to exam boards, so you will need to check with your school or college about the exact modules available to you.

There are many topics within sociology but you can only study a few of them for A level. As sociology is concerned above all with social groups and how they are related, you will be encouraged to examine the links between different aspects of sociology.

Methods – how sociologists obtain information about society; the advantages and disadvantages of different methods of research.

Social differentiation and stratification – social class, ethnicity, gender and age; how these affect an individual's access to work, wealth, education and other social resources.

The family – types of family structure and how families differ across social groups; marriage, divorce and gender roles; the position of children in the family and wider society.

Education – the relationship between social class, social mobility and education; how 'culture' is passed on through education; educational institutions; the curriculum; educational achievement between genders and different ethnic groups.

You are also likely to study topics from the following.

Deviance and control – how to define antisocial behaviour; the possible causes and outcomes of crime; how social order and control are achieved through laws and social 'norms' (generally agreed codes of behaviour); who has ultimate responsibility for social order, and what are its benefits or negative side effects? Suicide as a social issue; the role of the mass media in defining social deviance.

Development and underdevelopment – how to define these terms; imperialism and its effect on ideas about 'race' and ethnicity; urbanisation and industrialisation.

Health, welfare and poverty – definitions of poverty and the reasons for its continuation; distribution of wealth and income; poverty and exclusion; the role of the welfare state.

Mass media and popular culture – how the media reflects or influences culture and ideas; ownership and control of the media; selection and presentation of news and information. How the mass media presents age, social class and ethnicity.

'I enjoy sociology because it is relevant to everyday life. You can see the concepts involved in sociology every day, which makes it interesting. I'm looking forward to the crime and deviance unit next year as it will really help me with law.'
Lauren, aged 16, studying sociology, English, psychology and law

Communities and nations – the formation and maintenance of communities; urbanisation and its effect on communities; nationhood and relations between nations.

Power and politics – how political systems work; authority (positions of power and control) and ideology (political ideas and theories); states and governments; political parties and pressure groups; feminism, environmentalism and other social movements.

Global sociology – development and underdevelopment of different countries; cultural, political and economic relationships between societies; industrialisation and the environment.

Religion – the role of religion in society (as a conservative influence or agent of change); religious institutions and how they are changing; religions in a multicultural society.

You don't need GCSE sociology to take the A level, but it will obviously help you with your further studies. You will need good English skills, as the exams involve essay answers, and also maths, as there are lots of statistics to analyse.

HOW DO YOU STUDY?

Sociologists study the things of everyday life such as families, newspapers, schools and jobs. Sometimes people think that there isn't much to the study of sociology and that it's just common sense. However, much of what you do in studying sociology involves trying to get behind everyday ideas by challenging these commonsense assumptions and the things that people take for granted and understand them better. The course contains a lot of reading, essay writing and class discussion. DVDs, newspaper articles and the web are also used to show how sociology relates to the world around us. You may go on visits, for example to the public gallery of a court to see a variety of different cases. You may get speakers in the school such as the police or someone from a different religion talking about how it affects their life and how they live.

SUBJECT COMBINATIONS

Sociology could combine with and complement subjects such as government and politics, psychology or economics, and would also combine well with health and social care or arts subjects. If you are considering a BSc in sociology, it would be a good idea to combine sociology A level with a more numerate/quantitative subject such as maths, statistics or computing.

It is possible to combine all A and AS levels with other equivalent qualifications such as BTEC Nationals or OCR Nationals and they could form part of Diplomas.

HIGHER EDUCATION OPTIONS

It is not necessary to have studied A level sociology in order to study it at university, although the background knowledge provided by your A level would certainly help with the first year of your degree.

Degree-level study

A degree in sociology may be a BA or BSc. In some cases this indicates whether the approach is more on the arts or the science (specifically quantitative) side. This means you should check the content of each course carefully before applying.

The first year of a sociology degree course covers some of the topics you will already have looked at during your A level studies, but in much more depth. Many first-year courses are quite broad, offering you a general introduction to the social sciences. In your second and third years, you will be able to specialise in areas that particularly interest you, for example, gender and sexuality, culture, race relations, religion or social policy.

Degree subject combinations

You can combine sociology with many subjects, but the most widely available are history, politics, psychology, economics and

English. There are also combinations in related areas such as criminology and social policy.

Sociology is not part of the National Curriculum, and for entry to postgraduate teacher training a large amount of the content of your degree should be relevant to the school curriculum. There are a few social science PGCE courses, which are specific to the 14 to19 teaching age groups, and places on these courses are limited. These courses include sociology but may ask for another subject specialism such as history, religious education, economics or psychology. You might consider a joint degree in sociology and another subject, if you want to study sociology without jeopardising your chances of going into teaching later on. It is important to check the acceptability of your intended degree carefully with postgraduate teacher training providers before you start your degree course.

Other higher education qualifications

There are sociology foundation degrees combined with psychology or criminology. There are degrees in community regeneration, social and community studies, community engagement, and public and community services.

HND and HNC courses are available in social sciences or social studies with related courses in health and social care, and social care practice.

Relevance to other subjects?

One of the most popular alternatives is to take a degree in social work, and to qualify as a social worker. (It is possible to take a postgraduate qualification after other degrees for social work training.) Other popular options are public services management, community studies and counselling degrees. You could also look at criminology or criminal justice, cultural studies, politics, housing studies, development studies, economics, geography and history.

Important advice

If you are considering social work, you must build up a good portfolio of work experience and voluntary work. If you want to teach sociology, make sure you check that your degree course is acceptable for postgraduate training.

CAREER OPTIONS

Into work after A levels

Employers will value your understanding of human social behaviour as well as your research skills. Career opportunities include working for the government, market research, human resources, the police or prison service. If you want to go into social work later on, you could build up experience by working in a social services type job, e.g. as a care assistant.

Into work as a graduate

Working in sociology

Social researcher – working for market research organisations, charities, educational organisations, local or national government; may require getting further qualifications in information management or social research methods.

Social worker – supporting and advising people who experience health or social problems within the community; you would need to do further study for this.

Teacher – in a school or college, for which you would need a PGCE. See the important advice section for more information.

Administrator – for local government in departments such as education, housing or social services, central government or charities.

Counsellor, welfare worker or community advice worker – working in a variety of settings, providing support and advice to a range of clients. You would need further training.

Working outside sociology

You will have developed valuable research skills as well as your knowledge of society and could consider careers in advertising and marketing, human resources and the police.

SOURCES OF INFORMATION

The Social Research Association
www.the-sra.org.uk

British Sociological Association
www.britsoc.co.uk

Websites

www.socialworkcareers.co.uk

www.sociology.org.uk

Anthropology

Anthropology is a new A level developed by the Royal Anthropological Institute and the AQA examination board.

Anthropology is the study of mankind: where we came from, how we live differently in societies across the world, and how we interact with our environments.

Studying anthropology will help you to think critically about your own society. You will gain an understanding of your own society and also develop a broad knowledge about global politics, economic development, cultures and beliefs, and an insight into the realities of life in other regions of the world.

Anthropology has several different disciplines within it such as cultural, archaeological, linguistic, and biological or physical

'Anthropology really changes the way that you think about things. It challenges all your assumptions about the world.'
Emer, social anthropology degree student

'It's not a dusty old subject, it's alive and happening.'
David, recent graduate in anthropology, currently doing voluntary work

anthropology. The latter deals with the social behaviour and biology of different people and includes the study of evolution.

The new GCE has been designed to give A level students a grounding in anthropology including the biological and social/cultural branches – through exploration of themes such as being human, becoming a person, global and local processes, and practising anthropology. At A2 you will conduct a small-scale personal investigation on a topic of your choice.

Anthropology can have either a social sciences or scientific slant so combines well with many different A level subjects.

There are many different ways to study anthropology to either BA or BSc level. Some universities teach biological and social anthropology as separate degrees, others don't distinguish between the two. Anthropology is often taught together with another subject such as archaeology or a language but can be combined with many subjects. There are also specialised courses like forensic anthropology, where human remains are analysed for either medical or legal purposes. Some university courses specialise in different regions of the world.

Anthropologists are creative and critical thinkers, who are well equipped for a variety of careers. Possibilities include education, government, advertising, charities, international organisations such as the World Health Organisation, museums and the media. Anthropology graduates also go into journalism; it's very useful for foreign correspondents and for marketing and PR.

The Royal Anthropological Institute
www.therai.org.uk

Travel and tourism

Travel and tourism is very broad and includes not only package tours, special interest holidays, travel by train, boat, coach, car and plane, but also theme parks, zoos, historical sites, and houses and museums. If you think about your local area you are sure to identify some places of interest worth visiting. This course is aimed to give you an understanding and overview of the travel and tourism industry today. You learn to appreciate how it is always evolving as customers' needs and trends change. A good example of this is the trend towards 'staycations' – people holidaying in the UK rather than abroad. It is also a highly competitive industry. You also look at issues such as customer service, quality and responsible tourism.

This A level is available as a double or as a single award.

WHAT DO YOU STUDY?

The topics listed give an idea of what could be covered. The exact content of AS and A2 specifications differs according to exam boards, so you will need to check with your school or college about the exact modules available to you.

- **The travel and tourism industry** – looking at the industry and at how and why it grows and develops. You will learn what mix of organisations make up the UK travel industry and the significance of the industry to the UK economy. You will investigate the wide range of careers available in the industry and identify those jobs that will suit you. This might include looking at employment overseas and the types of skills and personal qualities required.

- **Customer service** – very important in a highly competitive business. You will find out how important it is that all staff in the industry receive comprehensive induction and training packages. You learn about different types of customers, how to deal with complaints and how to measure, monitor and evaluate customer service procedures and practices.

- **Travel destinations** – learning about the major continental European and long-haul destinations for UK tourists, studying their location and finding out what makes them attractive to different types of tourism. You will look at the different types of transport available, especially as customers are becoming more environmentally aware. You will study attractions in the UK for overseas visitors.

- **Range of holidays** – looking at the range of different types of holidays available; you may have the opportunity to undertake a specialised study of a particular type of holiday, which could include special interest and activity holidays, guided tours, sports tourism, ecotourism, adventure tourism or cultural tourism.

- **The impact of tourism and current issues in the industry** – this covers the ecological impact of tourism development and 'responsible tourism', as well as other issues such as the use of technology and how global tourism is developing.

'Get a part time job in the industry while you are studying. I worked part time as a hotel receptionist and that helped me get my first full time job in the same hotel.' Andrew, guest relations manager in a hotel, with a BA in hospitality and tourism management

It also covers the economic impact of tourism, and the trend of people having 'staycation' holidays in the UK rather than going abroad.

In addition, there are other units offered (according to the specification), which cover the following topics:

- business operations in travel and tourism
- management in travel and tourism
- event management
- marketing in travel and tourism
- human resources in travel and tourism
- travelling safely
- security in travel and tourism
- resort operations
- promotion and sales in travel and tourism
- hospitality, including corporate hospitality.

HOW DO YOU STUDY?

The course is a mixture of group assignments, group presentations and individual research-based assignments, alongside a series of practical tasks designed to help you to obtain the skills needed for working in the industry. You will undertake work experience, day and residential visits both in the UK and possibly abroad; you may learn practical skills (such as ticketing) and foreign languages. You will put on a real travel and tourism event for fellow students or the general public, and visit trade shows and exhibitions. You are likely to undertake a project for A2. You may have to pay towards any residential courses.

SUBJECT COMBINATIONS

Possible useful combinations include foreign languages, physical education, psychology, geography, media studies and business.

It is possible to combine all A and AS levels with other equivalent qualifications such as BTEC Nationals or OCR Nationals and they could form part of Diplomas.

HIGHER EDUCATION OPTIONS

Degree-level study

There are degrees in travel and tourism, and travel and tourism management. You will also find many related and specialist degrees, for example, adventure tourism management, business travel and tourism, cruise management, ecotourism, hospitality management, sports tourism, resort management, tourism marketing, leisure and recreation management. All these degrees would give you the opportunity to develop your skills further and are likely to include placements in the UK and/or abroad.

Degree subject combinations

It is popular to combine travel courses with a language or business studies (including marketing and public relations) although there are related combinations on offer such as spa management, outdoor recreation, events management, countryside management, cruise and travel operations, and tourism management (licensed premises). It is also possible to combine biological conservation and planning with tourism.

Other higher education qualifications

Travel and tourism foundation degrees are widely available and you will also find a variety of foundation degrees in specialist areas of the industry such as outdoor adventurous activities, business travel and tourism, airline and airport management, countryside recreation and tourism, heritage management, and venue and events management.

HND and HNC travel and tourism courses are available and again there are specialist courses such as international tourism management and business and tourism. You could also consider related HNDs such as hospitality or leisure and recreation management.

Relevance to other subjects?

Look at business studies or retail management, marketing or public relations courses.

Important advice

Keep up to date with innovations in travel and tourism as it is a fast-changing industry. Consider how swine flu, the credit crunch or threats of terrorism might affect tourism. Look at trends such as sustainable tourism, adult gap years and the opportunities that will be created by the 2012 Olympics. Attend travel shows and talk to travel companies. Work experience or work shadowing would be useful to help you decide if this type of work is for you. Also think about learning a foreign language.

CAREER OPTIONS

Into work after A levels

Your skills from this course could lead to a wide range of employment opportunities, especially if you have taken some extra vocational qualifications. You could consider jobs in travel agents, airline cabin crew, car rental, cruise ships, airport ground staff, hotel administration/reception, travel call centre work, conference planning and resort representative work. There could be Apprenticeships available in this area and there will be further opportunities created by the 2012 Olympics.

Into work as a graduate

Working in travel and tourism

Travel graduates often join large travel companies in head-office functions such as financial control, personnel or marketing. They may also work in travel agents, tourist attractions, tourist information or in specialist travel areas such as adventure, sports tourism or health and fitness holidays. If you are willing to travel and broaden your experience this can really help your career.

Working outside travel and tourism

Your customer service, business and organisational skills will be transferable to a lot of other careers such as hospitality and catering management and the leisure industry. You will also have options for working in general business, administration and management.

SOURCES OF INFORMATION

ABTA
www.abta.com

Association of Independent Tour Operators
www.aito.co.uk

Institute of Travel and Tourism
www.itt.co.uk

World Tourism Organization
www.unwto.org

VisitBritain
www.visitbritain.org

Website

www.atlapedia.com (online atlas)

'I started as an apprentice and have worked my way up while getting some extra qualifications. It's quite a stressful job but very interesting and what was surprising was that it is nearly all over the phone. I am going to learn some extra languages, which will really help me.'
Penny, business travel consultant with A levels in travel and tourism (double award) and French

World development

Are you concerned about poverty and discrimination here and around the world?

Do you know about the Jubilee Debt Campaign ('drop the debt')? Do you think Haiti should have its international debt cancelled in the wake of the earthquake? How can we help people to get out of poverty? Should the government provide more overseas aid, and what happens to it when it is given? How can we make trade fair? What about healthcare in other parts of the world? How would local health provision affect someone who is HIV positive?

World development A level will help you to gain an understanding of global issues and their impact on people and societies. It explores the need to develop a more just and fair society and considers the issues of poverty, inequality, aid and trade. These are issues that shape our and everyone's lives.

WHAT DO YOU STUDY?

World development AS/A2 is unique to WJEC, although other awarding bodies such as AQA and WJEC offer global development as an option in the sociology course.

In world development there are two main areas that are studied as part of the WJEC AS specification:

- development, resources and global citizenship
- poverty and inequality.

And at A2:

- theories and concepts of development
- one of the following themes: economic development, political development or social development.

You will study global issues, economic growth and the development of a sustainable, 'one world' vision. You will examine the forces at work in the processes of globalisation and interdependence. You will consider how development takes place and how a more just and equal society might be achieved; for some people, basic needs such as water supplies are important, for others it is their working conditions in a factory making fashion clothing. You will look at local, national as well as international issues, evaluating approaches such as fair trade, community action and government support. You will be challenged by issues of poverty and discrimination locally and globally. The course contains aspects of other subjects such as economics, geography, sociology, politics, economics, citizenship, history and business studies.

HOW DO YOU STUDY?

You will be taught through lectures, problem-solving and discussions. At AS this will be in the form of a portfolio of three articles in the national and international press, which you will summarise as well as giving your own views on the subject, plus an essay that compares one aspect of poverty. At A2 you will undertake an individual report based on any theme in the specification. You can choose a topic in an area of interest to you,

'The course is great but make sure you get some relevant experience to help you in the job market. You need the practical as well as the theory.'
Sandra, aged 20, on an international development degree

which could be an issue affecting your local community or economy or something further afield.

SUBJECT COMBINATIONS

The course combines well with many subjects, especially geography but also with business, sociology, economics, modern languages and politics. Languages could be particularly useful if you plan eventually to work abroad. There is no reason why world development cannot be combined with science and maths, especially if you are interested in sustainable technology or global challenges.

It is possible to combine all A and AS levels with other equivalent qualifications such as BTEC Nationals or OCR Nationals and they could form part of Diplomas.

HIGHER EDUCATION OPTIONS

Degree-level study

Relevant courses are available in international relations, international studies, international development and third world or development studies. There are combinations available with subjects such as languages and business. These courses may include work placements in the UK or abroad, sometimes included as an assessed module within the degree.

Degree subject combinations

Economics, peace studies, politics, modern world history, modern languages, English as a foreign language, human geography, international relations, law, physical geography, sociology, biological conservation, business studies and economics are possible combinations. There are also some more unusual combinations, such as journalism, theology and nutrition.

Other higher education qualifications

There are some related foundation degrees available in community development and development geography. An HND is available in world development.

Relevance to other subjects?

You will find world development options in some other degrees, such as business studies, economics and geography, and on modular degrees. There is a degree in business studies and globalisation, and you could look at international relations as another option. Citizenship, citizenship studies and global citizenship are other options, as is human rights.

Important advice

Start finding out about global issues from the media. Keep up to date with current issues and events. Find out what is going on in your local community, for example, is there a pressure group against a new road or airport expansion?

Are people being made unemployed? Be aware of national and global campaigns by aid agencies. Take note of leaflets and adverts that come through your door. Order your free copy of *Developments* magazine. A gap year could be useful to you, and you might like to investigate the many opportunities available for putting your concerns and understanding into practice. Be active. World development is for the sort of people who want to make a difference. Think about volunteering, joining a campaign group or doing something for a local charity.

CAREER OPTIONS

Into work after A levels

Although world development doesn't prepare you for a specific career, knowledge of world development issues would be invaluable in careers in local government or the Civil Service, and in financial services such as banks. Working for a global company would be another option, as would work with charities or voluntary organisations.

Into work as a graduate

Working in world development

You will have an understanding of the forces that drive modern societies and of global issues. This knowledge will prove useful in careers in government, law, public administration, commerce, financial services and public relations. You may be inspired to get involved in local or even national politics or work for a political party or campaign group.

There could also be careers in the development field with government and voluntary organisations, charities, aid agencies and transnational bodies, and you would be well placed to work anywhere in the world. If you want to work for a voluntary organisation (often called non-governmental organisations, or NGOs) as a field worker you will need overseas experience in development work. Look for internships and four- to six-month placements abroad. Many agencies look for specialists – people with particular expertise such as logistics, language skills, advocacy skills and fundraising skills. This is where a combined degree can be a definite advantage.

Working outside world development

World development gives you knowledge and skills that could be applied to many different careers. Local or national government are possibilities and you might also wish to consider training in social work or teaching. You could also consider a range of other graduate-level jobs in finance, retail management or administration.

SOURCES OF INFORMATION

United Nations
www.un.org

World Development Movement
www.wdm.org.uk

Development in Action
www.developmentinaction.org

Drop the Debt
www.jubileedebtcampaign.org.uk

GreenNet
www.gn.apc.org

One World
www.oneworld.net

Students Partnership Worldwide
www.spw.org

Directgov (UK government website)
www.direct.gov.uk

Bond (British Overseas NGOs for Development)
www.bond.org.uk

Developments **magazine (free)**
www.developments.org.uk

Department for International Development (has free publications)
www.dfid.gov.uk

'Be willing to take 'stepping-stone' jobs to get where you want to be. I started out as a packer with a charity but ended up in a secondment, which helped me a lot.'
Dan, emergency response officer with a leading charity

Part three
Alternatives to
A levels

Part three

Alternatives to A levels

There is a range of qualifications that you could consider instead of, or in combination with, A levels. Some of these qualifications, such as BTEC National and OCR National qualifications, are widely available. Other programmes of learning included, such as the International Baccalaureate or Cambridge Pre-U, are offered by some institutions. This section also includes qualifications that are only available in particular parts of the UK, including the new Diploma qualifications, which are available in England. These are described in detail, including descriptions for each of the available Diploma subjects.

See Appendix 1 for information about qualification frameworks, and how qualifications relate to each other.

BTEC NATIONAL QUALIFICATIONS

These are specialist vocational qualifications valued by both employers and higher education. They focus on applied knowledge and understanding of a specialised area. BTEC Diplomas are practical, work-related courses and are available at level 2 (BTEC First) and level 1 (BTEC Entry). You learn by completing projects and assignments that are based on realistic workplace situations, activities and demands. Students focus on a particular subject area and develop a range of specialist skills and knowledge. BTEC qualifications attract points on the UCAS tariff.

BTEC qualifications have recently been revised so the BTEC National Diploma is now known as the *Edexcel BTEC Level 3 Extended Diploma*, equivalent to three full A levels. It prepares students for direct entry into employment or for progression to higher education.

The BTEC National Certificate is now known as the Edexcel BTEC Level 3 Diploma (equivalent to two A levels), while the BTEC National Award is known as the *Edexcel BTEC Level 3 Subsidiary Diploma*. BTEC qualifications can be studied on a full-time or part-time basis and this new revision enables them to fit into many of the new Diploma courses.

These are the broad subject areas in which BTEC Diplomas are available:

- art and design
- business
- children and young people
- construction and the built environment
- engineering
- enterprise and entrepreneurship
- health and social care
- hospitality, travel and tourism
- ICT
- land based and environment
- media
- performing arts and music
- public services and uniformed services
- science
- physical education and sport.

To find out more about these and other subjects go to the Edexcel website: www.edexcel.org.uk.

OCR NATIONAL QUALIFICATIONS

OCR National Awards, Certificates and Diplomas are qualifications aimed at 16- to 19-year-olds in vocational areas and are available at levels 1 to 3. OCR National qualifications at level 3 attract points on the UCAS tariff.

The subjects available include:

- art and design

- business
- design
- health, social care and early years
- information technology
- media
- public services
- sport
- travel and tourism.

For further information go to the OCR website: www.ocr.org.uk.

INTERNATIONAL BACCALAUREATE (IB)

The International Baccalaureate Diploma programme is equivalent to other post-16 qualifications like A levels and Advanced Diplomas. It normally takes two years and covers a broader range of subjects than A levels. You study six subjects, which include mathematics, your own language, a foreign language, a humanities subject, a science and an arts subject. You could take a second language or science in place of the arts subject. The IB Diploma also includes an extended essay. The IB Diploma is accepted for university entry and attracts points on the UCAS tariff. To find out more see www.ibo.org.

CAMBRIDGE PRE-U

The Cambridge Pre-U is an alternative to A levels. It aims to prepare students with the skills and knowledge they need to be successful in higher education and attracts UCAS points. It consists of a number of principal subjects plus the core Global Perspectives and Research (GPR) element.

The Cambridge Pre-U Diploma is awarded to those completing three principal subjects and the core GPR component. Up to two A levels may be substituted for the principal subjects. The Cambridge Pre-U GPR element

can be taken as a freestanding package, and a separate qualification.

The Cambridge Pre-U Certificate is available in 26 individual principal subjects, certificated separately and assessed at the end of a two-year programme of study. One-year short courses are available in modern languages.

You can find out more at www.cie.org.uk.

AQA BACC

This consists of three A levels plus an AS in critical thinking, general studies or citizenship. It also includes an Extended Project Qualification (EPQ) and core enrichment activities, which include work-related learning, community or voluntary work, and personal development activities such as public speaking, first aid, photography, sport or performing arts. See www.aqa.org.uk for more information.

WELSH BACCALAUREATE

The Welsh Baccalaureate Diploma is formed of two parts.

Core – consists of the following components: key skills; Wales, Europe and the world (which includes a language option); work-related education, personal and social education and an individual investigation.

Options – consists of principal learning and a project together with other options such as GCSEs, AS/A levels, NVQs and BTECs.

Elements of the new Diplomas available in England are being added to the Welsh Baccalaureate (such as the principal learning elements and the project).

Principal learning and project qualifications are now offered in Wales in the following ten occupational areas:

- business administration and finance
- construction and the built environment

- creative and media
- engineering
- environmental and land-based studies
- hair and beauty studies
- hospitality
- information technology
- manufacturing and product design
- society, health and development.

By 2011 they will be available in a further four occupational areas: travel and tourism; public services; sport and leisure and retail.

The Welsh Baccalaureate Diploma is available at foundation, intermediate and advanced level. The advanced Diploma is accepted for entry into higher education and attracts UCAS points. For more information, visit www.welshbaccalaureate.org.uk.

SCOTTISH HIGHERS AND ADVANCED HIGHERS

Available in Scotland, Highers are the qualifications normally needed for entry into university or college to study for degrees and Higher National courses (HNCs and HNDs).

Four or five Highers are normally taken in Scotland in the fifth and sixth year of secondary school or at a college of further education and are studied in considerable depth, involving coursework and final examinations. Advanced Highers are taken in the sixth year at school, or at college, and are aimed particularly at students who have passed Highers. They extend the skills and knowledge gained at Higher level and are additional qualifications that are useful for entry into higher education or the workplace. Universities express their entry requirements in terms of Highers; entry profiles for Highers and Advanced Highers can be found on the UCAS website, www.ucas.com.

Scottish Baccalaureate

There are two available:

- the Scottish Baccalaureate in Languages
- the Scottish Baccalaureate in Science.

The Scottish Baccalaureate in Languages and the Scottish Baccalaureate in Science consist of a group of relevant Higher and Advanced Higher qualifications in languages and science respectively. In addition there is an Interdisciplinary Project. This is an Advanced Higher Unit in which you apply your subject knowledge in realistic contexts. The idea of the Interdisciplinary Project is to help you develop and show evidence of initiative, responsibility and independent working. These are skills that will help you in higher education and in employment. Find out more at www.sqa.org.uk/baccalaureates.

NATIONAL VOCATIONAL QUALIFICATIONS (NVQS)

NVQs have five levels,1 to 5. These qualifications relate to specific occupational areas. They are assessed on the skills and knowledge that you can demonstrate in the workplace. They are offered as part of courses in some schools or colleges where the course has a practical element. They can also be gained once you have started work. NVQ level 3 is equivalent to A level standard. NVQs are current being revised in the light of the new Qualifications and Credit Framework (QCF).

KEY SKILLS

Key skills are the skills that are commonly needed for success in a range of activities in education and training, work and life in general.

There are six key skills. *N.B. The first three are being replaced by functional skills (see functional skills entry).*

Communication. Taking in information by reading and listening; providing information by speaking and writing.

Application of number. Being confident in using, interpreting and manipulating numbers, quickly and accurately.

Information and communication technology. Using computers to source information; selecting, entering and presenting text, data and images.

Working with others. Playing a full part in a team and being clear about one's own responsibilities.

Improving own learning and performance. Being able to plan and monitor one's own work and learning.

Problem solving. Being able to analyse problems and make decisions.

There are five levels of key skills: levels 1 to 4 are levels likely to be used in schools, colleges and in Apprenticeships and other training; level 5 is a single combined personal skills development unit.

Key skills can provide UCAS points towards university entrance (at levels 3 and 4), but acceptance of these is at the discretion of the university.

FUNCTIONAL SKILLS

These are practical skills in English, information and communication technology (ICT) and mathematics, and are useful for anyone in their education and training as well as in their daily lives. They are already part of the Diplomas and will replace the three key skills of communication, application of number, and information and communication technology.

DIPLOMAS (ENGLAND)

Diplomas were designed with input from employers and higher education institutions.

They help you to develop a range of skills that will be useful both in the workplace and for future study. They are flexible and combine academic and practical learning. They provide you with detailed business knowledge that will help you to enter the workplace and also equip you with the skills and theoretical knowledge to progress into higher education.

Diplomas also include 'functional skills' in English, maths and ICT, which lead to a qualification within the Diploma. You may also have the opportunity to take other courses, such as A levels, GCSEs and vocational qualifications as part of the Diploma.

All Diplomas include:

Principal learning (PL)

This is the main part of the Diploma, focused on the subject area you choose for your course (e.g. hair and beauty, or hospitality). You'll learn the knowledge and skills specific to this type of industry.

Additional and specialist learning (ASL)

This is the part of a Diploma where you can choose to study a particular topic in more depth, or to study something different that widens your experience, such as another language. These might be additional A levels, BTEC National qualifications or specific industry-related qualifications.

Generic learning (GL)

Generic learning is there to help you develop and apply the skills and knowledge you need for learning, employment and your own development. At each Diploma level generic learning includes:

- a project
- functional skills in English, maths and ICT
- personal, learning and thinking skills
- work experience of a minimum of ten days.

Some of these vocational qualifications can be gained while you are working or on an Apprenticeship and they could lead to full-time or part-time higher education.

Diplomas are currently available in these industry areas:

- business, administration and finance
- construction and the built environment
- creative and media
- engineering
- environmental and land-based studies
- hair and beauty studies
- hospitality
- information technology
- manufacturing and product design
- public services
- retail business
- society, health and development
- sport and active leisure
- travel and tourism.

Diplomas are available at levels 1 (Foundation), 2 (Higher) and 3 (Advanced).

There is also a Progression Diploma, which is equivalent to two-and-a-half A levels.

The level 3 Advanced Diploma is equivalent to three-and-a-half A levels.

The Advanced and Progression Diplomas qualify for UCAS points, see Appendix two for more information.

Diploma subjects

The rest of Part 3 describes each of the Diploma subjects, as listed above, under the following headings:

- What do you study?
- How do you study?
- Options after your course

- Higher education entry
- Sources of information.

Business, administration and finance Advanced Diploma

Business plays a key role in the economy. There are over two million businesses, both large and small, registered in the UK. This Diploma gives you a solid introduction and understanding of the business world.

You will have the opportunity to set up and run your own business and learn how to survive and remain competitive while taking into account factors such as the environment, consumer trends, new technology and globalisation.

WHAT DO YOU STUDY?

All Diplomas include:

Principal learning: focusing on the subject area of the Diploma.

Additional or specialist learning: the opportunity to study in more depth, take additional courses like A levels or gain specialist qualifications.

Generic learning: a project, functional skills in maths, English and ICT, personal, learning and thinking skills, and work experience.

The topics listed give an idea of what could be covered. The exact content of Diploma specifications differs according to exam boards, so you will need to check with your school or college about the exact modules available to you.

At advanced level your principal learning covers three themes; you apply these themes to every topic that you study.

- **Business enterprise** – how businesses work, planning, setting up and running a business. Developing a business from the initial idea to the final product together with a marketing and sales plan.

- **Business administration** – information, project and event management, improving business performance and being a responsible and ethical employer.

- **Finance** – accounting, taxation, using and developing financial data. Drawing up financial plans for business. Skills in personal and business finance.

In addition you will look at different careers and ways of progressing in business.

You study the following topics.

Business enterprise: you will develop your entrepreneurial skills and link your study with the real world. This will help you gain an understanding of the business world both nationally and internationally.

Business communication: you will look at current communication practices and theories and develop your own communication skills through presentations, role play and real-life situations.

Business administration: you will examine the importance of effective administration, management principles and techniques.

Personal finance and financial services: looking at people's attitudes towards money, the financial services and products available, personal financial planning and protection available to consumers.

Business finance and accounting: learning about accounting, taxation, budgeting, auditing and interpreting simple financial statements.

Marketing and sales: how marketing works internationally, nationally and locally. Branding and other marketing techniques, and the role of advertising and the media.

Teams in business: working in teams, leadership and management techniques.

Customer service: what is good customer service? Examining the policies and practices, laws and regulations.

Corporate social responsibility: different types of responsible practice, the ethical issues businesses face, and the reasons behind business investment in the community.

Responding to change in business: what factors lead to change in business and how managers and staff respond? Learn the skills to survive change.

People at work: sources of information and advice about career pathways, the recruitment process, performance management, and statutory and contractual rights and responsibilities.

The additional or specialist learning could include qualifications like BTECs/OCRs, GCSEs or A levels. You may be able to study qualifications related to the industry such as marketing, HR, administration, IT specialist software or accounting. Languages would be another option.

It is not essential to have studied the subject before in order to take the Diploma.

HOW DO YOU STUDY?

You will study through a mixture of classroom lessons, practical assignments, presentations, individual and group work, private study and tutorials. You will learn and develop skills on your work experience placement and go on employer visits.

OPTIONS AFTER YOUR COURSE

The Advanced Diploma in business, administration and finance will give you the skills you need for either university or work, and can be a first step towards a career in this area. You might also go into a career in human resources, sales and marketing, financial services, learning and development or any one of the vast range of different businesses operating globally. If you are considering employment you may wish to consider an Apprenticeship or trainee post.

If you complete this Diploma you don't have to opt for a career in this area. The Diploma teaches a mix of subjects, knowledge and skills valued by colleges, universities and employers.

HIGHER EDUCATION ENTRY

If you are interested in studying a business degree, look at the information on business studies in Part two.

The Diploma in business, administration and finance can help you to get onto a higher education course such as a degree, foundation degree or HND/HNC, as well as other professional courses. Examples of degrees you could consider include business administration, marketing or management.

For entry onto some degree or higher level courses, specific subjects may be required. You must check with individual institutions.

SOURCES OF INFORMATION

The Diploma in business, administration and finance
www.baf-diploma.org.uk

'I've got a really good business idea that I can't tell you about! I'm going to use this course to see if it's worth me going it alone when I finish.'
Liam, aged 16, business, administration and finance Diploma with GCSEs in English and ICT

Construction and the built environment Advanced Diploma

Construction and the built environment is all around us and is one of the most important economic sectors of the UK. This sector includes jobs in design, structural work, surveying, environmental issues, sustainability of the built environment, town planning, conservation and much more.

You will get an overview of the whole industry and everything that has to be taken into account in a construction project. It's not just the economics and providing good value that matter in a construction project, but other factors such as the effect on the local community, the environment, transport systems, and cultural and historical considerations. You will learn some of the essential skills of the industry, like health and safety and teamwork, as well as learning how the industry works and the opportunities available. As well as studying theory, you will have an opportunity to develop practical construction skills.

WHAT DO YOU STUDY?

All Diplomas include:

Principal learning: focusing on the subject area of the Diploma.

Additional or specialist learning: the opportunity to study in more depth, take additional courses like A levels or gain specialist qualifications.

Generic learning: a project, functional skills in maths, English and ICT, personal, learning and thinking skills, and work experience.

The topics listed give an idea of what could be covered. The exact content of Diploma specifications differs according to exam boards, so you will need to check with your school or college about the exact modules available to you.

At advanced level your principal learning covers three themes; you apply these themes to every topic that you study.

- **Designing the built environment** – how the built environment is designed and constructed, how it impacts on people and communities, and how history,

politics and economics influence it. The stages in the design and planning processes and the legislation involved, as well as the health, safety and environmental factors that must be considered.

- **Creating the built environment** – the range of skills and knowledge needed in different parts of the industry. Tools, materials and modern construction techniques. Project management and other processes and techniques used to make sure a building project runs smoothly.

- **Valuing and using the built environment** – analysing the need for good management and maintenance of buildings, assessing the damage to

'The course has been really good. It has given me the chance to find out what construction is like and has made me more determined to get into it when I finish school.'
Katherine, construction and the built environment Advanced Diploma with A level maths

> *'Doing hands-on work is much better than being in a classroom. I find we learn much more.'*
> Stephen, construction and the built environment Advanced Diploma

a building from people as well as the outside environment. Understanding the importance of good design to create a sustainable building. How new developments affect local communities and how people have to be consulted about construction projects.

The additional or specialist learning could include qualifications like BTECs/OCRs, GCSEs or A levels. Examples could include units from a level 3 award in construction or an A level in environmental studies, geography or sciences. You might also take additional specialist learning that concentrates on a particular part of the industry, such as building services engineering, housing management, estate agency and valuation, or finance and management in the industry.

It is not essential to have studied construction before in order to study the Diploma.

HOW DO YOU STUDY?

The course will be a mixture of class work, project work and field work. Visits and trips are an important part of the course and there will be talks from people in the industry. There will be visits to a wide range of construction sites to get first-hand knowledge of the industry and real-life health and safety inductions. You will visit planning departments and architects. You will also go on visits to building exhibitions and places such as the Centre for Alternative Technology.

OPTIONS AFTER YOUR COURSE

The Diploma will give you the skills you need for further study, work or training and it is the first step towards a career in this industry.

If you are considering employment you may wish to consider an Apprenticeship or trainee post.

If you complete this Diploma you don't have to opt for a career in this area. The Diploma teaches a mix of subjects, knowledge and skills valued by colleges, universities and employers.

HIGHER EDUCATION ENTRY

The Advanced Diploma can help you to get onto a higher education course such as a degree, foundation degree or HND/HNC, as well as other professional courses. You might progress to university to study construction management, property asset management, building services engineering, civil engineering, housing, planning or architecture.

For entry onto some degree or higher level courses, specific subjects may be required. You must check with individual institutions. For example, an A level in mathematics could be useful if you want to study architecture and civil engineering courses at university.

SOURCES OF INFORMATION

The Diploma in construction and the built environment
www.cbediploma.co.uk

> *'The work placement was really good. I went out with staff who manage and maintain social housing developments, and had the chance to do things for myself rather than watching, which was good for getting experience.'*
> Pat, construction and the built environment Advanced Diploma

Creative and media Advanced Diploma

The creative and media industry is one of the UK's most vibrant and dynamic industries offering many opportunities. The Advanced Diploma covers 24 different disciplines from creative writing through to radio, TV, interactive media, computer games, design and performing arts. The course introduces you to the creative process and gives you a real understanding of the industry and what employers want.

WHAT DO YOU STUDY?

All Diplomas include:

Principal learning: focusing on the subject area of the Diploma.

Additional or specialist learning: the opportunity to study in more depth, take additional courses like A levels or gain specialist qualifications.

Generic learning: a project, functional skills in maths, English and ICT, personal, learning and thinking skills, and work experience.

The topics listed give an idea of what could be covered. The exact content of Diploma specifications differs according to exam boards, so you will need to check with your school or college about the exact modules available to you.

There are many different areas on offer and here is the full list, although not all the options may be available locally to you.

- **Art and design** – 2D and 3D art, craft, graphic design, product design, fashion, textiles, footwear, photo imaging.

- **Performing arts** – choreography, dance performance, drama performance, drama technical and production, music performance, music technology.

- **Media** – film, television, radio and audio, interactive media, animation, computer games.

- **Creative writing, advertising, publishing and printing**.

You usually study four disciplines (although you could specialise in one or two). Some schools and colleges offer specific pathways including certain disciplines, e.g. art and design, performing arts, fashion design and advertising, music technology, and interactive media.

At advanced level your principal learning involves four core themes; you apply these themes to every topic that you study.

Creativity in context – what influences the creative process, e.g. society, culture, the environment or other people's work?

Thinking and working creatively – ways of exploring, experimenting with and developing ideas, skills and techniques.

Principles, processes and practice – the skills, techniques and processes needed turn your ideas into reality.

Creative businesses and enterprise – an understanding of real situations and what is needed to succeed in the industry.

Whichever disciplines you choose, you will be taught how to apply them to real-life situations by following six units.

1. **Capture**: how to capture your ideas and turn them into reality.

2. **Show**: how to develop your skills in planning and preparing to show or perform your work, and then presenting and evaluating your exhibition or show.

3. **Interaction**: artists, designers, performers and producers often work with the community to support projects, initiatives

and campaigns. You will learn how to interact with others through community project work.

4. **Commission**: how to work to a client brief and how to identify, create and evaluate work for a target audience.

5. **Evaluation**: reflecting on your work, successes and areas for improvement. Exploring progression and careers.

6. **Investigation**: a research-based unit on a study of your own choice, together with a log tracking your research, planning and progress.

The additional or specialist learning could include qualifications like BTECs/OCRs, GCSEs or A levels or qualifications related to your discipline. This could include examinations in music, dance, speech and drama, qualifications in media techniques, sound engineering, photography or fashion skills like pattern cutting.

You will need to discuss your additional or specialist learning needs with your school or college.

It is not essential to have studied creative and media before in order to study the Diploma.

HOW DO YOU STUDY?

The course centres on a programme of assignments and activities, designed to put your skills to the test. Teaching is through small group work, workshops and lectures. There will be visits to places connected with the industry as well as work experience. You might visit a radio studio, fashion show, theatre rehearsal or computer games studio.

OPTIONS AFTER YOUR COURSE

The Diploma in creative and media will give you the skills needed for further study, work or training. If you are considering employment, there may be some Apprenticeships available.

Look at the sections covering creative and media subjects within this book to give you a fuller idea of the options available.

Remember the Diploma in creative and media doesn't mean you have to opt for a career in the sector. It gives you transferable skills as well as any specialist skills you will have learned.

HIGHER EDUCATION ENTRY

The Advanced Diploma in creative and media can help you to get onto a higher education course such a degree, foundation degree or HND/HNC, and other professional courses.

You might choose courses that are related to creative and media disciplines or broader courses like English, history or politics. Some Diploma students will have identified a clear vocational path and may opt to progress via a degree into careers such as film production, computer games, graphic design, dance, drama, screenwriting or journalism.

If you have studied the art and design pathway you might apply to an art foundation course leading to a degree in art and design. You can sometimes enter these degrees directly without the foundation course if you have an exceptional portfolio of work.

For entry onto some degree or higher level courses, specific subjects may be required. You must check with individual institutions.

SOURCES OF INFORMATION

The Diploma in creative and media
www.skillset.org/qualifications/diploma

Skillset
www.skillset.org

Creative and cultural skills
www.ccskills.org.uk

'I love English and want to write adverts. This course will get me started now, not after a degree.'
Ronan, creative and media Advanced Diploma with English language A level

Engineering Advanced Diploma

Engineers use their creativity and technical skills to solve problems: whether it is designing a robotic vacuum cleaner, installing a control system to help a disabled person in their home, or a pump to provide precious water in a developing country. Over 1.6 million people are involved in engineering in the UK and there is always a shortage of good engineers both here and overseas.

This course will help you understand how engineering works and includes IT, materials, production and manufacture. You will also find out about the range of careers available.

WHAT DO YOU STUDY?

All Diplomas include:

Principal learning: focusing on the subject area of the Diploma.

Additional or specialist learning: the opportunity to study in more depth, take additional courses like A levels or gain specialist qualifications.

Generic learning: a project, functional skills in maths, English and ICT, personal, learning and thinking skills, and work experience.

The topics listed give an idea of what could be covered. The exact content of Diploma specifications differs according to exam boards, so you will need to check with your school or college about the exact modules available to you.

At advanced level your principal learning covers four themes; you apply these themes to every topic that you study.

- **The engineered world** – how engineering businesses operate, career opportunities and career structures.

- **Discovering engineering technology** – basic engineering principles such as design, materials, electronic systems, maintenance and manufacturing, as well as how to use 2D and 3D computer software for modelling and for design, testing and manufacture.

- **Engineering the future** – future developments and new innovations, how new materials contribute to design and how to develop and launch new ideas.

- **Analytical methods for engineering** – how to apply mathematical and scientific principles in engineering; analysis, design and problem solving including algebra, geometry and trigonometry, calculus and statistics.

You study the following topics.

Investigating engineering business and the environment: you will gain insight into engineering businesses and the environmental impact of engineering activities.

Applications of computer aided design (CAD): using CAD to produce drawings and models to test or convey ideas.

Selection and application of engineering materials: exploring the link between the materials used for engineering products and the selection of processes used for their manufacture.

Instrumentation and control engineering: understanding the link between specification and design, and the implementation of individual engineering control systems.

Maintaining engineering plant, equipment and systems: planning and producing maintenance schedules and reports for systems and products.

Investigating modern manufacturing techniques used in engineering: exploring the types and methods of production and manufacturing processes and systems.

Innovative design and enterprise: understanding the role of innovation in engineering design.

Mathematical techniques and applications for engineers: using mathematics to model engineering problems and understand how mathematics is an essential tool in engineering.

Principles and application of engineering science: developing an understanding of the fundamental scientific principles that engineers use to carry out investigations into engineering problems.

The additional or specialist learning could include qualifications like BTECs/OCRs, GCSEs or A levels. You might take the level 3 certificate in mathematics for engineering, or a BTEC National award in engineering. You could also take a course related to a specialist interest such as robotics, electronics or automotive engineering.

It is not essential to have studied engineering before in order to study the Diploma.

HOW DO YOU STUDY?

You will study via a mixture of class work, project work (alone and in groups), workshop assignments and study visits. You will visit engineering companies and exhibitions. You might visit local projects to see engineering in action in the community; as well as visiting engineering projects from history, like bridges and railways, looking at engineers such as Thomas Telford or Isambard Kingdom Brunel and considering how you might improve on their work today.

OPTIONS AFTER YOUR COURSE

The Diploma will give you the skills you need for further study, work or training and it is the first step towards a career in this industry. If you are considering employment you may wish to consider an Apprenticeship or trainee post.

If you complete this Diploma you don't have to opt for a career in this area. The Diploma teaches a mix of subjects, knowledge and skills valued by colleges, universities and employers.

See also the information provided in the entry for engineering A level.

HIGHER EDUCATION ENTRY

The Advanced Diploma can help you get onto a higher education course such as a degree, foundation degree or HND/HNC, as well as other professional courses. You might progress to university to study an engineering degree in different areas of engineering such as manufacturing, electronic, mechanical, building services, automotive or aeronautical engineering. You might also consider product design or progress to more general courses such as physics.

For entry onto some degree or higher level courses, specific subjects may be needed. For example, Oxford University requires that engineering Advanced Diploma students must have physics A level and the level 3 certificate in mathematics for engineering as part of their additional specialist learning. You must check entry requirements with individual institutions.

SOURCES OF INFORMATION

The Diploma in engineering
www.engineeringdiploma.com

Website

www.enginuity.org.uk

Environmental and land-based studies Advanced Diploma

This sector is concerned with land management and production, animal health and welfare, and the environmental industries. Jobs in this sector cover a wide range from horticulture, farming, conservation, landscape design and working in animal care (including veterinary nursing) to game keeping, fisheries, arboriculture and floristry. It's a growing sector with an estimated 110,000 extra people needed over the next ten years.

WHAT DO YOU STUDY?

All Diplomas include:

Principal learning: focusing on the subject area of the Diploma.

Additional or specialist learning: the opportunity to study in more depth, take additional courses like A levels or gain specialist qualifications.

Generic learning: a project, functional skills in maths, English and ICT, personal learning and thinking skills and work experience.

The topics listed give an idea of what could be covered. The exact content of Diploma specifications differs according to exam boards, so you will need to check with your school or college about the exact modules available to you.

At advanced level your principal learning covers three main learning themes.

These themes are then applied to everything you study.

- **The productive and working environments** – the resources available in the natural environment, both renewable and non-renewable, the influences upon them, how they influence us and how these resources are used. The economics of this industry, the variety of jobs on offer and the practical skills required by environmental and land-based employers.

- **Plants and animals** – how plants are used for commercial, recreational and conservation purposes and animals for food, leisure, work or companionship. Includes the care of plants and the care and welfare of animals and how this relates to the commercial world.

- **Developing the sustainable environment** – explores the impact of people and businesses on our environment, the importance of the sustainable use of resources and how sustainable practices can be implemented. The role of people and organisations and the tools and techniques used to monitor and analyse our environments.

These are the topics studied.

The ecology of the natural environment and the importance of biodiversity: how ecosystems operate and interrelate, biodiversity and how the environment operates naturally and when managed.

The management of natural resources and resources for production: the factors that influence the productivity and sustainability of production systems, active intervention programmes, managing and maintaining the health of plants and animals, and pollutants. This topic highlights the need for good scientific knowledge and training in managing the environment.

Business management and careers in the environmental and land-based sector: how business is run and good ethical business practice within the industry, as well as the range of careers available.

Plant and animals (applied science): the structure, physiology and functions of plants and animals, the scientific principles underpinning their management and the interrelationships between them in the natural and managed environments.

Plants, animals and humans (how they relate): the role and uses of wild and domesticated animals, and of wild and cultivated plants, in the economy.

Plants and animals (safe working practices and relevant legislation): health and safety and the legal obligations of environmental and land-based enterprises.

Sustainable management and development of resources: the balance between environmental and economic viability. Sustainable development and the importance of environmental policy, planning, management and protection.

Global impacts and the environmental and land-based sector: what factors affect the environment globally, for example intensive farming or deforestation.

Research methodology, evaluation and environmental analysis: the value of environmental evaluation, impact assessments and the techniques and resources used to undertake valid research. The importance of research underpinning scientific practice.

The additional or specialist learning could include qualifications like BTECs/OCRs, GCSEs or A levels. You may be able to study qualifications related to the industry like a level 3 award in ecology, conservation, horticulture or equine management. Some courses offer specialised pathways through the Diploma.

It is not essential to have studied this subject before in order to study the Diploma.

HOW DO YOU STUDY?

You will work individually and in groups, and your coursework will be assessed.

You will work on projects such as assessing pollution levels or looking at local recycling schemes. You will go on study visits to employers and have visiting speakers. You will build up a portfolio, complete work experience and a project on a related topic.

OPTIONS AFTER YOUR COURSE

The Advanced Diploma in environmental and land-based studies will give you the skills you need for either university or work, and can be a first step towards a career in this area. If you are considering employment you may wish to consider an Apprenticeship or trainee post.

If you complete this Diploma you don't have to opt for a career in this area. The Diploma teaches a mix of subjects, knowledge and skills valued by colleges, universities and employers.

HIGHER EDUCATION ENTRY

The Advanced Diploma in environmental and land-based studies can help you to get onto a higher education course such as a degree, foundation degree or HND/HNC, as well as other professional courses. You might progress to university to study zoology, environmental science, horticulture or related subjects like biology, geography or economics.

For entry onto some degree or higher level courses, specific subjects may be required, such as A levels in sciences. You must check with individual institutions.

SOURCES OF INFORMATION

The Diploma in environmental and land-based studies
www.diplomaelbs.co.uk

Hair and beauty studies Advanced Diploma

The hair and beauty industry offers many opportunities. You could manage your own hair salon, run a spa or health club, become a fashion stylist or qualify in stage make-up or photography.

The Advanced Diploma in hair and beauty studies explores these opportunities and more. You will learn general management and business skills, as well as researching business location and design, events and product management. You will be able to explore the ways in which media and image influences the hair and beauty sector and look at topics ranging from spas to cosmetic science.
This Diploma will encourage you to develop your skills, be creative and learn all about the hair and beauty industry.

WHAT DO YOU STUDY?

All Diplomas include:

Principal learning: focusing on the subject area of the Diploma.

Additional or specialist learning: the opportunity to study in more depth, take additional courses like A levels or gain specialist qualifications.

Generic learning: a project, functional skills in maths, English and ICT, personal, learning and thinking skills, and work experience.

The topics listed give an idea of what could be covered. The exact content of Diploma specifications differs according to exam boards, so you will need to check with your school or college about the exact modules available to you.

At advanced level your principal learning covers four themes; you apply these themes to every topic that you study.

- **Employability** – how businesses are run, management, health and safety and hygiene.
- **Customer interaction** – effective communication and establishing good relationships with clients and colleagues, the importance of good personal presentation.
- **Creativity and innovation** – how the market is influenced by economic, social, environmental and ethical factors. The importance of the media and image. The importance of creativity and flair, for example in creating and launching new products.
- **The science of hair and beauty** – the chemical properties of products and understanding how scientific knowledge is important in this industry.

You will also examine the six industries in this sector and how they fit into the sector:

- hairdressing
- barbering
- African–Caribbean hairdressing
- beauty therapy
- spa therapy
- nail services.

You will also:

- develop management, finance and business skills in the hair and beauty industry
- learn about the factors influencing business location and the interior design

of new and refurbished commercial premises

- investigate how to select, match and create media suitable for an event

- explore marketing strategies for hair and beauty products and identify their impact on consumers

- understand a range of professional spa organisations

- discover the basic scientific principles and concepts of cosmetic chemistry and product research, design and development within the hair and beauty sector.

In addition you will study:

- the history of hair and beauty in society

- safe working practices

- communication and client care

- skin care and make-up

- hair care and styling

- hand care and nail art

- sales skills.

The additional or specialist learning could include qualifications like BTECs/OCRs, GCSEs or A levels. You may be able to study qualifications related to the industry like massage, media or camouflage make up, complementary medicine, anatomy and physiology.

It is not essential to have studied hair and beauty before in order to study the Diploma.

HOW DO YOU STUDY?

You will work individually and in groups and your coursework will be assessed.

You will build up a portfolio, complete work experience and a project on a related topic. The course may include visits to trade shows, museums and art galleries or cosmetic manufacturers.

OPTIONS AFTER YOUR COURSE

The Diploma in hair and beauty studies will give you the skills you need for either further study, work or training and it is the first step towards a career in this industry.

The Diploma doesn't qualify you as a hairdresser, beauty therapist or nail technician, but focuses on the skills and qualities necessary to pursue these or related careers within the sector. After your course you may wish to gain specific skills and complete an Apprenticeship in hair, beauty, nails services, spa therapy or fashion. Alternatively you could go into related job areas like health and fitness, retailing, cosmetic science, paramedical careers, complementary medicine, care or creative industries.

Remember the Diploma in hair and beauty studies doesn't mean you have to opt for a career in the sector. The Diploma will give you transferable skills, which may be especially relevant to business, finance, sales, customer care and science.

HIGHER EDUCATION ENTRY

The Advanced Diploma in hair and beauty studies can help you to get onto a higher education course such as a degree, foundation degree or HND/HNC, as well as other professional courses. You might progress to university to study salon management, business management or media studies. You could also consider degrees such as biology, beauty therapy, salon or spa management, fashion photography, journalism, fashion styling, cosmetic science or specialist make-up.

For entry onto some degree or higher level courses, specific subjects may be required. You must check with individual institutions.

SOURCES OF INFORMATION

The Diploma in hair and beauty studies
www.diplomainhairandbeautystudies.org

Hospitality Advanced Diploma

The hospitality industry offers a wide range of opportunities both in the UK and abroad. It includes jobs in hotels and catering, and includes events, conferences and business management. The course will give you an overview of the industry and the essential skills to gain employment, get into higher education or run your own business.

WHAT DO YOU STUDY?

All Diplomas include:

Principal learning: focusing on the subject area of the Diploma.

Additional or specialist learning: the opportunity to study in more depth, take additional courses like A levels or gain specialist qualifications.

Generic learning: a project, functional skills in maths, English and ICT, personal, learning and thinking skills, and work experience.

The topics listed give an idea of what could be covered. The exact content of Diploma specifications differs according to exam boards, so you will need to check with your school or college about the exact modules available to you.

At advanced level your principal learning covers four themes; you apply these themes to every topic that you study.

- The hospitality industry.
- People in the hospitality industry.
- Business and finance in the hospitality industry.
- Hospitality operations.

'I want to travel and this course has given me lots of ideas as to possible careers. I am hoping to work for an international hotel chain.'
Abdullah, taking the Advanced Diploma in hospitality

You study the following topics.

Investigating the social and economic trends in the hospitality industry: introducing the breadth of businesses, activities and careers in the industry, its importance to the UK economy, and the key responsibilities of the industry.

Legislation and procedures in the hospitality industry: the key legislation and procedures affecting the industry, including health and safety, food safety, fire regulations, licensing, equal opportunities and discrimination.

Customer service in the hospitality industry: developing good customer service skills for front and back of house, emphasising the link between customer service and the success of the business.

Communication and information sharing: how effective teamwork and communication helps the business and customer experience. Looking at how good and effective teams are built.

Managing people in the hospitality industry: how to identify good practice, improve your own practice, and plan your professional development, based on a real workplace setting.

Finance and budgetary control: how the financial side of the industry works and how budgets and budgetary control are vital to commercial success.

Running a hospitality business: acquiring the basic knowledge and transferable skills to set up a small business, of any type, within the sector.

Sales and marketing: how the sector identifies customer needs and then promotes its products and services to maximum effect.

Managing a food operation: building on basic food service and general hospitality skills, focusing on the management and teamwork elements involved in running a large kitchen, looking at food safety, the diversity of customer need, and costings.

Hospitality services: managing hospitality services in different establishments and learning how all the different sections work together.

The additional or specialist learning could include qualifications like BTECs/OCRs, GCSEs or A levels. You may be able to study qualifications related to the industry such as a specialist subject to develop your particular interests in the hospitality sector. This could be a level 3 certificate or award in food preparation and cooking, food and drink service, guest services, or business and administration, including ICT. Studying languages could also be worth considering.

It is not essential to have studied hospitality before in order to study the Diploma.

HOW DO YOU STUDY?

You will learn through a series of lectures, workshops, study visits and practical exercises and be assessed using a variety of methods such as assignment work, realistic work-based practical tasks, multiple choice tests and role plays. The practical assignments might involve researching, collating and interpreting data from surveys about the industry, carrying out a health and safety risk assessment in a restaurant, preparing financial accounts, costing menus or writing a marketing plan for a hotel.

OPTIONS AFTER YOUR COURSE

The Advanced Diploma in hospitality will give you the skills you need for either university or work, and can be a first step towards a career in this area. You might also go into a career in hospitality as a trainee or Apprentice in catering, hotels or leisure outlets.

If you complete this Diploma you don't have to opt for a career in this area. The Diploma teaches a mix of subjects, knowledge and skills valued by colleges, universities and employers.

HIGHER EDUCATION ENTRY

The Advanced Diploma in hospitality can help you to get onto a higher education course such as a degree, foundation degree or HND/HNC, as well as other professional courses. You might progress to university to study specialist degrees such hospitality, hotel or event management, or go into related areas like finance, languages or marketing.

For entry onto some degree or higher level courses, specific subjects may be required. You must check with individual institutions.

SOURCES OF INFORMATION

The Diploma in hospitality
www.hospitalitydiploma.co.uk

'The work placement in a restaurant was really good. You might think it is calm and relaxing but it is mental in the kitchens!'
Sarah, Advanced Diploma in hospitality

Information technology Advanced Diploma

The IT industry is a fast-moving sector of the economy and this Diploma will give you hands-on experience of the industry and of key IT activities, like project management, IT support, website development and business solution design.

WHAT DO YOU STUDY?

All Diplomas include:

Principal learning: focusing on the subject area of the Diploma.

Additional or specialist learning: the opportunity to study in more depth, take additional courses like A levels or gain specialist qualifications.

Generic learning: a project, functional skills in maths, English and ICT, personal, learning and thinking skill, and work experience.

The topics listed give an idea of what could be covered. The exact content of Diploma specifications differs according to exam boards, so you will need to check with your school or college about the exact modules available to you.

At advanced level your principal learning covers three themes; you apply these themes to every topic that you study.

- **Business** – how business works and the skills required.

- **People** – understanding the people involved in IT, this includes the types of staff in the industry and the different sorts of customers. Career paths available in the industry.

- **Technology** – the ever-changing and evolving technology in the industry and how to anticipate the changes it brings as well as how to adapt to them.

You study the following topics.

The potential of technology: how technology helps businesses achieve their goals, what role it plays in the global economy, and what benefits and risks come with technology.

Understanding organisations: how organisations are structured, and measuring the factors that influence the success or failure of an organisation.

Professional development: communication techniques in business, dealing with clients. Developing IT-based solutions to understand how statistical techniques are used to analyse business practices.

Making projects successful: what factors cause a project to succeed or fail, how to use industry-standard software to create detailed project plans to manage, monitor and report on the progress of a project.

Creating technology solutions: using industry-standard approaches to investigate, create, test and implement a technological solution that meets a particular organisation's requirements and needs.

> *'I didn't realise how much a new IT system costs, so you really need to know your stuff when recommending new systems or you could really get into trouble. I was so glad I helped on an implementation team for my work experience.'*
> Stuart, Advanced Diploma in IT

Multimedia and digital projects: how different types of digital media work in business in, for example, computer games, virtual worlds and the internet, and how to make maximum use of this technology. You will work on your own multimedia project.

Managing technology systems: how network systems are maintained on a daily basis. How problems are anticipated and solved; how systems are upgraded and tested without disruption; and testing and documenting all changes.

The additional or specialist learning could include qualifications like BTECs/OCRs, GCSEs or A levels. You may be able to study qualifications related to the industry like a level 3 award in software design, interactive media or image generation and manipulation. You might wish to study a subject that could help you get into a specific degree course, for example mathematics, which may be required for some computer science courses.

It is not essential to have studied information technology before in order to study the Diploma.

HOW DO YOU STUDY?

You will work individually and in groups and your coursework will be assessed.

You will build up a portfolio, complete work experience and a project on a related topic. The course may include visits to exhibitions, trade shows and IT employers, and there will be talks from outside speakers from industry. You will develop your own real-life IT solutions for business and create your own multimedia product such as an interactive website.

OPTIONS AFTER YOUR COURSE

The Advanced Diploma in information technology will give you the skills you need for either university or work, and can be a first step towards a career in this area.

If you are considering employment you may wish to consider an Apprenticeship or trainee post.

See also the information provided within the ICT and ICT (Applied) A level entry.

If you complete this Diploma you don't have to opt for a career in this area. The Diploma teaches a mix of subjects, knowledge and skills valued by colleges, universities and employers.

HIGHER EDUCATION ENTRY

The Advanced Diploma in information technology can help you to get onto a higher education course such as a degree, foundation degree or HND/HNC, as well as other professional courses. You might progress to university to study a course such as computing, IT, computer network technology, computer games development, business information technology, information and communication technology, business systems, internet business development, e-commerce and internet systems, or multimedia technology and design.

For entry onto some degree or higher level courses, specific subjects may be required. You must check with individual institutions.

See also the information provided in the entries for computing, and IT and IT (Applied) A levels.

SOURCES OF INFORMATION

The Diploma in information technology
www.e-skills.com/diploma

'I found the problem solving really challenging. They give you a real life situation and you have to work out a solution. We looked at the weaknesses in a charity's IT systems and had to suggest cost effective ways to make them more efficient.' Davina, taking Advanced Diploma in IT with A level business

Manufacturing and product design Advanced Diploma

The manufacturing and product design industry is a large, fast-moving industry and the Diploma allows you to study in any of the five sub-sectors: food, textiles, processing, chemicals and engineering. You will look in detail at the different development techniques used in manufacturing, the properties of materials and how to assess safety and environmental risks. You will develop vital business skills, including budgeting, cost management and profitability. You will work in a team developing your own products as well as learning all about the different careers available.

WHAT DO YOU STUDY?

All Diplomas include:

Principal learning: focusing on the subject area of the Diploma.

Additional or specialist learning: the opportunity to study in more depth, take additional courses like A levels or gain specialist qualifications.

Generic learning: a project, functional skills in maths, English and ICT, personal, learning and thinking skills, and work experience.

The topics listed give an idea of what could be covered. The exact content of Diploma specifications differs according to exam boards, so you will need to check with your school or college about the exact modules available to you.

At advanced level your principal learning covers three themes; you apply these themes to every topic that you study.

- **Production design and materials science** – the process of manufacturing a product, from purchasing raw materials to selling the finished product.

- **Business and enterprise** – manufacturing as a business, how it works and the skills required for a profitable enterprise.

- **Production systems** – working practices and how to get the best product at the right price while considering factors like sustainability and health and safety.

You study the following topics.

Customer needs and market requirements: how manufacturers gather and use data about customers, competitors and markets; how networking can promote sales; and how businesses respond to their ethical and legal responsibilities. The importance of good customer service.

Supply chain management: how it works effectively across a company.

Managing resources and working practices: the different roles within a business. Working practices and responsibilities. The importance of teamwork, entry requirements, training and skills needed for different roles within this industry.

Research, development and introduction of new products: development of new products including design specifications and the issues that effect innovation of new products, such as sustainability and continuous improvement.

Materials science: properties of materials and how they are used in different products and manufacturing processes, how to investigate these properties safely, and how science and technology are used to increase productivity.

Production and processing systems: different manufacturing processes, the role of advanced technology and control systems in the manufacturing process.

Management of production and processing operations: maximising plant efficiency using maintenance and problem-solving techniques. The different organisational and management techniques that are used.

Quality in manufacturing: the importance of quality in every aspect of a manufacturing business. Total quality management, and how it works. Different ways of monitoring the quality of a product.

The additional or specialist learning could include qualifications like BTECs/OCRs, GCSEs or A levels. You may be able to study qualifications related to the industry like level 3 awards in food technology, process manufacturing, engineering or a business application like accounting or marketing. You could consider a subject that is required for a particular degree course, such as art and design or design and technology A level, for product design, or A level physics or maths, for engineering.

It is not essential to have studied manufacturing and product design before to study the Diploma.

HOW DO YOU STUDY?

You will work individually and in groups, and your coursework will be assessed.

You will build up a portfolio, complete work experience and work on projects in workshops or design studios. You will visit trade shows and different manufacturing companies, depending on your specialism.

OPTIONS AFTER YOUR COURSE

The Advanced Diploma in manufacturing and product design will give you the skills you need for either university or work, and can be a first step towards a career in this area. If you are considering employment you may wish to consider an Apprenticeship or trainee post.

If you complete this Diploma you don't have to opt for a career in this area. The Diploma teaches a mix of subjects, knowledge and skills valued by colleges, universities and employers.

HIGHER EDUCATION ENTRY

The Advanced Diploma in manufacturing and product design can help you to get onto a higher education course such as a degree, foundation degree or HND/HNC, as well as other professional courses. You might progress to university to study a subject such as textiles, printing and publishing, food manufacturing management, ceramics, process technology and management, or manufacturing systems engineering.

See the entry for A level design and technology (product design) for more information.

For entry onto some degree or higher level courses, specific subjects may be required. You must check with individual institutions.

SOURCES OF INFORMATION

The Diploma in manufacturing and product design
www.manufacturingdiploma.co.uk

> *'I enjoyed the food and drink schools challenge, where we developed a new pizza. It was good to work as a team and be creative, as well as learning all the business bits involved.'*
> Sharon, aged 18, Advanced Diploma in manufacturing and product design

Public services Advanced Diploma

This Diploma gives you an insight into how public services work and how they help individuals, the community and the business world. The Diploma covers a wide range of public services and includes the services available from local authorities, national government as well as the Armed Forces, fire and ambulance services, prison services and the police. The course includes the investigation of public services available locally. Careers options are explored, including some 'behind the scenes' jobs that aren't as well known as other progression routes in this sector.

WHAT DO YOU STUDY?

All Diplomas include:

Principal learning: focusing on the subject area of the Diploma.

Additional or specialist learning: the opportunity to study in more depth, take additional courses like A levels or gain specialist qualifications.

Generic learning: a project, functional skills in maths, English and ICT, personal, learning and thinking skills, and work experience.

The topics listed give an idea of what could be covered. The exact content of Diploma specifications differs according to exam boards, so you will need to check with your school or college about the exact modules available to you.

The Diploma covers the seven sectors in this sector of work: justice, defence, business, central and local government, health, administration and finance, and general public sector management.

At advanced level your principal learning is made up of these units.

Public services and the importance of collaborative working: public services perform many different functions and sometimes they have to work collaboratively, e.g. if there were a serious incident or some other emergency. You will learn about the range and level of public services available both in the UK and in other countries, how they work and how they all fit in to work together.

Community engagement and partnership working: how public services engage with the community to identify their needs and meet them effectively. How public services work in partnership with local communities so that citizens have a say in the services provided to them.

Accountability and public service funding: how public services are funded and how they must offer good value for money. How public service organisations have to be accountable for their budget and how it is used.

Leading effective public services: you will learn about different management theories and how they are used in different public service organisations. The key principles of motivating and supporting teams to deliver public services.

People management and public service values: people are the most important resource in the delivery of good quality public services. You will learn how approaches to managing staff vary across the range of public services, including uniformed services, and understanding the importance of good working relationships in delivering essential services.

> *'I recommend the Diploma because it tells you what is going on in the real world and not just theory.'*
> Rita, Advanced Diploma in public services

Managing public service projects: implementing and managing projects in the different public services. Learning different project management processes, tools and techniques.

Marketing and public relations in public services: understanding how marketing and public relations work in this sector, and the importance of the media and communication to publicise services and make the public aware of them.

The additional or specialist learning could include qualifications like BTECs/OCRs, GCSEs or A levels. You may be able to study qualifications related to the industry like level 3 modules from BTEC qualifications such as exercise, health and lifestyle, custodial care services, or enhancing public service delivery through the use of ICT. You could also study first aid, keyboard skills or administration. Alternatively you could choose an A level in a subject like languages, history, politics or sociology to help you with university entrance.

It is not essential to have studied public services before in order to study the Diploma.

HOW DO YOU STUDY?

You will work individually and in groups, and your coursework will be assessed.

You will build up a portfolio, complete work experience and a project on a related topic. You will carry out study visits in different areas of the public services, for example a placement in the Armed Forces, living in an army training centre and undergoing endurance tests and exercises to get a taste of what army life is like.

OPTIONS AFTER YOUR COURSE

The Advanced Diploma in public services will give you the skills you need for either university or work, and can be a first step towards a career in this area. You may be able to enter some careers directly after the Diploma like the police, fire service, the Armed Forces or jobs in local and national government. There may be Apprenticeships or trainee jobs available. For some careers in the public services, further study at a higher level may be required.

If you complete this Diploma you don't have to opt for a career in this area. The Diploma teaches a mix of subjects, knowledge and skills valued by colleges, universities and employers.

HIGHER EDUCATION ENTRY

The Advanced Diploma in public services can help you to get onto a higher education course such as a degree, foundation degree or HND/HNC, as well as other professional courses. You might progress to university to study public services, social work, youth work, housing, or community development. You might also study a more general course such as politics, law or business.

For entry onto some degree or higher level courses, specific subjects may be required. You must check with individual institutions.

SOURCES OF INFORMATION

The Diploma in public services
www.diplomainpublicservices.co.uk

'There are so many different opportunities in this area and it covers really important jobs like the army, police, and ambulance and fire service.'
Mandeep, Advanced Diploma in public services

Retail business Advanced Diploma

The retail business industry offers a wide range of opportunities. It's not just working in or managing a shop, but covers areas like buying, supply chain management, visual merchandising, marketing, accounts, IT and logistics. This sector provides about three million jobs and is a competitive and fast-changing industry that has to respond quickly to market forces to survive.

WHAT DO YOU STUDY?

All Diplomas include:

Principal learning: focusing on the subject area of the Diploma.

Additional or specialist learning: the opportunity to study in more depth, take additional courses like A levels or gain specialist qualifications.

Generic learning: a project, functional skills in maths, English and ICT, personal, learning and thinking skills, and work experience.

The topics listed give an idea of what could be covered. The exact content of Diploma specifications differs according to exam boards, so you will need to check with your school or college about the exact modules available to you.

Your principal learning covers these topics.

Examining the world of retail: learning how the retail business works and how it survives both in the UK and globally. The importance of innovation and identifying emerging trends. The wide range of career opportunities in this sector.

Developing retail channels: looking at the different ways of successfully getting a product to the customer (e.g. the internet). How this impacts on the business, for example the financial and staffing implications. Skills needed to work successfully in this area.

Buying practices of retail businesses: buying practices play an important role in retail business so must be done effectively in order to have the right products at the right time. How to develop product ranges, supported by effective market research, to meet customer needs. The skills needed to develop networks, gain market knowledge and negotiate successfully.

Retail supply chain management and logistics: supply chain management includes all the movement and storage of products, whether they are raw or finished goods, from the point of origin to the point of consumption. How the supply chain works and the careful planning involved to ensure efficiency, sustainability and profitability.

Marketing in retail businesses: using market research and good marketing strategies to market products. Learning how to interpret market intelligence and market conditions to get the right products at the right price to the right customers.

Merchandising in retail businesses: merchandising is about getting the right product to the right person at the right time. Developing stock control systems based on data from sales forecasts. Ways of analysing financial performance, assessing and minimising risk and also methods of monitoring and improving systems.

Management of sales in retail: all sales activities have to be planned and managed

'We did a project on how new products are launched. You wouldn't believe the planning and research that is involved.'
Aaron, Advanced Diploma in retail business

to keep costs down and profits up. You will learn about designing a sales plan to increase sales. The relationships between customer service, the retail environment and the customer experience, and the impact these have on sales. Understanding your customers, customer behaviour, buying patterns and sales targets.

Visual merchandising for retail: window and in-store displays, product positioning and effective promotional techniques are all important parts of visual merchandising. You will learn the skills needed to interpret a design brief, and how to design and safely install visual merchandising installations. How visual merchandising has to be attractive and appropriate and how to use space cost effectively to stimulate customer desire to buy in accordance with changing market needs.

The additional or specialist learning could include qualifications like BTECs/OCRs, GCSEs or A levels. You may be able to study qualifications related to the industry like a level 3 in road freight logistics, customer service, buying and merchandising for fashion retail, or visual merchandising for retail. You may be able to take a qualification in a particular area of retail like floristry.

It is not essential to have studied retail business before to study the Diploma.

HOW DO YOU STUDY?

You will work individually and in groups, and your coursework will be assessed.

You will build up a portfolio, complete work experience and a project on a related topic.

> 'My placement in a freight forwarding company at the airport was really good. It's amazing to see what goods come into the country by plane, as well as all the paperwork that is involved.'
> Mattie, Advanced Diploma in retail business

You will visit retail employers and attend trade shows and exhibitions.

OPTIONS AFTER YOUR COURSE

The Advanced Diploma in retail business will give you the skills you need for either university or work, and can be a first step towards a career in this area. If you are considering employment you may wish to consider an Apprenticeship or trainee post and go straight into the retail industry.

If you complete this Diploma you don't have to opt for a career in this area. The Diploma teaches a mix of subjects, knowledge and skills valued by colleges, universities and employers.

HIGHER EDUCATION ENTRY

The Advanced Diploma in retail business can help you to get onto a higher education course such as a degree, foundation degree or HND/HNC, as well as other professional courses. You might progress to university to study retail management, retail marketing, fashion buying management, licensed retail or more general courses like business, finance or IT.

For entry onto some degree or higher level courses, specific subjects may be required. You must check with individual institutions.

SOURCES OF INFORMATION

The Diploma in retail business
www.diplomainretailbusiness.com

Society, health and development Advanced Diploma

This Diploma covers a vast industry offering a wide range of opportunities and a major UK employer. It's all about people and the range of services that they need. You will look at all the different services available in this sector, including healthcare, social care, social work, day care and community justice. You'll find out in detail how these services work and the range of opportunities and careers available to you in this sector.

WHAT DO YOU STUDY?

All Diplomas include:

Principal learning: focusing on the subject area of the Diploma.

Additional or specialist learning: the opportunity to study in more depth, take additional courses like A levels or gain specialist qualifications.

Generic learning: a project, functional skills in maths, English and ICT, personal, learning and thinking skills, and work experience.

The topics listed give an idea of what could be covered. The exact content of Diploma specifications differs according to exam boards, so you will need to check with your school or college about the exact modules available to you.

At advanced level your principal learning covers the main four sectors in this industry: services for children and young people; health; community justice; and social care.

You will study the following topics.

The sectors in context: the similarities and differences in the political, social and economic factors that influence the sectors covered by this Diploma. Understanding how support and services are provided in these areas.

Principles and values in practice: how the principles and values that can be found in key legislation, regulations and codes of practice underpin working approaches in these sectors.

Partnership working: how individuals, colleagues, teams and organisations need to work effectively and efficiently to improve their services.

Communication and information sharing: how effective communication, information sharing and record keeping are vital to providing effective and appropriate services in and across these sectors. Effective interaction with people who may have a range of different communication needs.

Personal and professional development in the work environment: how to identify good practice, improve your own practice, and plan for professional development, based on expectations in an actual workplace setting.

Safeguarding and protecting individuals in society: understanding the importance of promoting and protecting the health, safety and security of individuals and society. The study of risk and the individual's right to choose to take risks.

> *'The visits to different employers are really interesting. We've been to a hospital and a nursery and I hope to do a placement in the children's ward of a hospital.'*
> Donna, Advanced Diploma in society, health and development with A level biology

The additional or specialist learning could include qualifications like BTECs/OCRs, GCSEs or A levels. You may be able to study qualifications related to the industry like a level 3 award in management, health and social care, children's care, learning and development, or health sciences. You might take a specialist unit from a BTEC like prevention control and impact of infection, public health, supporting adults through transition, physiological disorders, nutrition for health and social care, or teamwork in the public services.

You might also choose a first aid course, ICT or administration qualifications.

You could consider a subject to help with a future application to a particular higher education course, such as an AS or A level in biology, chemistry, psychology or sociology.

It is not essential to have studied society, health and development before in order to study the Diploma.

HOW DO YOU STUDY?

You will work individually and in groups, and there will be role play and practical work. You will build up a portfolio, complete work experience and a project on a related topic. You will go on study visits to employers to find out about the reality of work in this sector.

OPTIONS AFTER YOUR COURSE

The Advanced Diploma in society, health and development will give you the skills you need for either university or work, and can be a first step towards a career in this area. You might go into a career as a care worker, play leader, nursery nurse or administrator at this level. There could be Apprenticeships available leading to further qualifications.

If you complete this Diploma you don't have to opt for a career in this area. The Diploma

teaches a mix of subjects, knowledge and skills valued by colleges, universities and employers.

HIGHER EDUCATION ENTRY

The Advanced Diploma in society, health and development can help you to get onto a higher education course such as a degree, foundation degree or HND/HNC, as well as other professional courses. You might progress to university to study a degree in dietetics, childhood studies, nursing, midwifery, educational psychology, physiotherapy, occupational therapy, social work or probation.

For entry onto some degree or higher level courses, specific subjects may be required. A level biology is likely to be required for physiotherapy, for example. You must check with individual institutions.

SOURCES OF INFORMATION

The Diploma in society, health and development
http://shd.skillsforhealth.org.uk

'I really want to help make a difference and become a probation officer. I hope to do a work experience with the local youth offending team. If I decide it's not for me then I can go and do something completely different but at least I will have tried.' Brian, aged 17, Advanced Diploma in society, health and development

Sport and active leisure Advanced Diploma

The sport and active leisure industry offers a wide range of opportunities, especially with the emphasis on healthy lifestyle choices and the 2012 Olympics. The industry includes sport and recreation, health and fitness, playwork and outdoor pursuits. Sport and leisure currently contributes over eight billion pounds annually to the UK economy and continues to grow. You will gain a thorough understanding of this sector, the skills needed and the careers available.

WHAT DO YOU STUDY?

All Diplomas include:

Principal learning: focusing on the subject area of the Diploma.

Additional or specialist learning: the opportunity to study in more depth, take additional courses like A levels or gain specialist qualifications.

Generic learning: a project, functional skills in maths, English and ICT, personal, learning and thinking skills, and work experience.

The topics listed give an idea of what could be covered. The exact content of Diploma specifications differs according to exam boards, so you will need to check with your school or college about the exact modules available to you.

At advanced level your principal learning covers three themes; you apply these themes to every topic that you study.

- **Sport and active leisure and the individual** – the positive steps people can take to improve their lifestyle and the implications these choices have on society.

- **Sport and active leisure and the economy** – the industry's impact on the economy and how the industry promotes itself nationally and globally.

- **Sport and active leisure and the community** – the implications of equality and diversity legislation, and the principles of inclusion to respond appropriately and fairly to all customer needs.

You study the following topics.

Impact of an active and healthy lifestyle: examining your own lifestyle and finding out how lifestyle choices affect your mind, body and overall well-being. Evaluating the impact of lifestyle choices on individuals and how to help them improve their health and well-being.

Effective management and leadership in sport and active leisure: learning to become an effective manager who can identify business opportunities. Examining different business models and how they function within an organisation to make it successful.

Applying science and technology to sport and exercise: understanding how knowledge of anatomy, physiology and technology, for example, in equipment or clothing, can be used to improve performance and the experience of sport and active leisure.

Applying scientific principles to enhance performance: different approaches to performance enhancement used in sport and active leisure. Analysing and measuring the effects of methods of performance enhancement on performance and suggesting how performance can be improved.

The sport and active leisure workforce and the economy: looking at the types of staff that make up the industry, and the careers and career paths available. Analysing the impact of the global sport and active leisure industry and commercialisation on the UK economy and its environment.

Politics and policies in sport and active leisure: analysing the extent to which the sport and active leisure industry has influenced government policy, evaluating the legacies of a major sport and active leisure event.

Promoting opportunities for all in sport and active leisure: promoting opportunities for everyone to take part in sport and active leisure, and understanding how to respond to the needs of different communities.

Developing community cohesion through sport and active leisure: how sport and active leisure can be used to influence or challenge behaviour patterns in society through providing positive role models and bringing communities together.

The additional or specialist learning could include qualifications like BTECs/OCRs, GCSEs or A levels. You may be able to study industry-related qualifications in coaching or instructing.

It is not essential to have studied sport and active leisure before in order to study the Diploma.

HOW DO YOU STUDY?

Study will involving work in the classroom as well as in gyms and sports centres.

You will build up a portfolio, complete work experience and a project on a related topic. You will go on visits to employers and sports and leisure centres and have outside speakers from the industry.

OPTIONS AFTER YOUR COURSE

The Advanced Diploma in sport and active leisure will give you the skills you need for either university or work, and can be a first step towards a career in this area. You might go into jobs like leisure centre assistant, play worker or personal trainer and there may be Apprenticeships available.

See also information in the entries for leisure studies and physical education A levels.

If you complete this Diploma you don't have to opt for a career in this area. The Diploma teaches a mix of subjects, knowledge and skills valued by colleges, universities and employers.

HIGHER EDUCATION ENTRY

The Advanced Diploma in sport and active leisure can help you to get onto a higher education course such as a degree, foundation degree or HND/HNC, as well as other professional courses. You might progress to university to study a degree in sports studies, sport and exercise science, outdoor adventure leadership, physical education, sport and exercise psychology, sports development, or leisure management. You could also consider degrees in health promotion, occupational therapy, physiotherapy, osteopathy or related subjects like business and marketing.

For entry onto some degree or higher level courses, specific subjects may be required such as biology for sports or paramedical courses. You must check with individual institutions.

SOURCES OF INFORMATION

The Diploma in sport and active leisure
http://saldiploma.skillsactive.com

Travel and tourism Advanced Diploma

Travel and tourism covers many different industries and is a fast-changing, dynamic industry. It includes tourism services, passenger transport, visitor attractions, conferences and events, and accommodation services such as holiday parks and caravans. Customer service is key in this industry and the Diploma will encourage you to develop your skills in all areas, be creative and learn about the varied career opportunities in this sector.

WHAT DO YOU STUDY?

All Diplomas include:

Principal learning: focusing on the subject area of the Diploma.

Additional or specialist learning: the opportunity to study in more depth, take additional courses like A levels or gain specialist qualifications.

Generic learning: a project, functional skills in maths, English and ICT, personal, learning and thinking skills, and work experience.

The topics listed give an idea of what could be covered. The exact content of Diploma specifications differs according to exam boards, so you will need to check with your school or college about the exact modules available to you.

At advanced level your principal learning covers three themes; you apply these themes to every topic that you study.

- **Destinations** – looking at the wide range of destinations available to different groups of travellers.

- **Customer experience** – learning that in a customer focused industry like travel and tourism, the customer experience is key to running successful travel businesses.

- **Changes and trends** – understanding that the industry is fast moving, and tastes and trends change quickly for many reasons. Learning that the customers'

preferences may change, and there could also be political, economical and environmental factors that influence the industry.

Topics studied include:

Travel and tourism destinations and cultures: looking at leading tourist destinations, how they attract tourists, and the impact and ethics of tourism.

Changes and trends: examining technological and socio-economic changes and how they affect the industry.

Promotion, image and perception: how travellers are influenced by their perception and image of a place and how that can be influenced.

Products and services: looking at ideas for business start-ups, how to set objectives, use project planning techniques, work to a budget, and how to negotiate for resources.

The UK travel and tourism sector: how this people industry operates in the UK. Socio-cultural awareness in a global context, and leadership and communication styles.

Political and economic influences: the role of global organisations, governments, trade

> *'We are doing a project on the 2012 Olympics; you don't realise all the different jobs involved and how much this will help tourism in the whole country.'*
> Solli, Advanced Diploma in travel and tourism with A level geography

and professional bodies and their influence on the sector. How tourism contributes to the UK economy.

Environmental influences: environmentally friendly tourism and how the various forms of transport impact on the environment, both nationally and locally.

Technology: looking at the software that is key to the industry, how technology influences the customer experience and how it impacts on transport developments.

The additional or specialist learning could include qualifications like BTECs/OCRs, GCSEs or A levels. You may be able to study qualifications related to the industry like a ticketing or reservations or you might consider an extra language.

It is not essential to have studied travel and tourism before in order to study the Diploma.

HOW DO YOU STUDY?

You will work individually and in groups, and your coursework will be assessed.

You will build up a portfolio, complete work experience and a project on a related topic. The course may include visits to trade shows, travel companies and exhibitions.

OPTIONS AFTER YOUR COURSE

(See also the entry for travel and tourism A level)

The Advanced Diploma in travel and tourism will give you the skills you need for either university or work, and can be a first step towards a career in this area. You might also go into a career in a travel agency, tourism or transport company and there may be Apprenticeships available.

If you complete this Diploma you don't have to opt for a career in this area. The Diploma teaches a mix of subjects, knowledge and skills valued by colleges, universities and

employers.

HIGHER EDUCATION ENTRY

The Advanced Diploma in travel and tourism can help you to get onto a higher education course such as a degree, foundation degree or HND/HNC, as well as other professional courses. You might progress to university to study travel and tourism or a related course, such as leisure and recreation, or hospitality management. You could also consider related degrees in business, finance and marketing.

For entry onto some degree or higher level courses, specific subjects may be required. You must check with individual institutions.

SOURCES OF INFORMATION

The Diploma in travel and tourism
www.tandtdiploma.co.uk

> *'It's such a fast moving industry and has to change and adapt, sometimes within 24 hours. You wouldn't think that a little bit of volcanic ash would cause so much trouble. We have to have the customer service skills to cope with anything.'*
> Bella, reservations manager for a major airline

Appendix 1

QUALIFICATIONS FRAMEWORKS

There are three qualifications frameworks, which group together qualifications at different levels.

- The **National Qualifications Framework (NQF)** categorises 'academic' qualifications, such as GCSEs and A levels.
- The **Qualifications and Credit Framework (QCF)** is the new framework for vocational or work-related qualifications.
- The **Framework for Higher Education Qualifications (FHEQ)** shows how different types of higher education qualifications compare to one another.

The three different frameworks, and qualifications at each level, are shown below.

QCF/NQF levels	FHEQ levels	Examples of qualifications at that level
8	D (doctoral	Doctorates
7	M (masters)	Masters degrees
6	H (honours)	Bachelors degrees
5	I (intermediate)	Diplomas of Higher Education, foundation degrees, Higher National Diplomas
4	C (certificate)	Certificates of Higher Education
3		A levels, BTEC Nationals, Advanced Diplomas, Progression Diplomas, International Baccalaureate
2		GCSEs grades A*-C, BTEC Firsts, Higher Diplomas
1		GCSEs grades D-G, BTEC Introductory qualifications, Foundation Diplomas
Entry level		Entry level Awards and Cerificates

Appendix 2

THE UCAS TARIFF

The UCAS Tariff is a system for allocating points to qualifications to report achievement for entry to higher education. It gives numerical values to qualifications, establishes agreed equivalences between different types of qualifications, and provides comparisons between applicants with different types of achievement.

A and AS level UCAS Tariff points

A level (A2)	A level double award	AS	AS double award
	A*A* 280		
	A*A 260		
	AA 240		
	AB 220		
	BB 200		
	BC 180		
	CC 160		
A* 140	CD 140		
A 120	DD 120		AA 120
			AB 110
B 100	DE 100		BB 100
			BC 90
C 80	EE 80		CC 80
			CD 70
D 60		A 60	DD 60
		B 50	DE 50
E 40		C 40	EE 40
		D 30	
		E 20	

Diplomas

The Progression Diploma is worth up to 350 UCAS points and the Advanced Diploma is worth up to 490 UCAS points (3.5 A levels).

Other qualifications

Many other qualifications also attract UCAS Tariff points, including: BTEC Nationals, OCR Nationals, Cambridge Pre-U qualifications and the International Baccalaureate. Some specialist qualifications in subjects such as music, drama, childcare, fashion and finance are also included. More qualifications are being incorporated into the Tariff all the time. Further details are available on the UCAS website.

Appendix 3

GLOSSARY

A2 level	Advanced level (represents the second half of the full A level)
A level	Advanced level
Apprenticeships	Developed by the government and industry to allow young people to train while in a job and attain work-related qualifications at levels 2 and 3
AQA	Assessment and Qualifications Alliance (examination board)
AS level	Advanced Subsidiary level (represents the first half of the full A level)
BA	Bachelor of Arts degree
BEd	Bachelor of Education degree
BEng	Bachelor of Engineering degree
BMus	Bachelor of Music degree
BSc	Bachelor of Science degree
BTEC	BTEC qualifications are vocational qualifications offered by Edexcel
CACHE	Council for Awards in Childcare and Education
CCEA	Council for the Curriculum, Examinations and Assessment (Northern Ireland examination board)
Degree	A qualification that can be studied for at a college or university: awarded by a university. A degree shows that you have attained a preset level of knowledge and understanding, usually over a three- or four-year period of study
DipHE	Diploma of Higher Education
Diploma	A qualification often related to a job area. A Diploma shows that you have achieved a preset level of knowledge and understanding. In England, the Diploma for young people aged 14 to 19 is a new qualification offered in a range of work-related subjects, at several levels
Dissertation	An essay of specified length, which forms part of a higher education degree course
Edexcel	Examination board that offers a range of qualifications, including BTEC qualifications
FdA	Foundation degree (Arts)
FdSc	Foundation degree (Science)
Fieldwork	Practical work or research, which is undertaken away from an education establishment
Foundation course	A one-year course that is usually required for entry to higher education courses, usually covering the subjects required to bring students up to standard to start on the first year of a degree. There are special Foundation courses in art for entry to art and design courses
Foundation degree	A degree lasting two years (full time, longer part time) with a mix of work-based experience and study. It can lead to employment or progression to an honours degree course. Courses are designed to tackle local skills shortages

Gap year	A year away from education, often taken after leaving school and before going to college or university
GCE	General Certificate of Education
Highers and Advanced Highers	Scottish alternatives to A levels
HNC	Higher National Certificate (Edexcel)
HND	Higher National Diploma (Edexcel)
IB	International Baccalaureate
JCQ	Joint Council for Qualifications
MA	Master of Arts degree
MPhys	Master of Physics degree
MRes	Master of Research; this has a strong emphasis on learning through research experience
MSc	Master of Science degree
Modular course	A course taken in sections called modules. These courses allow you to take exams at the end of each module instead of doing all your exams at the end of the course
National Curriculum	Sequences of study and attainment set by the Government, which are used in all state schools
NVQ	National Vocational Qualification
OCR	Oxford, Cambridge and Royal Society of Arts Examining Board
PGCE	Postgraduate Certificate in Education
PhD	Doctor of Philosophy
QCA	Qualifications and Curriculum Authority
QTS	Qualified Teacher Status
Sandwich course	Course that includes a work placement in Britain or abroad
Specifications	A designation of both the areas to be covered and the skills to be attained in a course of study
Syllabus	A designation of the content of a course of study
Synoptic	A level courses have a synoptic part, which represents a summing up, either of the knowledge learned during the course and/or of the skills developed during the acquisition of such knowledge. You may find that the examination boards vary somewhat in their interpretation of this word
UCAS	Universities and Colleges Admissions Service, which handles applications to full-time higher education courses
Vocational courses	Courses geared towards areas of work
WB	Welsh Baccalaureate
WJEC	Welsh Joint Educational Committee (examination board)

Appendix 4

USEFUL CONTACT POINTS

Qualifications and Curriculum Development Agency
www.qcda.gov.uk

Joint Council for Qualifications (publish national exam results)
www.jcq.org.uk

Examination boards

AQA
www.aqa.org.uk

Cambridge Pre-U
www.cie.org.uk

CCEA
www.ccea.org.uk

Edexcel
www.edexcel.org.uk

International Baccalaureate Organisation
www.ibo.org

OCR
www.ocr.org.uk

Scottish Baccalaureate
www.sqa.org.uk/baccalaureates

Welsh Baccalaureate
www.welshbaccalaureate.org.uk

WJEC
www.wjec.co.uk

Index